Advertising Management: Concepts and Cases

Advertising Management: Concepts and Cases

Abhishek Gupta

CYBER TECH PUBLICATIONS
4264/3, Ansari Road, Daryaganj, New Delhi-110002 (India)
Ph.: 011-23244078. Fax: 011-23280028
E-Mail: cyberpublicationsdelhi@yahoo.com

ADVERTISING MANAGEMENT: CONCEPTS AND CASES

Abhishek Gupta

First Edition 2009

Published by :

G.S. Rawat for **Cyber Tech Publications**
4264/3, Ansari Road, Daryaganj, New Delhi-110002 (India)
Ph.: 011-23244078. Fax: 011-23280028
E-Mail: cyberpublicationsdelhi@yahoo.com

Printed at : Asian Offset Printers

Preface

The subtle force of advertising reaches out and touches everyone living and working in the modern world today. In fact, at some time in their lives, most people even become creators of advertising-whether they design a flier for a school car wash, write a classified ad for a garage sale, or develop a whole campaign for some business, charity, or political endeavor.

Today, our voices are no longer limited by the scope of 20th-century media. Thanks to the Internet and a variety of online database services, people and organizations can now send advertising messages to millions of people around the world-instantly. Advertising is undergoing a transformation of historic proportions-from a monopolistic corporate monolog to a totally democratic dialog. Suddenly everybody has a voice.

That makes the study of advertising more important today than ever before, not only for students of business or journalism-who may be contemplating a career in the field-but also for students of sociology, psychology, political science, economics, history, language, science, or the arts. Most of these people will become users of advertising; all will be lifetime consumers of it.

The study of advertising gives students, regardless of their major field of study. Many valuable tools to use in any subsequent profession. It helps them learn to: think and plan strategically: gather and analyze primary and secondary research data; compute and evaluate the potential of alternative courses of action; cooperate with a team in developing creative solutions to a problem; analyze competitive proposals; understand why people behave the way they do; express themselves and their ideas with clarity and simplicity; persuade others to their point of view; appreciate and assess the quality of different creative endeavors; and use data to speak with knowledge, confidence, and conviction.

—Author

Preface

CONTENTS

1

Introduction

Advertising is a management function. While advertising is the event, advertising management is the whole process - a function of marketing starting from market research continuing through advertising leading to actual sales or achievement of objective. It goes further in regard to evaluation of the whole cost-benefits that were involved in the whole exercise.

This means that if there is a public service ad with an objective to increase domestic saving, the evaluation would take place in terms of the actual increase in domestic savings as can be found from banks and other financial institutions. If it's about launch of a new product, then the evaluation would be in terms of benefits derived from the cost sunk in the advertising campaign.

Advertising management incorporates various specialised sub-functions like media strategy, message strategy, media planning, media buying etc.

While advertising management is an inseparable part of the marketing department, usually, the marketing department of an organisation is concerned more with market research and evaluation of results. All the critical processes of advertising management are generally outsourced to specialised advertising agencies. For example the media buying is done in bulk by these ad agencies on which they receive discount / commission, that goes into their earning. It involves designing the strategies to be adopted for influencing the public ie media selection and deciding on the aspect to be advertised based on the image of the company and the present marketing objective.

HOW DATA MINING CAN HELP ADVERTISING MANAGEMENT

Data Mining is a relatively new set of analytical techniques designed to provide management information for decision-making purposes. The distinguishing characteristic of data mining is the application of techniques and rules designed to extract information from very large databases. These databases are often developed in the course of ordinary business both online and offline. This paper addresses the question of the relevance of data mining techniques to the field of advertising management. First, the definition of data mining is explored followed by an exposition of the core concepts in data mining. Second, an example of data mining developed by the first author is explained. Finally, the applicability of data mining to advertising management problems is addressed.

HOW DATA MINING CAN HELP ADVERTISING MANAGEMENT

In the current advertising and marketing business and in the press, data mining has been and continues to be the focus of a great deal of attention (Small 1997;Elder & Ridgeway 1999; Abbott, Matkovsky & Elder 1998; Condon 1997; Foley, John & Bruce Caldwell 1996; Miller 1997; Mitchell 1997; Novack 1996; O'Harrow 1998; Stone 1997). But care must be taken to separate fact from myth. Data mining is a useful tool, a new approach that combines discovery with analysis. Data mining is not a newly discovered branch of mathematics embodied in software that will, when hooked-up to a large database, inexplicably and inevitably reveal the business insights contained in the millions of records stored therein. Yet it is a tool that will increasingly become important for competitive businesses.

The past two decades has seen a dramatic increase in the amount of information or data being stored in electronic format. This accumulation of data has taken place at a dramatic rate. It has been estimated that the amount of information in the world doubles every 20 months and the size and number of databases are increasing at an even faster rate. The increase in use of electronic data gathering devices such as point-of-sale or remote sensing devices has contributed to this explosion of available data (Dilly 1995).

Data mining is one way to extract predictive information from these large databases. The focus of this paper is to show how data mining may become a major tool for the advertising industry. This discussion will address the following areas: what data mining is, what technologies data mining uses, what ways data mining can be used, some examples of successful data mining applications in businesses, what is holding back data mining in advertising, and, finally, ways to develop a successful data mining project.

DEFINITIONS OF DATA-MINING

Data mining is a powerful new technology with great potential to help companies focus on the most important information in their data warehouses. Data mining tools predict future trends and behaviors, allowing businesses to make proactive, knowledge-driven decisions. The automated, prospective analyses offered by data mining move beyond the analyses of past events provided by retrospective tools typical of decision support systems. Data mining tools can answer business questions that traditionally were too time-consuming to resolve. They scour databases for hidden patterns, finding predictive information that experts may miss because it lies outside their expectations (White Paper 1997).

The expression "Data Mining" sometimes refers to the whole process of knowledge discovery and sometimes to the methods that are used in the knowledge discovery phase. The SAS institute has adopted a defińition that is more orientated towards methods. According to the SAS institute, data mining consists of "Methods used to explore and model relationships in large amounts of data."

Here are some more useful definitions for data mining:

Data mining is the process of discovering meaningful new correlations, patterns and trends by sifting through large amounts of data stored in repositories, using pattern recognition technologies as well as statistical and mathematical techniques.

Data mining is the exploration and analysis, by automatic and semiautomatic means, of large quantities of data in order to discover meaningful patterns and rules (M.J.A. Berry, G. Linoff 1997).

Data mining the use of advanced statistical tools to reach into a company's existing databases to discover patterns and relationships that can be exploited in a business context.

Data mining is a combination of powerful methods that help reducing costs and risks as well as increasing revenues, by extracting information from the available data.

Data mining is the non trivial extraction of implicit, previously unknown, and potentially useful information from data. (William J Frawley, Gregory Piatetsky-Shapiro and Christopher J Matheus 1991)

Why Do We Need Data Mining?

There are a number of factors that have combined to bring data mining to the attention of the business community. First, there is a general recognition that there is untapped value in large databases. Second, there is a consolidation of database records tending toward a single customer view. Third, there is huge storage of databases, including the concept of an information warehouse. Fourth, there is a reduction in the cost of data storage and processing providing for the ability to collect and accumulate detailed data. Fifth, there is intense competition for a customer's attention in an increasingly saturated marketplace. Finally, there is movement towards the de-massification of business practices.

De-massification is a term from Alvin Toffler (1970). During the industrial revolution economies of scale led businesses to mass manufacturing, mass marketing and mass advertising. The information revolution is providing the capability to custom manufacture, to market and advertise to small segments and ultimately to the individual. This is de-massification and it is a strong force in business today.

Data mining is evolving as an essential segment in the decision-support marketplace. Like data warehousing, data mining is experiencing rapid change and growth as major corporations around the world begin to implement new and enhanced systems for leveraging corporate data. The META Group, a Stamford, Connecticut research firm, reports the market for data mining software and services to be \$3.2 billion in 1996. The firm anticipates growth to \$10 billion in 2000 (About Data Mining,1997).

A recent Gartner Group Advanced Technology Research Note listed data mining and artificial intelligence at the top of the five key technology areas that "will clearly have a major impact across a wide range of industries within the next three to five years." Gartner also listed data mining as one of the top 10 new technologies in which companies will invest during the next five years (White Paper 1999).

If data mining is understood and applied, it can generate new revenue, increased profits, and have significant cost savings. However, those "ifs" speak volumes about a set of technologies that is still in its infancy. (Gerber 1998).

"Data mining is an immature, unstable market today. We have to perfect the technology and the understanding of it by business analysts. However, it is necessary for survival. If you don't use it to predict a trend before your competitors, you're dead," says Erick Brethenoux, Paris-based research director for advanced technologies at the Gartner Group (Gerber 1998).

"Indeed, there's been a frenzy of interest in datamining, which has captured corporate America's imagination-and budgets-with one simple value proposition: Get to know your customers better, and you'll keep them longer. That can translate into bigger profits over longer periods" (McCarthy 1998).

It executives will likely triple the size of their existing data stores in the next two years, predicts a recent study by the San Francisco-based Sentry Technology Group. Moreover, to make the most of all those terabytes of data, they will probably need to invest heavily in advanced OLAP (Online Analytical Processing) products and algorithm-intensive datamining technologies. So, before they gear up to embark on this latest technology adventure, they had better prepare themselves for the fact that datamining projects can consume millions of dollars and years of effort. But the alternative could be just as costly: then upper management, may wonder why the competition always seems so much better at spotting sales trends, developing smarter marketing campaigns, and accurately predicting customer loyalty (McCarthy 1998).

Data mining is emerging as the major solution to solve a series of critical, fast growing business issues. In particular, with the effects of globalization and deregulation, major corporations are facing new pressure from increased competition on a worldwide basis. Effectively responding to this challenge requires faster marketing cycles to produce a greater number of campaigns to attract and retain the best customers. As a result, tools are required in the hands of marketers to help them stay on top of corporate data that provides the foundation of any good marketing program. These tools must go beyond simply reporting data records or historical sales performance - they must ultimately provide the business professional with deep insight into customer actions. This insight is best achieved with a combination of hindsight as well as foresight (About Data Mining 1997).

Data mining offers a rich capability for modeling historical performance and then using this model to predict likely future outcomes. This combination of hindsight and foresight is unique to data mining and provides business professionals with a new understanding of factors, which truly contribute to business success or failure (About Data Mining, 1997).

Data Mining Technologies

The primary technologies which comprise data mining are neural networks, decision trees, rule induction, genetic algorithms, and nearest neighbor.

Neural Networks

A neural network is patterned after the neurons in the human brain. It's made up of a web of electronic neurons that send signals to each other through thousands of connections, which are adjusted up or down as the machine learns particular applications. A neural network can be taught voice recognition, for example, simply by having a trainer speak words into the machine, reinforcing some connections and not others (Darling 1998).

Neural networks are an approach to computing that involves developing mathematical structures with the ability to learn. The methods are the result of academic investigations to model nervous system learning. Neural networks have the remarkable ability to derive meaning from complicated or imprecise data and can be used to extract patterns and detect trends that are too complex to be noticed by either humans or other computer techniques. A trained neural network can be thought of as an "expert" in the category of information it has been given to analyze. This expert can then be used to provide projections given new situations of interest and answer "what if" questions (Dilly 1995).

Neural networks have broad applicability to real world business problems and have already been successfully applied in many industries. Since neural networks are best at identifying patterns or trends in data, they are well suited for prediction or forecasting needs including: sales forecasting, industrial process control, customer research, data validation, risk management, and target marketing etc. (Dilly 1995).

Neural networks use a set of processing elements (or nodes) analogous to neurons in the brain. These processing elements are interconnected in a network that can then identify patterns in data once it is exposed to the data, i.e. the network learns from experience just as people do. This distinguishes neural networks from traditional computing programs that simply follow instructions in a fixed sequential order. The picture to the right is a simple neural network (Dilly 1995).

Decision Trees

A tree-shaped structure that represents a set of decisions that can be used to predict which records in a new (unclassified) dataset will have a given outcome. Decision trees are simple knowledge representation and they classify examples to a finite number of classes, the nodes are labeled with attribute names, the edges are labeled with possible values for this attribute and the leaves labeled with different classes. Objects are classified by following a path down the tree, by taking the edges, corresponding to the values of the attributes in an object (Dilly 1995).

The following is an example of objects that describe the weather at a given time. The objects contain information on the outlook, humidity etc. Some objects are positive examples denote by P and others are negative i.e. N. Classification is in this case the construction of a tree structure, illustrated in the following diagram below, which can be used to classify all the objects correctly (Dilly 1995).

There are two classifications of decision trees: they are Classification and Regression Tree (CART), and Chi Square Automation Interactive Detection (CHAID).

Classification and Regression Tree (CART)

A decision tree technique can be used for classification of a dataset. Provides a set of rules that you can apply to a new (unclassified) dataset to predict which records will have a given outcome. It segments a dataset by creating 2-way splits and it requires less data preparation than CHAID (White Paper 1997).

The CART method derives its name from the tree-like structure that it builds as a model. These trees work much like the child's game of twenty questions, where one child asks questions to determine the kind of object another child has in mind. In this case, the tree asks questions about card members to determine which are likelier to attrite than others. Each question in the tree represents a choice between values of a particular variable that break a large group of card members into two smaller groups (Big Data - Better Returns Leveraging Your Hidden Data Assets to Improve, 27 Apr 1998).

For instance, there might be a choice between those members with more than $1,000 of monthly balance and those with less than that amount. Those with less than a thousand dollars could be transactors while those with more could be revolvers. As with the child's game, each question's answer provides a bit of information about card members and leads to other, more appropriate questions. For revolvers, the next-best question to determine whether someone will attrite might be whether their monthly balance has been decreasing, but for transactors, those who always pay off their monthly balance, the next-best question might be whether the monthly volume of transactions has been decreasing. Eventually, enough questions have been asked of the card members to place each in a group of people who will reliably do much the same as one another: stay or attrite (Big Data - Better Returns Leveraging Your Hidden Data Assets to Improve, 27 Apr 1998).

Because CART uses tests on the database to find its questions, it can be robust in the face of outliers, by isolating them with a single question. And because it searches for the best variable to use in the groups created by answers to questions based on other variables, it automatically finds combinations of variables (Big Data - Better Returns Leveraging Your Hidden Data Assets to Improve, 27 Apr 1998).

Chi Square Automation Interactive Detection (CHAID)

A decision tree technique used for classification of a dataset. Provides a set of rules that you can apply to a new (unclassified) dataset to predict which records will have a given outcome. It segments a dataset by using chi square tests to create multi-way splits. Preceded, and requires more data preparation than, CART (White Paper 1997).

Rule Induction

The extraction from data of useful if-then rules based on statistical significance. A data mine system has to infer a model from the database. That is, it may define classes such that the database contains one or more attributes that denote the class of a tuple i.e. the predicted attributes while the remaining attributes are the predicting attributes. Class can then be defined by condition on the attributes. When the classes are defined, the system should be able to infer the rules that govern classification, in other words the system should find the description of each class (Dilly 1995).

Production rules have been widely used to represent knowledge in expert systems and they have the advantage of being easily interpreted by human experts because of their modularity i.e. a single rule can be understood in isolation and doesn't need reference to other rules (Dilly 1995).

Genetic Algorithms

Genetic algorithms are a relatively new software paradigm inspired by Darwin's theory of evolution. A population of individuals, each representing a possible solution to a problem, is initially created at random. Then pairs of individuals combine to produce offspring for the next generation. A mutation process is also used to randomly modify the genetic structure of some members of each new generation (Genetic Algorithms 1996).

Genetic algorithms also generate rules from data sets, but do not follow the exploration-oriented protocol of rule induction. Instead, they rely on the idea of "mutation" to make changes in patterns until a suitable form of pattern emerges via selective breeding. The genetic crossover operation is in fact very similar to the operation breeders use when they crossbreed plants and/or animals. The exchange of genetic material by chromosomes is also based on the same method (A Characterization of Data Mining Technologies and Processes, 2 May 1998). Genetic algorithms are not just for rule generation and may be applied to a variety of other tasks to which rules do not immediately apply, such as the discovery of patterns in text, planning and control, and system optimization, etc. (Holland 1995).

Nearest Neighbor

Nearest neighbor is a technique that classifies each record in a dataset based on a combination of the classes of the k record(s) most similar to it in a historical dataset (where k is greater than or equal to 1). Nearest Neighbor is sometimes called the k-nearest neighbor technique (White Pape 1997).

Implications of Data Mining for Advertising Management

This discussion will focus on two areas of advertising management: Direct Response Advertising and Interactive Advertising and the related area of Customer Service.

Direct Response Advertising

The direct advertising and marketing industry is focused on choosing from millions of potential clients or prospects the people who are most likely to respond to an offer and then targeting a specific mailing or telesales campaign to them. By better targeting the candidates, not only does the response rate increase, but also the cost for each positive response goes down. A credit card company can leverage its vast warehouse of customer transaction data to identify customers most likely to be interested in a new credit product. Using a small test mailing, the attributes of customers with an affinity for the product can be identified. Recent projects have indicated more than a 20-fold decrease in costs for targeted mailing campaigns over conventional approaches (Hodel 1998).

Interactive Advertising

Interactive marketing and advertising are interested, among other things, in predicting what each individual accessing a Web site is most likely interested in seeing. A pharmaceutical company can analyze its recent sales force activity and their results to improve targeting of high-value physicians and determine which marketing activities will have the greatest impact in the next few months. The data needs to include competitor market activity as well as information about the local health care systems. The results can be distributed to the sales force via a wide-area network that enables the representatives to review the recommendations from the perspective of the key attributes in the decision process. The ongoing, dynamic analysis of the data warehouse allows best practices from throughout the organization to be applied in specific sales situations like selling the drugs on the World Wide Web (White Paper 1997).

Because of the Web's tracking ability, banner advertising can be exactly aimed to the target audience or potential customers who are most likely to click or respond using log file analysis process. Specifically data mining can help to discover a particular group of consumers with specific characteristics and behavior patterns. First of all, with server log files, geographic location, prior purchases browser type or past banner clicking can be obtained. From cookie files, an additional data component can be assembled and mined in order to discover the inclination for click-through and actual online sales. After this information is gathered, data mining can be used to infer customer composites about lifestyle similarity and characteristics. Based on all this information and data mining techniques, the advertising and marketing campaign will launch. Therefore the more targeted the ads, the higher the response will likely be obtained.

Customer Service

Whether they are shopping for toothpaste, a checking account or computers, consumers can choose from a range of products and services offering similar features for similar prices. Often, the only differentiator among suppliers is the quality of customer service they provide. Better understanding of customer's requirements through data mining holds the promise of helping companies to develop more attractive, focused service and support offerings (Data Mining for Competitive Advantage, 1997).

ADVERTISING MANAGEMENT CASE STUDY

The first author analyzed a data-set gathered by a Chicago mail-order company dealing with men's, women's, and children's shoes and home furnishing catalogs over several years. The objective of the company was 1) to reduce cost of mailing catalogs and 2) to increase the hit rate of mailings. The default model for women's catalogs is as follows: A total of 31,140 catalogs were sent out; from these, 6,545 made orders. So the hit rate was 21% as the default model (6,545/31,140=21%). The default model for home furnishing catalogs is as follows: A total of 31,140 catalogs were sent out; from these, 5,240 made orders. So the hit rate was 16.8 % as the default mode for home furnishings. A model was selected to satisfy the two objectives noted above. Coincidence Matrix Methodology was used because it is suitable to minimize the possibility of missing potential customers and to minimize the number of mailings needed to reach the majority of customers.

Generally speaking, Coincidence Matrix is a method to detect two or more unique events that occur almost simultaneously. Coincidence counting involves two or more event counters exposed to the same source of events and shows if there exists the relationship among events.

1) Women's catalog Model (Neural Net Model, Coincidence Matrix)

The results showed that if a total of 1,715 copies were sent out to the exact target audience, the hit rate would be 29.33%. So the hit rate is increased by 40 % (21% Vs 29.33%)

When the default model and the current model were compared, there is an interesting result. The total profit was increased by 37.3%. ((69,340- 50,498)/ 50,498)

Default model:

COGS: (31,140 X 5) + (6,546 X (63/2)) = $361,900

Revenue: 6,546 X $63 = $412,398

Profit: $ 50,498

Current Model:

COGS: (17,374 X 5) + (4,959 X (63/2)) = $243,078

Revenue: 4,959 X $63 = $312,417

Profit: $ 69,340.

2) Home's catalog Model (Neural Net Model, Coincidence Matrix)

The results in this case showed that if a total of 1,254 copies were sent out to the exact target audience, the hit rate would be 22.64%. So the hit rate is increased by 35 % (21% Vs 29.33%)

When Default model and the Current Model were compared, there is an interesting result. The total profit was increased by 56.36 %. ((50,498-33,192)/33,192)

Default model:

COGS: (31,140 X 5) + (5,240 X (82/1.7)) = $408,452

Revenue: 5,240 X $82 = $429,680

Profit: $ 50,498

Current Model:

COGS: (12,540 X 5) + (2,840 X (82/1.7)) = $199,688

Revenue: 2,840 X $82 = $232,880

Profit: $ 33,192

Profit increase by 56.36%.

CONCLUSION AND IMPLICATIONS

Data Mining is gaining wider acceptance in the general business community. To gain a competitive advantage in today's markets, data mining must be used to get the combination of hindsight and foresight to make proactive and knowledge-driven decisions a business needs to succeed. Success can be measured in increased profits, generating new revenue and providing a significant cost savings. However, data mining, with it strengths, has one down side.

The business must have knowledge people on its staff and the project could cost over a million dollars. The consequences of not doing data mining could be more disastrous with lost revenue, less customers or a market not being fully realized. There are many ways to do data mining through its various technologies. Now and in the future it will be coupled with other technologies such as OLAP (Online Analytical Processing) that will give businesses, a one-two punch for market success. The myths of data mining are just that: myths. As long as one does not expect results overnight, data mining may provide results. Finally, the application of data mining will continue to find answers where answers have not been found before. And this may be particularly true in the field of advertising where its application has not been universally adopted at the rate in some other areas of business.

ADVERTISING LAW

Advertising and promotions is bringing a service to the attention of potential and current customers. Advertising and promotions are best carried out by implementing an advertising and promotions plan. The goals of the plan should depend very much on the overall goals and strategies of the organization, and the results of the marketing analysis, including the positioning statement.

The plan usually includes what target markets you want to reach, what features and benefits you want to convey to them, how you will convey it to them (this is often called your advertising campaign), who is responsible to carry the various activities in the plan and how much money is budgeted for this effort. Successful advertising depends very much on knowing the preferred methods and styles of communications of the target markets that you want to reach with your ads. A media plan and calendar can be very useful, which specifies what advertising methods are used and when.

For each service, carefully consider: What target markets are you trying to reach with your ads? What would you like them to think and perceive about your products (this should be in terms of benefits to them, not you)? How can you get them to think and perceive that? What communications media do they see or prefer the most? Consider TV, radio, newsletters, classifieds, displays/signs, posters, word of mouth, press releases, direct mail, special events, brochures, neighborhood newsletters, etc.

What media is most practical for you to use in terms of access and affordability (the amount spent on advertising is often based on the revenue expected from the product or service, that is, the sales forecast)?

You can often find out a lot about your customers preferences just by conducting some basic market research methods.

Basic Methods to Get Feedback from Customers

Far too often, we think we know what our customers think and want because -- well, we just know, that's all. Wrong! Businesses can't be successful if they don't continue to meet the needs of their customers. Period. There should be few activities as important as finding out what your customers want for products and services and finding out what they think of yours. Fortunately, there are a variety of practical methods that businesses can use to feedback from customers.

The methods you choose and how you use them depend on what the type of feedback that you want from customers, for example, to find out their needs in products and services, what they think about your products and services, etc.

Employees

Your employees of usually the people who interact the most with your customers. Ask them about products and services that customers are asking for. Ask employees about what the customers complain about.

Comment Cards

Provide brief, half-page comment cards on which they can answer basic questions such as: Were you satisfied with our services? How could we provide the perfect services? Are there any services you'd like to see that don't exist yet?

Competition

What is your competition selling? Ask people who shop there. Many people don't notice sales or major items in stores. Start coaching those around you to notice what's going on with your competition.

Customers

One of the best ways to find out what customers want is to ask them. Talk to them when they visit your facility or you visit theirs.

Documentation and Records

Notice what customers are buying and not buying from you. If you already know what customers are buying, etc., then is this written down somewhere?

It should be so that you don't forget, particularly during times of stress or when trying to train personnel to help you out.

Focus Groups

Focus groups are usually 8-10 people that you gather to get their impressions of a product or service or an idea.

Surveys by Mail

You might hate answering these things, but plenty of people don't -- and will fill our surveys especially if they get something in return. Promise them a discount if they return the completed form to your facility.

Telephone Surveys

Hire summer students or part-time people for a few days every six months to do telephone surveys.

Major Methods of Advertising and Promotion (Methods of External Communications)

First, A Word About Writing Ads

It's almost useless to review lists of alternatives for advertising if you haven't developed well-written ads. Writing ads is a skill. There are important aspects to think about, including the wording, graphics, arrangement of wording and graphics, coloring, how your audience will interpret the ads, their placement, etc. Poorly done ads can hurt you worse than not having ads at all. Therefore, very carefully consider getting help to write your first ads.

What Should You Write in Your Ads?

The answer to this question depends almost entirely on the reading and listening habits of your current and potential customers. This is where some basic market research can help you a great deal. A lot can be learned by using a few basic methods.

Before you write your ads, you should give careful thought to your unique selling position so you know what unique features and benefits to convey and to whom. Review information in Positioning.

Note that a common mistake among inexperienced ad writers is to write the ad to themselves, rather than to their current and potential customers. Your ads should clearly the benefits (of products and services) to customers, not the benefits to you -- clearly state the ads in terms that the customer will value, for example, easy access, low cost, easy to use, reliability, etc. Your ads should answer the customer's question: "What's it it for me?" Your ad should also specify what they are to do next. What action should they take and how do they take it, for example, who do they call and how.

Major Methods of Advertising (Repeatedly Getting Message Out)

Brochures or Flyers

Many desk-top publishing and word-processing software packages can produce highly attractive tri-fold (an 8.5 inch by 11-inch sheet folded in thirds) brochures. Brochures can contain a great deal of information if designed well, and are becoming a common method of advertising.

Direct mail -- Mail sent directly from you to your customers can be highly customized to suit their nature and needs. You may want to build a mailing list of your current and desired customers.

Collect addresses from customers by noticing addresses on their checks, asking them to fill out information cards, etc. Keep the list online and up-to-date. Mailing lists can quickly become out-of-date. Notice mailings that get returned to you. This should be used carefully and it can incur substantial cost, you don't want to inundate your stakeholders with information so make the most of your message. (See Using Direct Mail and Mailing Lists.)

E-mail messages -- These can be wonderful means to getting the word out about your business. Design your e-mail software to include a "signature line" at the end of each of your e-mail messages. Many e-mail software packages will automatically attach this signature line to your e-mail, if you prefer. (See Netiquette - Techniques and styles of writing e-mail messages and E-mail vs. voice mail.)

Magazines -- Magazines ads can get quite expensive. Find out if there's a magazine that focuses on your particular industry. If there is one, then the magazine can be very useful because it already focuses on your market and potential customers. Consider placing an ad or writing a short article for the magazine. Contact a reporter to introduce yourself. Reporters are often on the look out for new stories and sources from which to collect quotes.

Newsletters -- This can be powerful means to conveying the nature of your organization and its services. Consider using a consultant for the initial design and layout. Today's desktop publishing tools can generate very interesting newsletters quite inexpensively.

Newspapers (major) - Almost everyone reads the local, major newspaper(s). You can get your business in the newspaper by placing ads, writing a letter to the editor or working with a reporter to get a story written about your business. Advertising can get quite expensive. Newspaper are often quite useful in giving advice about what and how to advertise. Know when to advertise -- this depends on the buying habits of your customers.

Newspapers (neighborhood) -- Ironically, these are often forgotten in lieu of major newspapers, yet the neighborhood newspapers are often closest to the interests of the organization's stakeholders.

Online discussion groups and chat groups -- As with e-mail, you can gain frequent exposure to yourself and your business by participating in online discussion groups and chat groups. Note, however, that many groups have strong groundrules against blatant advertising. When you join a group, always check with the moderator to understand what is appropriate.

Posters and bulletin boards -- Posters can be very powerful when placed where your customers will actually notice them. But think of how often you've actually noticed posters and bulletin boards yourself. Your best bet is to place the posters on bulletin boards and other places which your customers frequent, and always refresh your posters with new and colorful posters that will appear new to passers by. Note that some businesses and municipalities have regulations about the number of size of posters that can be placed in their areas.

Radio announcements -- A major advantage of radio ads is they are usually cheaper than television ads, and many people still listen to the radio, for example, when in their cars. Ads are usually sold on a package basis that considers the number of ads, the length of ads and when they are put on the air. . A major consideration with radio ads is to get them announced at the times that your potential customers are listening to the radio.

Telemarketing -- The use of telemarketing is on the rise.

Television ads -- Many people don't even consider television ads because of the impression that the ads are very expensive. They are more expensive than most of major forms of advertising. However, with the increasing number of television networks and stations, businesses might find good deals for placing commercials or other forms of advertisements. Television ads usually are priced with similar considerations to radio ads, that is, the number of ads, the length of ads and when they are put on the air.

Web pages -- You probably would not have seen this means of advertising on a list of advertising methods if you had read a list even two years ago. Now, advertising and promotions on the World Wide Web are almost commonplace. Businesses are developing Web pages sometimes just to appear up-to-date. Using the Web for advertising requires certain equipment and expertise, including getting a computer, getting an Internet service provider, buying (usually renting) a Website name, designing and installing the Website graphics and other functions as needed (for example, an online store for e-commerce), promoting the Website (via various search engines, directories, etc.) and maintaining the Website. (See Building, Managing and Promoting Your Website and Online Advertising and Promotions.)

Yellow Pages --The Yellow Pages can be very effective advertising if your ads are well-placed in the directory's categories of services, and the name of your business is descriptive of your services and/or your ad stands out (for example, is bolded, in a large box on the page, etc.). The phone company will offer free advice about placing your ad in the Yellow Pages. They usually have special packages where you get a business phone line along with a certain number of ads.

Promotional Activities Through the Media (Reporters, Newspapers, etc.)

Articles that you write -- Is there something in your industry or market about you have a strong impression? Consider writing an article for the local newspaper or a magazine. In your article, use the opportunity to describe what you're doing to address the issue through use of your business.

Editorials and letters to the editor -- Often, program providers are experts at their service and understanding a particular need in the community; newspapers often take strong interest in information about these needs, so staff should regularly offer articles (of about 200 to 900 words) for publication.

Press kits -- This kit is handy when working with the media or training employees about working with the media. The kit usually includes information about your business, pictures, information about your products, commentary from happy customers, etc.

Press releases or news alerts -- They alert the press to a major event or accomplishment and requesting, e.g., it get included in the newspaper; they explain who, what, where, why and when; some include pictures, quotes, etc. to make it easier for the reporter to develop an announcement or story.

Public service announcements (PSA)s -- Many radio and some television stations will provide public service announcements for nonprofit efforts. Usually, these PSAs are free.

Other Promotional Activities and Events

Annual reports - Disseminate these to key stakeholders; they're ripe with information if they include an overview of your year's activities, accomplishments, challenges and financial status.

Collaboration or strategic restructuring-If you're organization is undertaking these activities, celebrate it publicly.

Networking-Spread the word to peers, professional organizations and those with whom you interact outside the organizations, e.g., educators, consultants, suppliers, clients, etc.

Novelties -- It seems more common to find ads placed on pens and pencils, coffee cups, T-shirts, etc. These can be powerful means of advertising if indeed current and potential customers see the novelties. This condition often implies additional costs to mail novelties, print T-shirts, etc.

Presentations -- You're probably an expert at something. Find ways to give even short presentations, for example, at local seminars, Chamber of Commerce meetings, trade shows, conventions, seminars, etc. It's amazing that one can send out 500 brochures and be lucky to get 5 people who respond. Yet, you can give a presentation to 30 people and 15 of them will be very interested in staying in touch with you.

Relationships with key stakeholders -- Identify at least one representative from each major stakeholder group and take them to lunch once a year. What seem as short, informal exchanges can cultivate powerful relationships of interest and concern.

Special events -- These tend to attract attention, and can include, e.g., an open house, granting a special award, announcing a major program or service or campaign, etc.

Special offers -- We see these offers all the time. They include, for example, coupons, discounts, sweepstakes, sales, etc.

PROCUREMENT, CONTRACTING AND ADVERTISING MANAGEMENT IN THE FEDERAL GOVERNMENT: LATEST DEVELOPMENTS

In the wake of the observations made by the Office of the Auditor General and the sponsorship scandal, many changes have been made to the federal government's procurement process and contracting rules in order to strengthen oversight, transparency and accountability. This document addresses these issues and consists of two parts. The first part highlights the reforms undertaken by the federal government with regard to the procurement of goods and services, and the recommendations of a task force that was established to study the subject. The second part describes progress made in the management of federal government advertising programs and sets out the main recommendations of the Gomery Commission on the subject. Both parts include a summary of the commitments on these issues made by the Conservative Party in the recent election campaign.

REFORM OF PROCUREMENT AND CONTRACTING

Current Situation

The Government of Canada buys approximately $14 billion worth of goods and services every year from thousands of suppliers. Among the 85 departments, agencies, Crown corporations and Special Operating Agencies, Public Works and Government Services Canada (PWGSC) is the government's largest purchasing organization, averaging 60,000 contracts totalling $10 billion annually. While PWGSC buys goods for most federal departments, the departments themselves buy most of the services they need.

On 12 December 2003, the Prime Minister named the Honourable Walt Lastewka as Parliamentary Secretary to the Minister of Public Works and Government Services, with special emphasis on procurement review. The Deputy Minister of PWGSC and the Assistant Deputy Minister of PWGSC's Acquisitions Branch established a Task Force to support Mr. Lastewka in his mandate. The Task Force was made up of staff from PWGSC, the Department of Justice, the Department of National Defence and the Treasury Board Secretariat (TBS), as well as a private-sector consultant. Task Force members had a broad background in procurement and significant experience in the public sector, and they were supported by an interdepartmental committee of Directors General. The Task Force was established at the same time as the Expenditure Review Committee, a new Cabinet committee responsible for reviewing all federal expenditures.

The federal government is committed to fundamental reforms in the way it procures goods and services. It is seeking a government-wide procurement system that is based on integrity, accountability and transparency, and that is faster, simpler, and reduces product and process costs. Significant savings can be achieved by eliminating overlap and duplication across government, and investing in a system that creates a competitive environment that is fair for all involved. These savings can then be reallocated to support the priorities that matter most to Canadians. The final report of the Task Force on the Government-wide Review of Procurement was tabled in January 2005; its main recommendations are presented in the following section of this paper.

In the interim, the Liberal government announced and implemented a series of measures:

1. On 23 March 2004, the government announced a new policy on the mandatory publication of contracts over $10,000. The TBS Web site provides information on contracts issued by or on behalf of the TBS. Since 31 October 2004, the Web site has been updated every three months to include information on new contracts awarded.
2. On 24 October 2005, the President of the Treasury Board announced an investment of up to $35 million per year for a new "learning and development initiative" for public servants, which includes training of specialists in the fields of finance, audit, and procurement.
3. On 25 October 2005, the President of the Treasury Board released a document entitled Management in the Government of Canada: A Commitment to Continuous Improvement, in which he unveiled a series of management reforms intended to improve management practices and enhance accountability.

Recommendations of the Task Force on the Government-wide Review of Procurement

Mr. Lastewka's Task Force made numerous recommendations aimed at clarifying the government-wide objectives of procurement, eliminating overlap and duplication across the government, and allocating and managing sufficient resources to ensure effective service delivery across government. Key recommendations are presented below.

Management of Procurement: The government should adopt a corporate approach to managing procurement, based on the best overall value for Canadians. Commodity plans, or appropriate portions thereof, should be made available as public documents to ensure transparency.

Dispute and Redress Mechanisms: The government should consider reviewing the existing dispute resolution mechanism in light of the findings included in the Task Force's report. There should be a robust government-wide approach to contract management, supplier performance and dispute resolution. For both contract award disputes and contract performance disputes, the procurement officer should remain the first point of contact to resolve disputes. For disputes over contract performance, any additional measure to address particular circumstance should be reflected in the commodity plan and contract.

Procurement Responsibilities: Where government-wide procurement tools and systems are available, their use should be mandatory and subject to continuous improvement. Requirements that cannot be met through these tools and systems should be handled in accordance with the applicable commodity management plan. Authority to use the tools should be widely delegated to departments, and within the tools, the only limitations on purchasing should be those associated with spending authority.

Commodity Management: The government should manage its procurement of all goods, services and construction based on government-wide, commodity management planning, taking into consideration the total cost of ownership and the risks associated with any given commodity.

Sourcing: The government should recognize that open competition is not necessarily the only measure of value, and, therefore, it should be replaced as the key performance measure. Each commodity plan should demonstrate which sourcing mechanism will achieve best value for money in procurement and adherence to the trade agreements: open competition; competition between qualified suppliers; or non-competitive or sole-source contracting.

Procurement Tools: PWGSC should develop appropriate corporate procurement tools that fully reflect value for money and meet the needs of departments. PWGSC should ensure that these tools are readily accessible and easy to use. Procurement terminology should definitely be standardized for use on a government-wide basis. Standardized plain language documents should be developed to contribute to the simplification and efficiency of the contracting process.

Working With Suppliers: To speed up procurement, and where appropriate, a pre-qualification process for suppliers should be created. Pre-qualification criteria should include performance history, professional and industry standards, business management systems and/or other applicable core requirements. Suppliers' performance should have a bearing on future business. PWGSC should develop common performance standards and measures for departments to use when evaluating suppliers during and after the selection process and the life of the contract. Resulting performance data, collected by departments, should be reported to PWGSC in a timely manner. Performance incentives, value engineering (i.e. sharing of innovation costs and savings), business guarantees, information sharing and other such approaches should be included in commodity plans and used to develop more effective relationships. In developing performance measures, PWGSC should develop a methodology that will reward superior performance and penalize poor performance.

Human Resources: All individuals who exercise procurement authority should have appropriate procurement training reflecting the qualifications needed to make informed decisions related to procurement.

A number of these recommendations have been implemented, including the development of a federal procurement policy based on government-wide product management, the mandatory use of existing procurement tools throughout government, where these are available, and human resources training in accordance with the new operational model.

The Conservative Party's Election Platform

In its platform for the recent election campaign, the Conservative Party of Canada promised to clean up the procurement of federal government contracts. It stated that it would:

- o Review and amend all contracting rules to make the government's procurement process free from political interference.
- o Appoint a Procurement Auditor to ensure that all procurements are fair and transparent, and to address complaints from vendors.
- o Permit smaller vendors and vendors outside of the National Capital Region to receive due consideration for government contracts.

REFORM OF ADVERTISING MANAGEMENT

Current Situation

In 2002, the government made far-reaching changes to its advertising policies and procedures. It subsequently responded to the November 2003 report of the Auditor General - which led to the creation of the Commission of Inquiry into the Sponsorship Program and Advertising Activities (the Gomery Commission) - by adopting a series of measures intended to improve the situation:

- An increase in the number of suppliers for advertising, the number of opportunities for firms to compete and the variety of procurement methods;
- Payments based on hourly remuneration, not commission-based remuneration (the source of frequent abuses in the past); other methods of payment - such as retainers and performance-based methods - may be considered when warranted;
- Selection of a new Agency of Record through a competitive Request for Proposals (RFP) process;
- Implementation of an amended requirement of 80% Canadian content;
- Ongoing strengthening of internal capacity; and
- Issuance of an annual report on government advertising activities, to increase transparency.

- These new policies and procedures have been accompanied by a number of structural and administrative changes:
- The elimination of Appendix Q of the Treasury Board Regulations on advertising, together with the integration of advertising into the standard contracting policy which came into effect on 1 January 2003;
- The strengthening of management oversight mechanisms through:
  * the centralization of decision-making on advertising in the Strategic Communications Planning section of the Privy Council Office; and
  * the establishment of two new organizations in PWGSC to manage and coordinate advertising projects: the Public Opinion Research and Advertising Coordination Directorate, and the Communication Procurement Directorate.

Key Recommendations of the Gomery Commission to Complete the Reforms Already Under Way

The Gomery Commission's first recommendation(5) on government advertising is that the current Government of Canada definition of "advertising" be amended to conform to accepted advertising industry standards, and be included in the government Communications Policy and other related documents.

The recent changes announced by the President of the Treasury Board include enhancements to the audit function that are intended to strengthen these oversight mechanisms. In the Commission's opinion, this system appears to be comprehensive and may well prove to be a success. However, the Commission also suggests that the government consider further measures, including:

- o an instruction by the Office of the Comptroller General to each department and agency to conduct an annual audit of departmental advertising programs and processes, foreseeing that, in due course, it will be possible to make an annual decision by modifying or eliminating this requirement;

- a comprehensive audit of government advertising initiatives by the Office of the Auditor General in either fiscal year 2006/07 or 2007/08, to verify that the new processes and policies in place are ensuring fairness, value for money, effectiveness, training and, above all, the elimination of political intervention in the management and administration of advertising activities; and
- independent assessments of the views of government departments and agencies, advertising firms and the public on the efficiency and effectiveness of the new advertising management systems and policies, and on any other impact or consequence.

Finally, the federal government should promote competent management of advertising and sponsorship activities through training and certification.

The Conservative Party's Election Platform

In the recent election campaign, the Conservative Party of Canada promised to clean up government advertising and contracting activities, to ensure that they are not used for partisan purposes by government, or for the private benefit of contract recipients. The Party stated that it would:

- Ensure that all government public opinion research is automatically published within six months of the completion of the project, and prohibit verbal-only reports.
- Ensure that an independent review is conducted of government public opinion research practices discussed in Chapter 5 of the Auditor General's November 2003 report to determine whether further action, such as a judicial inquiry, is required.
- Open up the bidding process for government advertising and public opinion contracts to prevent insider firms from monopolizing government business.

PROCUREMENT: GOVERNMENT-WIDE RESPONSIBILITIES

Governing Legislation

- o Federal procurement is carried out within a framework of more than 15 Acts of Parliament and more than 35 different policies.

Treasury Board

- o Sets government-wide procurement policies.
- o Sets limits on the project and contract approval authorities of ministers and approves projects and contracts above those limits.
- o Ensures government-wide overview.

Operating Departments and Agencies

- o Deliver programs and services for Canadians.
- o Develop operational requirements for goods and services.
- o Contract for goods (when delegated) and for services, within ministerial limits.
- o Use PWGSC services for other procurements.

International Trade/Industry Canada

- Negotiate government procurement provisions as part of trade agreements.

Program Departments

- Identify socio-economic programs/objectives that could be supported by procurement.
- Carry out program effectiveness evaluations.

Justice

- Provides legal advice on procurement transactions and issues.

Canadian International Trade Tribunal

- Reviews complaints about individual government procurements for compliance with trade agreements.

- Issues findings, recommends remedial actions; may award costs and other compensation.

Auditor General

- Reviews government operations to ensure compliance with policy and value for money.
- Recommends remedial action to the government.

PWGSC as a Common Service Organization (CSO)

- Carries out procurement for operating departments and agencies:
- mandatory for goods (unless delegated);
  - optional for services and construction.
  - Delegates goods procurement authority to departments.
  - Develops government-wide methods of supply.

In carrying out procurement for operating departments and agencies, the CSO through collaboration, is normally responsible for determining how services will be provided to meet the needs of its customers. The operating departments and agencies are generally responsible for determining what they need, where and when. Procurement, which includes market research, product planning and the soliciting, evaluating, selecting, negotiating, issuing, and administering of contracts, is the responsibility of the CSO which must ensure contracts are successfully executed in accordance with the agreed terms of time, cost and performance.

2

Advertising and Promotion

INTRODUCTION

You may have the finest product and the most attractive prices, but if potential customers don't know about your business, your chances of success are limited. Advertising and promotion refer to activities undertaken to increase sales or enhance the image of a product or business. Advertising is used primarily to inform the potential customer of:

(1) the availability of products or services,

(2) when they are in season,

(3) where you are located and

(4) anything special about your product.

Promotional activities are important for maintaining customer traffic throughout the market season-used early in the season to draw customers to your business and during the season to maintain customer traffic levels during slow periods.

Unfortunately, the benefits of advertising and promotion for direct farm marketers have yet to be consistently demonstrated. Promotion of farm products appears to be effective in some cases, but not in others. The potential for successful advertising and promotion is increased when products are clearly differentiated, are of exceptionally high quality, are very seasonal in nature or are new offerings. Research conducted on direct farm marketing indicates that advertising, with emphasis on product freshness and quality, is more likely to move produce than price cutting.

How much should you spend? It is considered good business in retail marketing to spend 2 to 3 percent of gross sales for advertising. A 1985 survey of direct farm marketers in the mid-Atlantic states showed that producers spent an average of 3 percent of sales on advertising. You may find you cannot afford to do as much advertising as you would like. Therefore, it is important to set priorities. A scattered shotgun approach with limited funds usually ends up with poor results. It is important to plan your advertising program, otherwise you may fritter away your hard earned dollars. Know your targeted customers and direct your appeals to them.

Be Honest and Factual

On-farm and roadside markets with that "something special" usually build their merchandising program around a distinguishing trademark-a unique sign, display, atmosphere or building design. Advertising is easier to remember and more appealing when backed up by a unique, easily illustratable business name or slogan that clearly and concisely states the nature of the business and/or the principle products sold, e.g., WILBER'S WATERMELONS, APPLE ANNE'S-Fruit, Cider, Bakery Goods, RATZLAFF'S CHEMICAL FREE PRODUCE. Avoid creative names that may serve to confuse your potential customer. Many successful on-farm businesses carry the owner's name, creating a more intimate and sincere relationship with the consumer.

In the summer of 1993, a survey was undertaken of the fresh farm produce outlets in Cochise County, Arizona. Visitors were asked how they learned about the direct farm market they were patronizing. A similar survey was completed in Michigan. The results, summarized as follows, give some indication of the effectiveness of different promotional activities. Let's now look at each of these promotional activities and how they might be used in your enterprise. To help you evaluate these advertising options, first ask yourself: Why am I considering doing this? What is it suppose to do? What are my goals? Then seek feedback from your customers, particularly new customers, as to how they heard about you, to determine which advertising media was most effective.

Word-of-mouth

What can you do to help your present customers spread the word? Provide visitors with your business card. Include fliers or coupons with each purchase and ask your customers to pass them on to family and friends. Develop and distribute "point of purchase" marketing materials and displays:

A "Fresh Farm Produce" buyers' guide and map (discussed later). Information on "how to" pick, reduce spoilage, can, freeze, dry produce, etc.

Recipes and Cooking Ideas

How to get to other farm outlets and community points of interest. Build repeat customers through customer satisfaction. Inquire into the customer's needs. Seek suggestions for improvement. If visitors have a bad experience or don't find what they were looking for, they not only don't return, but will also tell others where not to stop.

Maintain a guest register or ask customers to fill out a pre-printed card. Then mail them a postcard or flier at the start of next year's season thanking them for their business, indicating when different produce will be available and inviting them back. Hopefully they will also bring others. Consider having customers register directly on to a postcard. Later, print your message on the reverse side. This can save you a lot of time.

Media Coverage

The fresh farm produce outlets in the Willcox, Arizona area have been particularly successful in generating and receiving news coverage in local and regional newspapers and television. Not only has this media coverage been very effective in promoting the outlets, it is free.

The direct farm marketers in an area should consider banding together to generate media publicity. Name (contract with) a publicist to develop media opportunities and systematically generate positive publicity for the area's direct farm marketing outlets. This might be done through the local Chamber of Commerce. Organize a media tour of area outlets. Invite the media to special events.

(a) Classified ads in the food or for sale sections of the Want Ads of local and regional newspapers:

The ad should indicate what is for sale, when and where. Most direct farm marketers do not advertise price.

(b) Display ads in the entertainment or food section or in special supplements of regional newspapers: Such ads should be attractively designed and easy to read, with a limited number of words and a good use of white space. Incorporate a trademark or symbol in every ad so that it is quickly recognized by your regular customers. The advertising department of the newspaper can help you plan a layout. Since such ads are more expensive, cooperative funding should be explored with other area direct farm marketers. A group ad will convey to potential customers the wide variety of outlets, produce and experiences available, and assure visitors that they are likely to get what they want if they make the trip.

(c) Radio ads: Due to their higher cost, spot announcements on the radio must be short and to the point, 15 to 30 seconds. More frequent short announcements are believed to reach more people than less frequent longer ones. Frequent spot announcements can help create name recognition.

(d) Place information articles and/or advertising in area shopping guides, tourist publications, company and special interest news-letters targeted to specific audiences, e.g., Garden Clubs, health food, retirement communities, ethnic food.

(e) Yellow pages listing.

Roadside Signs

Road side signs are a particularly important information source once travelers are near your business or event. Road side signs can be hindrances if they are not done professionally and kept well maintained. If signs are unattractive, hard to read, home painted and unkept, your operation is likely to start with a bad impression. The entrance to you business should be clearly marked with a pull-off area on each side of the road.

Your initial road sign should, as a rule, be placed at least 2,500 feet from the entrance to your business to allow travelers a safe stopping distance. Then place several advance road signs out from your initial sign that state the distance to your business, e.g., JONES' PRODUCE, 2 MILES. Signage should start from the nearest Inter-state or major highway and clearly direct visitors to your business location. Roadside signs should contain six words or less, with a 1 or 2 word focal point to catch the traveler's interest. Use 7" to 12" letters and a good contrast of colors. The most easily read color combinations are black, dark blue, bottle green or scarlet red on white, yellow, orange or green. It is not always the size of the letters that make them readable, but the space or margins around them. Create a simple logo, such as the example provided, that provides easy recognition.

Media Advertising

There are a number of options for media advertising. Interviews with direct farm marketers indicate that the most commonly used mediums are:

Community Brochure/buyers' Guide

Many rural communities have developed an informational brochure or directory that lists all direct farm marketers in the area with a description of the products they offer. Also included is a map of the area with directions to each outlet and a harvest calendar indicating when different fruits and vegetables will be available. Such brochures are often developed with the aid of the county Cooperative Extension office and are funded through a subscription of those businesses listed. Printing and financial aid may also be available through a local utility or the state Department of Agriculture. Such directories will be effective, however, only if they are properly promoted and distributed to prospective customers. The printing cost of the brochure is small compared to the cost of promoting the directory, postage for mailing them and travel costs in placing the directory at travel information centers and brochure racks at strategic locations. This directory should also be distributed at the direct farm market outlets to assist with referrals and encourage return visitors and word-of-mouth promotion. This project might be coordinated by the local Chamber of Commerce.

The Willcox community has implemented a telephone service which out-of-town customers can call for a regularly updated recording indicating produce availability. The service is sponsored through subscriptions from the advertised businesses.

Referrals

Make sure that the employees of recreation and tourist facilities, motels, gasoline stations, restaurants, campgrounds, the Chamber of Commerce and other visitor oriented businesses are aware of your business. These people can help channel more customers to you. Make referrals.

Exchange customers. Help visitors find the products they are looking for. The Cochise County survey found that many visitors were not aware of the wide diversity of products available at other locations. Some returned home without purchasing sought-after items. When asked what other products or activities they would like to see offered, a significant number of visitors indicated a park/picnic area, swimming, horseback riding, a good place to eat-not knowing that those facilities were available in the Willcox community. A community brochure and map to local restaurants, museums, motels, retail shops, swimming and other recreational facilities should be available at the farm outlets.

Special Festivals

Agricultural festivals can be effective in attracting visitors to your community. They can generate additional sales if on-site activities are provided which bring potential customers in contact with your products. Such on-site activities might include things like hay rides, pick your own pumpkin (or watermelon), menudo cook-off, celebrity tomato pitch, watermelon seed spitting contest and farm tours. Unfortunately, the research indicates that limited spending on fresh farm products occurred at agricultural festivals mainly because such products (even those that the festival was named after) were not widely available. The festival activities often interfered with visitors getting to local businesses and on-farm outlets.

Special Tours

Field trips and special tours have proven effective in bringing people to the area and your business that might not have made it on their own. Such groups include garden clubs, residents of retirement communities, ethnic clubs, foreign visitors and company picnics. School tours have been effective in stimulating return visits by the children with their parents in tow.

Coupons, Special Discounts, Drawings

Experience indicates that general discounting can be counter productive in the direct marketing of farm produce. A discounted price suggests lower quality. The use of coupons can, however, help you track the effectiveness of different advertising media. In general it is recommended that discounts be expressed in whole dollars and cents rather than as a percent, and focus on increasing business during the slow seasons of the years. Giving your valued customers on unexpected benefit, e.g., free samples of new or slow moving produce may have a more positive impact than a discount.

Labels

Labels on bags, boxes, jars and containers reinforce your name to the consumer. Labels provide an opportunity for word-of-mouth advertising as guests to your customers' home observe your products. Generally, people will buy food items as gifts only when there is an attractive label indicating its origin and special qualities. Also labels can be effective in promoting the quality of your product, e.g., vine ripened, pesticide free, organic, high fiber, farm fresh, vitamin rich. Your name, logo and/or slogan can also be printed on T-shirts, aprons, hats and bags, for sale, to help your customers promote your business.

ADVERTISING AND PROMOTIONS MANAGER

- Prepare budgets and submit estimates for program costs as part of campaign plan development.

- Plan and prepare advertising and promotional material to increase sales of products or services, working with customers, company officials, sales departments and advertising agencies.
- Assist with annual budget development.
- Inspect layouts and advertising copy and edit scripts, audio and video tapes, and other promotional material for adherence to specifications.
- Coordinate activities of departments, such as sales, graphic arts, media, finance, and research.
- Prepare and negotiate advertising and sales contracts.
- Identify and develop contacts for promotional campaigns and industry programs that meet identified buyer targets such as dealers, distributors, or consumers.
- Gather and organize information to plan advertising campaigns.
- Confer with department heads and/or staff to discuss topics such as contracts, selection of advertising media, or product to be advertised.
- Confer with clients to provide marketing or technical advice.
- Monitor and analyze sales promotion results to determine cost effectiveness of promotion campaigns.
- Read trade journals and professional literature to stay informed on trends, innovations, and changes that affect media planning.
- Formulate plans to extend business with established accounts and to transact business as agent for advertising accounts.
- Provide presentation and product demonstration support during the introduction of new products and services to field staff and customers.
- Direct, motivate, and monitor the mobilization of a campaign team to advance campaign goals.
- Plan and execute advertising policies and strategies for organizations.

- Track program budgets and expenses and campaign response rates to evaluate each campaign based on program objectives and industry norms.
- Assemble and communicate with a strong, diverse coalition of organizations and/or public figures, securing their cooperation, support and action, to further campaign goals.
- Train and direct workers engaged in developing and producing advertisements.
- Coordinate with the media to disseminate advertising.
- Contact organizations to explain services and facilities offered.
- Direct and coordinate product research and development.
- Represent company at trade association meetings to promote products.
- Consult publications to learn about conventions and social functions and to organize prospect files for promotional purposes.

Requirements:

- Bachelor Degree in Commerce, Marketing or Administration.
- Minimum of 7 years experience.
- Strong English language skills. Including the meaning and spelling of words,
- Knowledge of principles and methods for showing, promoting, and selling products or services. This includes marketing strategy and tactics, product demonstration, sales techniques, and sales control systems.
- Knowledge of media production, communication, and dissemination techniques and methods. This includes alternative ways to inform and entertain via written, oral, and visual media.
- Knowledge of principles and processes for providing customer and personal services. This includes customer needs assessment, meeting quality standards for services, and evaluation of customer satisfaction.

- Knowledge of business and management principles involved in strategic planning, resource allocation, human resources modeling, leadership technique, production methods, and coordination of people and resources.
- Knowledge of design techniques, tools, and principles involved in production of precision technical plans, blueprints, drawings, and models.
- Knowledge of raw materials, production processes, quality control, costs, and other techniques for maximizing the effective manufacture and distribution of goods.
- Knowledge of administrative and clerical procedures and systems such as word processing, managing files and records, stenography and transcription, designing forms, and other office procedures and terminology.

3

Principles of Advertising

In the next five sections of the Principles of Marketing we begin an in-depth look at each promotional mix item. In this tutorial we present the first of a two-part examination of advertising with a discussion of basic concepts and trends. Our coverage of advertising continues in our next tutorial, Managing the Advertising Campaign, where we look at what decisions are needed to carryout a successful advertising campaign.

In this chapter we cover several fundamental issues in advertising including examining what advertising is and why it is important to the marketing organization. We also look at managing the advertising effort by comparing in-house management to that offered by advertising professionals, such as advertising agencies. Finally, the tutorial identifies different types of advertising and addresses trends facing the advertising industry.

WHAT IS ADVERTISING?

Advertising is a non-personal form of promotion that is delivered through selected media outlets that, under most circumstances, require the marketer to pay for message placement. Advertising has long been viewed as a method of mass promotion in that a single message can reach a large number of people. But, this mass promotion approach presents problems since many exposed to an advertising message may not be within the marketer's target market, and thus, may be an inefficient use of promotional funds. However, this is changing as new advertising technologies and the emergence of new media outlets offer more options for targeted advertising. Advertising also has a history of being considered a one-way form of marketing communication where the message receiver (i.e., target market) is not in position to immediately respond to the message (e.g., seek more information). This too is changing. For example, in the next few years technologies will be readily available to enable a television viewer to click a button to request more details on a product seen on their favorite TV program. In fact, it is expected that over the next 10-20 years advertising will move away from a one-way communication model and become one that is highly interactive.

Another characteristic that may change as advertising evolves is the view that advertising does not stimulate immediate demand for the product advertised. That is, customers cannot quickly purchase a product they see advertised. But as more media outlets allow customers to interact with the messages being delivered the ability of advertising to quickly stimulate demand will improve.

IMPORTANCE OF ADVERTISING

Spending on advertising is huge. One often quoted statistic by market research firm ZenithOptimedia estimates that worldwide spending on advertising exceeds (US) $400 billion. This level of spending supports thousands of companies and millions of jobs. In fact, in many countries most media outlets, such as television, radio and newspapers, would not be in business without revenue generated through the sale of advertising.

While worldwide advertising is an important contributor to economic growth, individual marketing organizations differ on the role advertising plays. For some organizations little advertising may be done, instead promotional money is spent on other promotion options such a personal selling through a sales team. For some smaller companies advertising may consist of occasional advertisement and on a very small scale, such as placing small ads in the classified section of a local newspaper.

But most organizations, large and small, that rely on marketing to create customer interest are engaged in consistent use of advertising to help meet marketing objectives. This includes regularly developing advertising campaigns, which involve a series of decisions for planning, creating, delivering and evaluating an advertising effort.

MANAGING ADVERTISING DECISIONS

Delivering an effective marketing message through advertising requires many different decisions as the marketer develops their advertising campaign. For small campaigns, that involve little creative effort, one or a few people may handle the bulk of the work. In fact, the Internet has made do-it-yourself advertising an easy to manage process and has especially empowered small businesses to manage their advertising decisions. As we will see, not only can small firms handle the creation and placement of advertisements that appear on the Internet, new services have even made it possible for a single person to create advertisements that run on local television. For instance, a company called SpotRunner allows users to select from a list of high-quality television ads that can be customized and then placed within local cable television programming.

For larger campaigns the skills needed to make sound advertising decisions can be quite varied and may not be easily handled by a single person. While larger companies manage some advertising activities within the company, they are more likely to rely on the assistance of advertising professionals, such as those found at advertising agencies, to help bring their advertising campaign to market.

ADVERTISING AGENCY FUNCTIONS

Professionals at advertising agencies and other advertising organizations offer a number of functions including:

Account Management-Within an advertising agency the account manager or account executive is tasked with handling all major decisions related to a specific client. These responsibilities include locating and negotiating to acquire clients. Once the client has agreed to work with the agency, the account manager works closely with the client to develop an advertising strategy. For very large clients, such as large consumer products companies, an advertising agency may assign an account manager to work full-time with only one client and, possibly, with only one of the client's product lines. For smaller accounts an account manager may simultaneously manage several different, though non-competing, accounts.

Creative Team-The principle role of account managers is to manage the overall advertising campaign for a client, which often includes delegating selective tasks to specialists.

For large accounts one task account managers routinely delegate involves generating ideas, designing concepts and creating the final advertisement, which generally becomes the responsibility of the agency's creative team. An agency's creative team consists of specialists in graphic design, film and audio production, copywriting, computer programming, and much more.

Researchers-Full-service advertising agencies employ market researchers who assess a client's market situation, including understanding customers and competitors, and also are used to test creative ideas.

For instance, in the early stages of an advertising campaign researchers may run focus group sessions with selected members of the client's target market in order to get their reaction to several advertising concepts. Researchers are also used following the completion of an advertising campaign to measure whether the campaign reached its objectives.

Media Planners-Once an advertisement is created, it must be placed through an appropriate advertising media. Each advertising media, of which there are thousands, has its own unique methods for accepting advertisements, such as different advertising cost structures (i.e., what it costs marketers to place an ad), different requirements for accepting ad designs (e.g., size of ad), different ways placements can be purchased (e.g., direct contact with media or through third-party seller), and different time schedules (i.e., when ad will be run). Understanding the nuances of different media is the role of a media planner, who looks for the best media match for a client and also negotiates the best deals.

TYPES OF ADVERTISING

If you ask most people what is meant by "type" of advertising, invariably they will respond by defining it in terms of how it is delivered (e.g., television ad, radio ad, etc.). But in marketing, type of advertising refers to the primary "focus" of the message being sent and falls into one of the following four categories:

Product-Oriented Advertising

Most advertising spending is directed toward the promotion of a specific good, service or idea, what we have collectively labeled as an organization's product. In most cases the goal of product advertising is to clearly promote a specific product to a targeted audience. Marketers can accomplish this in several ways from a low-key approach that simply provides basic information about a product (informative advertising) to blatant appeals that try to convince customers to purchase a product (persuasive advertising) that may include direct comparisons between the marketer's product and its competitor's offerings (comparative advertising). However, sometimes marketers intentionally produce product advertising where the target audience cannot readily see a connection to a specific product. Marketers of new products may follow this "teaser" approach in advance of a new product introduction to prepare the market for the product. For instance, one week before the launch of a new product a marketer may air a television advertisement proclaiming "After next week the world will never be the same" but do so without any mention of a product or even the company behind the ad. The goal is to create curiosity in the market and interest when the product is launched.

Image Advertising

Image advertising is undertaken primarily to enhance an organization's perceived importance to a target market. Image advertising does not focus on specific products as much as it presents what an organization has to offer. In these types of ads, if products are mentioned it is within the context of "what we do" rather than a message touting the benefits of a specific product. Image advertising is often used in situations where an organization needs to educate the targeted audience on some issue. For instance, image advertising may be used in situations where a merger has occurred between two companies and the newly formed company has taken on a new name, or if a company has received recent negative publicity and the company wants to let the market know that they are about much more than this one issue.

Advocacy Advertising

Organizations also use advertising to send a message intended to influence a targeted audience. In most cases there is an underlying benefit sought by an organization when they engage in advocacy advertising. For instance, an organization may take a stand on a political issue which they feel could negatively impact the organization and will target advertisements to voice their position on the issue.

Public Service Advertising

In some countries, not-for-profit organizations are permitted to run advertisements through certain media outlets free-of-charge if the message contained in the ad concerns an issue viewed as for the "greater good" of society. For instance, ads directed at social causes, such as teen-age smoking, illegal drug use and mental illness, may run on television, radio and other media without cost to organizations sponsoring the advertisement.

ADVERTISING TRENDS

Like most areas of marketing, advertising is changing rapidly. Some argue that change has affected advertising more than any other marketing function. The more important trends in advertising include:

DIGITAL CONVERGENCE

While many different media outlets are available for communicating with customers, the ability to distinguish between outlets is becoming more difficult due to the convergence of different media types. In advertising convergence, and more appropriately digital convergence, refers to a growing trend for using computer technology to deliver media programming and information. Convergence allows one media outlet to take advantage of features and benefits offered through other media outlets. For instance, in many areas around the world television programming is now delivered digitally via cable, telephone or satellite hookup. This delivery method uses the same principles of information delivery that is used to allow someone to connect the Internet.

The convergence of television and Internet opens many potential opportunities for marketers to target customers in ways not available with traditional television advertising. For example, technology may allow ads delivered to one household to be different than ads delivered to a neighbor's television even though both households are watching the same program. But convergence is not limited to just television.

Many media outlets are experiencing convergence as can be seen with print publications that now have a strong web presence. The future holds even more convergence opportunities. These include outdoor billboards that alter displays as cars containing geographic positioning systems (GPS) and other recognizable factors (e.g., GPS tied to satellite radio) pass by or direct mail postcards that carry a different message based on data that matches a household's address with television viewing habits.

FOCUS ON AUDIENCE TRACKING

The movement to digital convergence provides marketers with the basic resources needed to monitor user's activity, namely, digital data. Any media outlet that relies on computer technology to manage the flow of information does so using electronic signals that eventually form computer data. In simple form, electronic data is represented by either an "on" or "off" electronic signal.

In computer language this is further represented by two numbers "0" and "1" and, consequently, is known as digital information. All digital information can be stored and later evaluated. For media outlets delivering information in digital form, the potential exists for greater tracking and matching this with information about the person receiving the digital data. And tracking does not stop with what is delivered; it also works with information being sent from the customer. For instance, as we noted earlier, by clicking on their television screen viewers will soon be able to instantly receive information about products they saw while watching a television show. This activity can be tracked then used in future marketing efforts.

AUDIENCE CONCERN WITH TRACKING

While media convergence offers marketers more options for tracking response to advertisements, such activity also raises ethical and legal concerns. Many consumers are not pleased to learn their activities are being monitored when they engage a media outlet. Yet consider the following examples of how marketers are tracking users:

- *Television Viewing*-As we noted, the advent of digitally delivered television allows cable, telephone and satellite providers to track user activity through the set-top boxes connected to a subscriber's television. Future innovation will make the user television experience even more interactive and, consequently, open to even more tracking.
- *Television recording*-The days of television videotape recording are quickly coming to an end, replaced by recording using computer technology. A digitial video recorder (DVR), such as TiVo, can track users recording habits and, based on a viewer's past activity, make suggestions for programs they may want to record. Additionally, advertising services can program the DVR to insert special advertisements within a program targeted to a particular viewer.
- *Internet Spyware*-Downloading entertainment from the Internet, such as games, video and software, may contain a hidden surprise-spyware. Spyware is a special program that runs in the background of a user's computer and regularly forwards information over the Internet to the spyware's company. In some cases spyware keeps track of websites the user has visited. The information is then

used to gain an understanding of the user's interests, which then results in delivery of special ads when a user visits a certain site.

Ad Skipping and Blocking

As noted above, television recording devices offer marketers tremendous insight into viewers' habits and behavior. Yet from the consumer side, the DVR is changing how people view television programs by allowing them to watch programming at a time that is most convenient for them.

Viewer convenience is not the only advantage of the DVR. The other main reason consumers are attracted to the DVR is their ability to quickly skip over commercials. Of course this presents major issues for advertisers who are paying for advertisements. As more DVR devices with ad skipping or even ad blocking features are adopted by mainstream consumers the advertiser's concern with whether they are getting the best value for the advertising money becomes a bigger issue. Advertisers who feel frustrated with television ad-skipping may opt to invest their promotional funds in other media outlets where consumers are more likely to be exposed to an advertisement.

Changing Media Choices

There is a major cultural shift occurring in how people use media for entertainment, news and information. Many traditional media outlets, such as newspapers and major commercial television networks, are seeing their customer base eroded by the emergence of new media outlets. The Internet has become the major driver of this change. In particular, a number of important applications tied to the Internet are creating new media outlets and drawing the attention of many, mostly younger, consumers. Examples include:

- *Podcasting Audio*-This involves delivering programming via downloadable online audio that can be listened to on music players, such as Apple's iPod. Many news websites and even other information site, such as blogs, offer free downloadable audio programming.

- *Podcasting Video*-While audio downloading has been available for some time, the downloading of video to small, handheld devices, including cellphones, is in its infancy. Many television networks are now experimenting with making their programming available for download, albeit, for a fee.
- *RSS Feeds*-This is an Internet information distribution technology that allows for news and content to be delivered instantly to anyone who has signed up for delivery. Clearly those registering for RSS feeds represent a highly targeted market since they requested the content.
- *Networked Gaming*-While gaming systems have been around for some time, gaming systems attached to the Internet for group play is relatively new and becoming more practical as more people move to faster Internet connections. This type of setup will soon allow marketers to insert special content, such as advertising, within game play.

For marketers these new technologies should be monitored closely as they become accepted alternatives to traditional media outlets.

While these technologies are currently not major outlets for advertising, they may soon offer such opportunity. As these technologies gain momentum and move into mainstream acceptance marketers may need to consider shifting advertising spending.

Marketers should also be aware that new media outlets will continue to emerge as new applications are developed. The bottom line for marketers is they must stay informed of new developments and understand how their customers are using these in ways that may offer advertising opportunities.

In 1923, there were 26 metropolitan daily newspapers in Australia owned by 21 proprietors.

By 1950, the number had fallen to 15 metropolitan dailies having 10 owners. By 1987, there were three major proprietors of the metropolitan dailies-the Herald and Weekly Times Limited

(HWT), News Limited (News), and John Fairfax Holdings Limited (Fairfax)-as well as a small number of independent publishers with newspapers in one city, which shrank to two when News Limited took over HWT that year.

Metropolitan Press

Five companies own most of the newspapers of Australia. By far the biggest is News Limited which controls 68 per cent of the market (70 per cent of metropolitan newspapers and 30-35 per cent of all Australian newspapers measured by circulation). The next biggest, Fairfax, owns 21 per cent. They control all of the metropolitan press except for West Australian Newspapers (The West Australian, eight per cent) and Rural Press (Canberra Times, three per cent).

Regional Dailies

As with the metropolitan newspapers the majority of regional dailies are owned by the five biggest companies. Only four are owned by independent family-owned companies.

Table. Ownership and circulation of regional dailies 2004

Company	Titles	Circulation	% of total
APN	13	162,496	27.2
Fairfax	3	95,030	15.9
News Limited	4	137,028	23.0
Rural Press	9	127,292	21.3
WA Newspapers	1	5,746	0.9
Independent	6[16]	68,382	11.5
Total	36	595,974	99.8

Source Communication Update: Communications Law Centre June 2005

SUBURBAN, RURAL AND COMMUNITY NEWSPAPERS

Newspapers in these categories are also predominantly owned by the main companies, News Limited, APN and Rural Press. Details of the circulation and ownership of each paper are listed in Communication Update a publication of the Communications Law Centre and in the appendix of the Australian Press Council Annual Reports.

Ownership Restrictions

The existing laws, restricting cross-media ownership between television and newspapers, have been in force since 1992. They were introduced with the intention of maintaining diversity in all forms of media and enhancing public access to a variety of viewpoints. Several failed attempts to reform these laws have been made since.

The controls are embodied chiefly through the Broadcasting Services Act. Where it impacts on the print media, that legislation restricts the holder of a commercial television licence or a commercial radio broadcasting licence from owning a newspaper in the same licence area. In essence, that means a television or radio station owner in a city such as Sydney or Melbourne cannot own a newspaper that also services that same area. There are additional laws that restrict foreign ownership. They restrict aggregate foreign ownership of national and metropolitan newspapers to 30 per cent. Ownership by foreign individuals is capped at 25 per cent.

Shareholdings of portfolio investors are restricted to 5 per cent, but there is provision for applications to be made to allow higher levels. Aggregate foreign shareholding of provincial and suburban newspapers is held to 50 per cent. There are no cross-media or foreign shareholding restrictions placed on magazines, the ethnic community press or online information sites.

Because of the cross media rules, the owners of the major broadcast networks are separate from the metropolitan newspaper owners. The three major network owners are PBL (Nine Network, except Perth & Adelaide); Kerry Stokes's group (Seven); and Canwest (Ten). APN as well as owning newspapers is a major owner of radio stations. Some other radio network owners (such as Southern Cross) also have small television interests. The only restrictions on concentration of press ownership are contained in the Trade Practices Act, which sets out Australian anti-trust law and applies to all industries. Section 46 proscribes the abuse of monopoly power through predatory practices. Section 50 proscribes the attainment or increase of a dominant position in a market. However, these may be authorised if there is a public benefit in the take-over.

The Australian Competition and Consumer Commissioner's view is that the product market for the press is the newspaper industry, not all media, and that for most metropolitan newspapers the market is limited to the state concerned.

A report of a parliamentary committee in 1992 found no abuses of concentration and made no recommendations concerning initiatives to create new newspapers. However, all members of the committee agreed that "...concentration of ownership is potentially harmful to plurality of opinion and increases the potential risk that news may be distorted" and accordingly urged that the risk of further concentration "...should be minimised'.

The report seemed to accept that, if new newspapers were created, there would be a market battle that would result in only one newspaper emerging. It recommended that the test in Section 50 of the Trade Practices Act be amended to return to the pre-1977 proscription of takeovers that would result, or be likely to result, in a substantial lessening of competition.

Proposed Changes to Ownership Restrictions

In 2006, the Federal Government released proposals that would result in substantial changes in laws that govern control and ownership of print media companies and assets. At the time of writing, the new rules have yet to be framed and placed before the Parliament.

Pressure to amend the laws has mounted because of the emergence of new forms of media-especially digital media that can be made available online or in mobile form-from convergence of different mediums and from increased diversity in some areas.

The centrepiece of the proposed new laws for print media is the removal of cross-media restrictions and the imposition of new rules that set minimum limits to the number of independent voices in any given market. The limit would be five independent newspaper, television and radio operators in metropolitan markets and four in regional markets. The proposal allows considerable room for consolidation, and could result in significant media industry takeovers.

Any such actions would be regulated by the Australian Competition and Consumer Commissioner under the general merger provisions of the Trade Practices Act. The Australian Communications and Media Authority would be charged with ensuring that transactions comply with diversity requirements and the minimum limits.

The plan would result in foreign ownership limits being scrapped, but the media industry would still be subject to the "sensitive sector" provisions of the government's foreign investment policy. Sensitive sectors have tighter restrictions for requiring permission from the Federal Treasurer to exceed a 15 per cent shareholding and also involve more rigorous examination processes for approval.

ECONOMIC HEALTH NEWSPAPERS

Print media companies have enjoyed five years of growing revenues. The largest impact has come from a marked increase in advertising sales.

Published financial accounts show that metropolitan newspaper publishers had, by 2005, fully recovered from less favourable conditions in the wake of the introduction of the Goods and Services Tax in July 2000 to reach a level where their operating margins generally were running near the peak levels of previous economic cycles. Gross profits typically were in the range 25 per cent to 30 per cent of revenues, up from low levels of under 20 per cent.

Regional newspaper groups have returned a steadier pattern of growth and margin maintenance during that period, not having suffered to the same degree in 2001 and 2002 after the introduction of the GST. Margins are in a 30 per cent to 40 per cent range.

A study by PricewaterhouseCoopers (Australian Entertainment and Media Outlook 2006-2010, August 2006), shows that total newspaper industry revenues were $5.1bn in 2005, 14 per cent higher than the level of 2001. They had slumped to $4.35bn in 2002. The survey predicts an annual rise of three per cent to $5.84bn in 2010. About three-quarters of revenues come from advertising, which is predicted to increase at an average annual rate of four per cent-amounting to between $150m per annum (see section below on advertising trends).

Desirable but missing data for future editions would be trends in the employment of journalists, both for the print and internet activities of the paper, and trends annually in pagination, that is, the average size of newspapers in terms of number of pages for particular days of the week.

Circulation revenues on an industry basis now amount to $1.3bn. They have experienced considerable fluctuation as the sales of newspapers decline and aggressive promotional subscription offers are made. After a drop of 9.9 per cent in 2001, circulation revenues have slowly turned around to be running about one per cent annual growth, a trend predicted to continue through 2010. There is considerable variance between metropolitan and regional newspapers, brought about by migration of people to Queensland and to coastal towns on the east coast. This spurs greater growth in many regional areas. The other main reason for the current circulation revenue rise is increase in cover price.

Magazines

Magazine publishers have also been recovering from a downturn that started five years ago, but they have rebounded faster than newspaper companies. PricewaterhouseCoopers reports that this segment grew by 6.1 per cent in 2005, when revenues exceeded $2bn for the first time. It expects future revenue growth until 2010 to run at an average annual rate over four per cent. Revenues streams are evenly divided between advertising and circulation, although advertising is expanding slightly more rapidly. The main causes of circulation revenue growth are increased unit sales, revitalised categories, new titles and cover price rises.

The magazine industry covers a broad range of interests, from fashion to celebrity, special interest to news. The performance of any given category can vary significantly from year to year, with celebrity and fashion being two of the recent high growth areas. There has also been sizeable expansion in magazines that are inserted in newspapers. They enjoy wide distribution and have quickly attracted advertising support. It is a trend that is likely to continue.

The Industry

The improvement in the industry's financial health has resulted in an increased investment in news rooms, but the extent to which this occurring is difficult to quantify. Funds are being spent on newspaper and magazine websites in an attempt to capitalise on the rapid expansion in advertising through this medium.

Newspapers now frequently update their websites, with news stories written by members of staff through the day rather than running articles supplied by wire services. A considerable number of staff are devoted to the production of inserted magazines and lifestyle sections, some of which add to staff levels. Available total headcounts often show strong rises, but these are misleading because most major publishers in recent years have expanded by making acquisitions within Australia and overseas.

Advertising Revenue Trends

Advertising revenue has rebounded strongly in recent years, but its continued strength depends directly on domestic economic conditions. Some print media companies have recently cautioned that the outlook is weakening because of factors such as increased fuel costs. Consumer sentiment and retail spending are both displaying weakening trends, and they have a considerable impact on both advertising and circulation.

Newspapers

Total advertising expenditure in newspapers has been growing since 2002 at an annual amount reaching $300m. That reflects high single digit growth. PricewaterhouseCoopers predicts that this will moderate, but still continue at an annual rate around 3.5 per cent until 2010. About two-thirds of the growth comes from display advertising.

Display advertising makes up 57.6 per cent of the advertising stream, up from 52.3 per cent in 2002. To be most effective, display advertising requires full colour printing. That has become more widely available in recent years, allowing colour advertisements to run on many pages of a newspaper. Publishers are also focusing on inserts and the development of lifestyle sections and premium magazines, which open doors to new display advertisers. This trend should continue as newspaper companies sell more, higher margin colour display advertising. To this end, the major publishers have recently formed a new industry body to promote their colour printing capacities to advertisers.

Classified advertising, long known as "the rivers of gold" for newspapers such as The Age and The Sydney Morning Herald, is diminishing in importance as advertisers are attracted to online sites and specialist publications. According to the 2006 survey, Classified revenue grew by 1.4 per cent to $1.6bn (compared with the 2.2 per cent overall growth in newspaper advertising). In 2002 classifieds accounted for 47.7 per cent of advertising in newspapers; this share is now down to 42.4 per cent.

Magazines

Magazine advertising grew by 9.3 per cent in 2005. One reason for this was the strong increase in circulation, enhancing magazines' attractiveness as an advertising medium. The 2006 survey predicts growth at about five per cent for the rest of the decade, outpacing the predicted growth in newspaper advertising revenue.

The Industry

The largest threat for advertising comes in the form of competing online sites. Consumers are spending more time using the internet and advertisers are finding new ways to reach them, either by placing advertisements on those sites or by supporting search engines. A global report by Boston Consulting Group (Finding the Sweet Spot in Online Search, July 2006) says that the time consumers spent between 1999 and 2004 on newspapers, magazines, radio and television rose or fell by just a couple of percentage points. But time spent on the Internet escalated by 24 per cent. Online advertising expenditure rose by 22 per cent, whereas traditional media spending declined.

A similar trend is evident in Australia. Price water house Coopers says that Internet advertising in 2005 topped $500m for the first time, reaching $620m, compared with $160m in 2001. It expects annual growth exceeding 20 per cent for the rest of the decade, with revenues reaching $1.78bn by 2010. The annual dollar expansion in the near term is predicted to be around $200m. That is about the same dollar growth expected for newspapers. On the other hand, UK media buyer Group M has recently estimated that Internet advertising this year will beat for the first time advertising in national newspapers in that country.

The online trend is particularly impacting print media's grip on classified advertising. The three core categories of internet advertising, general, classifieds and search & directories, each experienced strong growth in 2005 and now have a relatively even share of revenue. Search & directories had the greatest growth and now surpass classifieds as the main category.

With the widespread adoption of broadband, the Internet could also have a negative effect on display revenues. Estimates provided by stockbroking company ABN Amro suggest that employment advertisements online currently account for an estimated 20 per cent of the market, and it is the largest single classified advertising sector. Real estate comes next, with online accounting for about 10 per cent, and cars come third at around eight per cent.

4

Basics of Advertising

Advertising and promotions is bringing a service to the attention of potential and current customers. Advertising and promotions are best carried out by implementing an advertising and promotions plan. The goals of the plan should depend very much on the overall goals and strategies of the organization, and the results of the marketing analysis, including the positioning statement.

The plan usually includes what target markets you want to reach, what features and benefits you want to convey to them, how you will convey it to them (this is often called your advertising campaign), who is responsible to carry the various activities in the plan and how much money is budgeted for this effort.

Successful advertising depends very much on knowing the preferred methods and styles of communications of the target markets that you want to reach with your ads. A media plan and calendar can be very useful, which specifies what advertising methods are used and when.

For each service, carefully consider: What target markets are you trying to reach with your ads? What would you like them to think and perceive about your products (this should be in terms of benefits to them, not you)? How can you get them to think and perceive that? What communications media do they see or prefer the most? Consider TV, radio, newsletters, classifieds, displays/signs, posters, word of mouth, press releases, direct mail, special events, brochures, neighborhood newsletters, etc.

What media is most practical for you to use in terms of access and affordability (the amount spent on advertising is often based on the revenue expected from the product or service, that is, the sales forecast)?

You can often find out a lot about your customers preferences just by conducting some basic market research methods. The following closely related links might be useful in preparation for your planning.

Positioning

Deciding and Conveying Your Unique Selling Position

Positioning includes identifying the unique market position, or "niche", for your organization. Positioning is accomplished through market analysis. Market analysis includes finding out what groups of potential customers (or markets) exist, what groups of customers you prefer to serve (target markets), what their needs are, what products or services you might develop to meet their needs, how the customers might prefer to use the products and services, what your competitors are doing, what pricing you should use and how you should distribute products and services to your target markets. Various methods of market research are used to find out information about markets, target markets and their needs, competitors, etc.

Various Perspectives

positioning,market segementing, etc.

Unique Selling Proposition

products, positioning and market segmentation

Unique Selling Proposition

Unique Selling Proposition: What's In It For Me?

Your Unique Selling Proposition

Simply, positioning is how your target market defines you in relation to your competitors.

A good position is:

1. What makes you unique
2. This is considered a benefit by your target market

Both of these conditions are necessary for a good positioning. So what if you are the only red-haired singer who only knows how to play a G minor chord? Does your target market consider this a good thing? Positioning is important because you are competing with all the noise out there competing for your potential fans attention. If you can stand out with a unique benefit, you have a chance at getting their attention.

It is important to understand your product from the customers point of view relative to the competition.

Environment

In order to begin positioning a product, two questions need to be answered:

1.What is our marketing environment?

2.What is our competitive advantage?

The marketing environment is the external environment. Some things to consider:

- How is the market now satisfying the need your software satisfies?
- What are the switching costs for potential users for your market?
- What are the positions of the competition?

The competitive advantage is an internal question. What do you have that gives you advantage over your competitors. Some things to consider:

- Is your company small and flexibility?
- Do you offer low cost and high quality?
- Does your product offer unique benefits?
- Are you the first on the market with this product (First mover advantage)?

Positioning Strategies

There are seven positioning strategies that can be pursued:

- *Product Attributes*: What are the specific product attributes?

- *Benefits*: What are the benefits to the customers?
- *Usage Occasions*: When / how can the product be used?
- *Users*: Identify a class of users.
- *Against a Competitor*: Positioned directly against a competitor.
- *Away from a Competitor*: Positioned away from competitor.
- *Product Classes*: Compared to different classes of products.

Segmentation

There are three types of segmentation:

- *Mass Marketing or Undifferentiated Marketing*: Go after the whole market with one offer and focus on common needs rather than differences
- *Product-variety Marketing or Differentiated Marketing*: target several market segments and design separate offers for each
- *Target Marketing or Concentrated Marketing*: Large share of one or a few sub-markets. Good when company's resources are limited

To identify a niche market, a series of 2 by 2 matrixes can be used to identify an area that is being overlooked by larger competitors. The competitors are mapped on this matrix and you can see where there may be some opportunities.

Positioning Differences

The differences that are promoted for a product must be:

- *Important*: The difference delivers a highly valued benefit to the target buyers
- *Distinctive*: Competitors do not offer the difference, or the company can offer it in a more distinctive way
- *Superior*: The difference is superior to other ways that the customer might obtain the same benefit
- *Communicable*: The difference can be explained and communicated to the target buyers

- *Preemptive*: Competitors cannot easily copy the difference
- *Affordable*: Buyers can afford to pay the difference
- *Profitable*: Company can introduce the difference profitably

Marketing-Place or Distribution

Place

Place, or distribution channel, is the method for making your product available to the consumer.

Functions

There are eight main functions for distribution channels:

- *Information*: gathering and distributing marketing research
- *Promotion*: developing and communicating offers
- *Contact*: communicating with prospective buyers
- *Matching*: fitting the offer to the buyer's needs
- *Negotiation*: reaching agreement on price and terms
- *Physical distribution*: transporting and storing the goods
- *Financing*: getting and using funds to cover the costs of channel work
- *Risk taking*: assuming the risks the channel work.

  Example-Selling a CD

Place is simply where your fans buy your CD. You can also call it distribution. There are many ways to distribute your CD.

Retail

Probably the most difficult is retail (selling your CD in music stores). This is difficult for independent musicians or bands because you usually need to have a relationship with a distributor.

Online

Isn't the Web wonderful? You can easily and cheaply set up a web page with your information, sample audio files, show dates, and how to order your CD.

In Person

Whenever you perform, you should sell your CDs. You can mention that you are selling CDs and where to buy them while you are performing. It is easier if you have a friend to help you. This person can collect the money, hand out the CDs, etc. so you don't have to worry about it during a show.

In Home

There is nothing wrong with telephone orders!

Price

Price is the amount of money charged for a product or service or the value exchanged for the benefits of the product or service.

For a new product, you must understand your positioning before you set a price. Make sure it is not too low, or the product will not be taken seriously. If it is too high, the potential customer will not take the risk.

Pricing Strategies

There are five general pricing strategies:

- *Product Line*: Setting price steps between product line items
- *Optional Product*: Pricing optional or accessory products
- *Captive Product*: Pricing products that must be used with the main product
- *By-Product*: Pricing low value by product to get rid of them
- *Product Bundle*: Pricing bundles of products sold together

New Product Pricing

There are two new product pricing strategies:

Market-Skimming: Initially set high prices to "skim" revenue layer by layer from the market. Works when:

- Quality and image support the higher price
- Enough buyers want the product at that price

- Cost of producing a small volume cannot be high
- Competitors should not be able to enter the market easily

Market Penetration: Set a low initial price in order to penetrate the market quickly and deeply to win a large market share. Works when:

- Market is highly price sensitive
- Production and distribution costs fall as sales volume increases
- Low price must help keep out the competition

Price Adjustment

The following are price adjustments based on changing situations:

- *Discount & Allowance*: reduced prices to reward customer responses such as paying early or promoting the product
- *Discriminatory*: adjusting prices to allow for differences in customers, products, and locations
- *Psychological*: adjusting prices for psychological effects. Ex: $299 vs. $300
- *Value*: adjusting prices to offer the right combination of quality and service at a fair price
- *Promotional*: temporarily reducing prices to increase short-run sales
- *Geographical*: adjusting prices to account for geographic location of customer.
- *International*: adjusting prices in international markets

Promotion

Promotion is the specific mix of advertising, personal selling, sales promotion, and public relations a company uses to pursue its advertising and marketing objectives.

If you are an entrepreneur, you most likely have limited resources and you are still learning about the market. Information gather is extremely important at this stage of the game. The trick is the start the revenue stream without spending too much money.

Objectives

The objectives that are met by promoting are to move the target market through the following phases:

Unawareness-> Awareness-> Beliefs/Knowledge-> Attitude-> Purchase Intention-> Purchase

It is believed that consumers cannot skip over a phase, but they need to move through them. Promotion is used to move the target market from one phase to another to finally purchase.

The Offer

The offer needs to be identified before you begin any promoting. What are you offering the target customer? What do you want the target market to do?

One mistake that can be made is to create a promotional advertisement and not tell the customer what to do. You should prompt the customer and tell them to "call this number to place an order" or "download this software from our web site".

Measuring Response

Testing different offers, advertisements, direct mail letters, lists, and promotion techniques can tell you what method is most effective. There is a trade-off. Testing is expensive. You need different versions of promotions, which raises production expense. You need to track the results, which takes time. But the information you gather could help you reduce wasteful, ineffective spending in the future.

If you decide to test, make sure you have a method for measuring response. You can do this by first asking the customer where they heard about you when taking the order, if it is a telephone order. If it is an order form that they mail back to you, you can code the order form with a tracking number that lets you know exactly what promotion the customer is responding to. This information can then be entered into the customer database for future analysis.

World Wide Web

The Web allows for a cheap way of promoting your product. It is a great tool because it allows the target customers to educate themselves about your product by reading about it, seeing a demo, and download a copy (and therefore serve as your distribution channel).

Remember, you are trying to reduce the perceive risk of purchasing your product. By providing a Web page, you are moving the target market through the communication cycle from unawareness to purchase.

Also, you are trying to reach innovators and early adopters. These people are actively searching for better ways to meet their needs. The Web is a natural place for them to go to look for you.

The difficulty with the Web is all of the noise out there. It is very crowded and difficult to be noticed. Register with all of the search engines, such as Yahoo and Alta Vista. Make sure that there are keywords in your web site that will attract your target audience.

Direct Mail

An average response rate for direct mail is about 1%. This depends on the offer, the mailing list, the target audience, the creative (how the direct mail piece looks), and the timing of the mailing. There is a whole industry built around direct mailing.

This promotional activity involves many steps. For more detail on how to execute a direct mailing, refer to Direct Mail.

Classified Advertisements

Although it may nice to be able to take out a full color, full page advertisement in an industry magazine, it is very expensive and will not reach your target market of the innovators and early adopters.

This target market will read the classified ads in the magazines looking for and willing to try new things.

The key for classified advertisements is frequency. Running an ad once will create awareness, but not necessarily action.

Request a media kit from the magazine you are considering. This should contain circulation information, subscriber profiles, and prices. This will help you determine if your target market reads this magazine.

Press Releases

A press release is an announcement of a new product release. Editors may take this information and publish it as news in their magazine or newspaper. This is a great way to get free publicity.

To send a press release, you should prepare a press kit that includes:

Cover letter to the editor

Press release product announcement

Product features sheet

Corporate background sheet

Evaluation product

Technical specifications sheet (if any)

Reprint of any past articles

Names of end user contacts and comments

Picture of your product

The editor may take your product announcement, make some modifications to it by hand, and send the original to be printed. In general, editors like to have the press releases double spaced with plenty of margin room.

There can be a 3-4 month lead time before your press release is published.

If possible, tie your press release into current events or human interest. It has a better chance of being published.

Don't write your press release like an advertisement. Any claims you make, be sure to back them up with user testimonials.

Tailor your press release to each publication, or at least each type of publication. Mass mailing press releases don't usually get published. Also, send your press release to one person at each magazine. If you are unsure of the person, contact the magazine for a contact name. Include in your press release the product name, the price, a company contact name, the company name, address, phone number, fax number, and e-mail address. Be prepared to take questions.

Your opening sentence should be clear and concise. "The first (product) capable of (doing this benefit) is now available from (your company) for people who need to (this need)".

Product Reviews

Magazines have product review editors that review it in an article or column. This can provide great exposure. However, it can also be risky. What damage will it do if you get a bad review? Before pursuing this promotional activity, it may be safest to fully complete testing, and have contacted many new customers to get their feedback on the product. Make sure there are no surprises.

Choose a magazine your target market is reading. You can always use quotes from the review in your promotional material for other promotions.

With more people accepting the product, the faster you will move past the early adopters and innovators. Call the magazine for the name of the correct person to send the product to. Ensure that this person gets a full product.

Be available for questions. If a reviewer has problems, there will usually be a phone call to the company first.

Example-Promotion Your Music

Shows

Direct Mail

Web Page

Posters

Event Listings

Reviews

Radio

Word of Mouth

Press Releases

Unique Selling Proposition

The Art of Finding Your Unique Selling Proposition

Positioning is about making your offering different from, and more valuable than, your competitors' offerings--and placing that idea in the minds of a target group of customers. Positioning attracts customers by creating a positive and unique identity for your company and its offerings. Positioning is vital for distinguishing your offering from everybody else's. In a world where there are more and more products and services every day, your customers are on advertising overload all the time. So they pick something to believe and hold that notion until a message breaks through and persuades them to change.

People can't hold warring ideas in their heads. They can't believe that the Norton Anthology is the best study guide for English literature, then study from a set of Cliffs Notes and believe they're doing the best they can to pass their exams. They can't believe that all paper towels are pretty much alike, buy one that costs more than most, and think that they are wise shoppers. The point is, positioning is your effort to claim a high ground in that overloaded prospect's head and hold it against competition.

There may be very little difference between your product and your competitors'--but if you can't find a way to communicate uniqueness and connect it to a need of your target, you might as well quit fighting your competition and sell out to them. There are many different ways to stake out a position. Just remember, your position reflects your unique selling proposition, and it is what makes your offering more valuable to your customers than what's being offered by your competition.

Perception of Your Business

How will your business be perceived as different from your competition in the minds of your targeted customers? To figure this out, you must look for your best customer and then design a position that matches his or her wants and needs to an advantage that only you can offer. Remember, you can't be all things to all people, but you can be the vendor of choice for a group of them.

Positioning Affects Every Aspect of Your Communications-And Your Business

Positioning is the basis for all your communications--your packaging and product design, sales promotions, advertising, and public relations. Everything you do must reinforce that position--otherwise you just undermine your marketing efforts and sow confusion instead of confidence. Positioning is serious business.

You must choose the right position, for now and down the road. Do the work now to develop a clear position for your business vis-à-vis your competitors. You'll ensure that you get the most from your advertising budget.

The truth is that with enough money, you can buy success in advertising. Mediocre, unfocused messages from a company without a clear position will generate sales surprisingly well if that company buys enough time or space to pound the message home. But think how much farther that budget could take you if you had a focused message, a unique selling proposition, and a target audience for your offering. Positioning--and the creative approach that grows from it--make the difference.

Developing the Positioning Statement and the Tagline

To begin creating your own sense of positioning for your business, answer the following questions with short, articulate answers that relate your offering to your customers' needs.

1. What does your business do?
2. For whom?
3. What is your biggest benefit to them?
4. Prove your claim. To what do you attribute that benefit?
5. How will your customers perceive this benefit, relative to the competition?

Once you've chosen your target customer and the needs you plan to fill, the next step is to create a unique selling position, or USP, for your product or service. In order to zero in on an effective and useful USP, we need to look at three types of market criteria. They are:

- WIIFM (What's In It For Me)
- The Four Ps
- The Big Five

We'll talk at the end of this chapter on how the integration of the customer niche and market niche criteria, if done properly, will give your USP more than just the sum of its parts. For the USP must be designed into the online storefront, not after it's up and running.

What's in it for Me?

The last thing you want visitors to say to themselves when they view your carefully constructed offer at your online storefront is "So what? What's in it to me?" It could be that you're not answering the ever-present question of the online shopper, "What's in it for me?" And you have to answer it in less than 10 seconds or they're off to your competitor.

Many years ago, a company called Federal Express came up with a new concept: delivering packages overnight. Until FedEx came along, if you wanted to ship a small package to the next city or state or even across the country, you had to go down to either the local bus station, post office, or airport and hand the small package over to the bus company, post office, or airline for them to deliver it. You were pretty much at the mercy of these shipping companies who would deliver the package on their schedule, not yours. Back then it might take up to several days to have your package delivered because the bus companies and airlines were in the business of moving people or, in the case of the airlines, people and large cargo, not small packages. Then, it had to be picked up at the package's final destination! And though the post office would deliver small parcels, you never really knew when they would be delivered.

FedEx saw an opportunity here. All they had to do was convince the public that they could deliver packages in a convenient and speedier fashion. But they needed a slogan that would say that their package delivery service was better than those of the airlines and bus companies. And they needed to say it in one simple phrase.

Free Info

After much thought, they decided that what differentiated them from their competitors was that they owned their own planes. This meant that customers could ship and receive products on the customer's schedule, and not the schedule of the airlines or buses. So what was the unique selling position that FedEx chose? We have our own planes.

It didn't fly with the public.

People didn't get it. "So you have your own planes," they said. "What does that mean to me?"

So, FedEx went back to the drawing board and came up with this: "When you absolutely, positively have to have it overnight." That worked. The public responded, and the rest is commerce history. Consumers didn't care if FedEx had their own planes. They didn't care if their packages were delivered by plane, train, bus, car, or Pony Express. The benefit to the consumer was that the package was delivered overnight, right to the recipient's door. Another good example is Domino's Pizza. How do you differentiate one pizza service from another? Domino's differentiated itself when it first got started from the competition by promising to deliver your pizza in record time: "30 minutes or less, or it's free!"

There's a lesson here, one that you can use when creating your own unique selling position (USP). You need to always remember WIIFM: "What's in it for me?" This is what a customer is looking for when he or she buys. Phrase your USP in those terms and you'll go a long way in creating an effective and successful unique selling position.

Differentiating Yourself from Your Competition

It's a competitive world out there, and getting more so every day. Your business is faced with the challenge of differentiating itself from your competitors and giving the consumer a reason why they should buy from you rather than your competition. But that's not as easy as it seems. For example, ask a random sample of business owners to tell you what makes them different from their competition, and you'll get a blank stare, or perhaps a response like one of these:

"My prices are the lowest."

"I guarantee satisfaction."

"My products are of high quality."

"I give great customer service."

But none of these responses sets them apart from the competition. Many businesses can claim the same things. A business must know what they offer a customer besides general statements and why they think a shopper should buy from them. That is, what makes the business unique in the market and in the eyes of a potential customer? To do that, you need to ask yourself the following questions.

- What gives your company a unique advantage over your competition?
- What is the distinct reason for consumers to buy from you?
- Can you portray in the consumer's mind a compelling image of what your business will do for them that others can't?

Notice those highlighted words: advantage, reason, and image. That's your objective when creating a solid, exact, and usable unique selling position that both positions you in the marketplace and convinces a consumer to buy from you. A good USP creates the framework and lays the foundation for your compelling product or service offer.

If that isn't enough, a good USP also keeps your business pointed in the right direction.

One of the things that made both FedEx and Domino's a success was a measurable and beneficial USP. They were measurable (overnight and 30 minutes, respectively) and carried a unique benefit (FedEx delivers to the recipient's door; Domino's promises it's free if not delivered on time).

Getting the picture? A good USP is specific, measurable, and conveys a customer benefit. Let's review.

So how do you differentiate yourself from the competition? How do you answer the consumer questions of WIIFM? Start with this: Using a pad and pencil, ask yourself the following questions and answer them as simply as you can. Remember, you're not creating a corporate mission statement here, so keep your responses simple.

"Why is my business special?"

"Why would someone buy from me instead of my competition?"

"What can my business provide to a consumer that no one else can?"

"What's a benefit to the consumer that I can deliver on?"

Keep your answers simple, specific, and measurable, and show a benefit to the buyer. If you're confused by what you offer, your customers will be, too.

Keeping Your Eye on the Competition

Ignorance may be bliss, but in the knock-down, drag-out world of business, ignorance of your competition can be a deadly mistake.

Keeping track of your competitors can be a difficult and time-consuming task. You can hire a corporate spy to infiltrate your competitor's organization; do a little dumpster-diving for useful discarded memos, manuals, and correspondence; or work smart by monitoring your competition's activities right from your desk, using the Internet. The Internet is filled with resources that can provide your company with media sources, web directories, clipping services, and competitive intelligence to keep you up to date on who the competition is and what they're doing.

By using these online sources, you can discover the answers to questions such as:

"Who are the leading companies in your industry?"

"What information on your competition is available?"

"Which of your competitors are most likely threats?"

Positioning Your Business-The Marketing Mix

If you've been anywhere near a marketing course, you would have heard of the Four Ps of Marketing. They are price, place, product and promotion. The Four Ps is another set of criteria that can help you choose a market niche. Let's look at price first.

Mix & Max: Tip

Think of the criteria of the Four Ps as variables that you can control. The Four Ps are interdependent upon each other, and taken together they form a marketing mix. Your objective is to come up with a mix of these Ps that will clearly differentiate you from the competition.

If you're going to compete on price, don't just say you're the lowest-say why. Customers will not accept a blanket statement unless you can prove it. For instance, perhaps you can sell at such a low price because of your ability to source product from the closeout industry, buying products at pennies on the dollar. Or perhaps you have an exclusive arrangement with a distributor or manufacturer that no one else has, allowing you to sell at the lowest price. On the other hand, you may sell at the highest price but offer some added value, such as free shipping or free 24/7 support. Play up these unique factors in your USP. Next is place. The Marines are a good example of this P.

The Marines are looking for a few good men-not all men, just a few, and only good ones. This is a great positioning statement, which makes their "business" unique and differentiates them among the other services of the armed forces. Another example was the tagline "The Pepsi Generation."

Look for a similar positioning with your business. Perhaps your focus is gender-based. Perhaps it's age-based. Sell to a unique segment of the population, not to all of it.

Following place is product. Take a common product that others sell and repackage it in a new way. For instance, take the iMac. It's just a PC, but look at the packaging. Not only does it sell, but it sells at a premium price! It also has a great positioning statement. Think Different! The iPod is another example. There are portable music devices at a lesser price, but Apple has learned that a sexy package goes a long way in differentiating the product, plus carrying a higher price tag.

Caution: Promises, Promises

Whatever you promise in your unique selling position, be sure you can deliver on it. Don't make the mistake of adopting a USP that you can't fulfill. This means making sure that everyone in your entire organization knows and understands your USP and can act on it!

Then there's promotion. Study the promotional possibilities of your product or service. Can you tie your product or service with a season or holiday where you can benefit from the promotional activities and mindshare of consumers that already exist at that time of year? Targeting your promotional message at the right time is the key to acceptance. So sit down and make a list of the popular seasonal events, including religious and cultural events other than those with a Euro-Christian focus, such as the Jewish and Asian religious holidays and ethnic holidays like Kwanzaa.

Finally, remember this very important fact when constructing your USP. Your USP is not about you nor is it about your business-it's about your customer.

The Big Five of eCommerce

Shoppers don't care about your site, your business, or your life. What they care about is themselves. When they come to your site, they want to see if there's anything there that interests them. They want to know, "What's in it for me!" They come to your web store with a certain set of expectations. Your job as a web merchant is to meet those expectations.

Caution: It's the Customer, Stupid

Everything on your site should be about the customer and designed from the customer's point of view. Your customer not only needs a reason to buy, but to buy easily and safely.

Your customers expect to find what they came for: a fair price, a good selection of product, great service, and a secure and safe place to shop. In other words, they're looking for the Big Five of online shopping. And if they're from "out of town"-that is, another country-they're also looking for a site that speaks their language!

The Big Five are:

- Selection
- Price
- Service
- Convenience
- Security

Consumers want to know right away if their visit to your site is going to save them time and money and if their shopping experience will be a pleasant one. Can they find what they want easily? Can they place an order in a variety of ways? Can they find your customer service pages, shipping and handling fees, and return policies without spending a large amount of time digging through your site looking for them?

These are the customer's expectations and you have to meet them if you want your online business to be a success. If your site is designed with the Big Five of online shopping in mind, you'll provide your customers a pleasant shopping experience and a reason to buy from your online store again.

Let's take a look at them. The Big Five of online shopping are selection, price, service, convenience, and security.

Selection: Do You have what they Want?

Shoppers come to the Net for the vast selection of product and services that are available at the click of a mouse. Whether shoppers find you through search engines, store directories, or through your own marketing and promotion, after they arrive at your site, they want to know you have what they're looking for. Don't build an impression in the shoppers' mind that you sell computer software or have an online bookstore and then offer only a small selection of titles.

When building a small-to medium-sized business, you need to focus your product or service offering. Look at your unique selling position. If done correctly, it tells you the market you're targeting and the unique product or service you're selling. If you've done your homework and created a compelling unique selling position, the shopper will feel that your web store offers the best selection on the Net.

Store Examples

Offering a good selection to shoppers is not necessarily a numbers game. The quality of your selection is much more important for a small web business than the quantity. The following are some good examples of small sites that work in large product categories yet deliver a good selection of product offerings for their market.

Music Stores

You don't have to be a CDNow.com or an Amazon.com to be successful selling music CDs on the Web. Acres of Videos & CDs at Click4Stuff at stores.yahoo.com/ggroup sells hard-to-find CD sets. Shoppers who come to their web store will find a good product selection specializing in hard-to-find classic music CD sets.

Software Stores

You don't have to be a CompUSA to competitively sell software on the Net. You can offer a specialized selection of software to shoppers and still give them a good selection in the category you choose. Accounting Shop at stores.yahoo.com/2020software sells only accounting software, whereas Natara Software at shop.store.yahoo.com/natara/ sells productivity software for the Palm handheld platform.

Pet Stores

The large pet stores on the Net such as PetsMart carry a wide variety of pet supplies for all kinds of pets. But a small store such as BunnyLuv-Essentials at shop.store.yahoo.com/shopbunnyl/ offers a nice selection of rabbit care supplies, toys, hay, food, and grooming tools. A shopper who comes to their site would be pleased with the selection of products in that subject area. As you can see, you can run with the big dogs of eCommerce if you choose your product or service well and deliver the best selection in that category.

Is Your Price Right?

What kind of price animal is your eBusiness? That's a question you need to answer. And after you answer it, your web store must demonstrate it. Do you sell products or services at a discount? Do you want to be a low-cost leader in your market niche? Or are you a value-added reseller? Do you add additional value to products in the form of some kind of service charging a higher price? Do you set the price of the products and services you sell, or does the consumer?

Whatever pricing model you decide on, you need to make it very clear to the shoppers who come to your site. Consumers do not like surprises. If you promoted your site as the low-price leader, your prices should show it. If you're a boutique shop and charge better-than-average prices, show the value you've added to your products or service. Make it very clear what you charge and why, and be sure it fits the expectations of your site visitors.

Another important point is not to hide your prices. Nothing annoys a shopper more than going through the process of ordering from you, entering their credit card number, and then being told what the total shipped price is. Be sure that you give your shoppers all the information they need to make a buying decision, up front, before they buy. Don't draw the customer into the buying process with low prices and then surprise them after they place their order with exorbitant shipping and handling charges on the order confirmation page. If you want to see a shopper bolt for the door, this is the way to do it.

So how do you inform the shopper of your shipping and handling charges? You can do it in one of two ways.

- Provide an easy-to-find section on your site that lists and easily explains your shipping rates and policies in general and your handling charges.
- Present an order review page to the buyer that lists the price of the product and all applicable shipping and handling charges. Give the buyer the total shipped price before you request his or her credit card number.

We suggest that you do both. That way the shopper fully understands the total amount of the sale before he or she completes the purchase. Don't forget to include any and all applicable taxes in the total of the sale.

Service: How Do You Measure Up?

You've put a lot of effort into building your web store. You've created a good selection of product for your market category and priced your product or service to sell. But that's not enough to earn a customer sale. Customers expect to be serviced, so customer service is a top priority for your website. Because you're not dealing with customers face-to-face, your service policies must instill a sense of trust in your shoppers.

Many current eCommerce companies on the Net today don't understand this simple fact. Consumers expect service. Your web store must deliver it. Good customer service includes

- Email confirmations
- Multiple means of contact
- Support outside business hours
- Guarantees and return policies

Email Confirmations

After a customer clicks the Place My Order button, he or she immediately wonders what will become of his or her order. It's only natural that sending an order into the vastness of cyberspace can cause a certain amount of consternation. You can relieve much of your customer's worries, and avoid frustrations, by sending a series of email confirmations that informs the customer of the status of his or her order right through the sales and shipping process.

As soon as the order is placed, an email confirming that the order was received should be sent to the customer. The Yahoo! store offers this service. The email message should include a complete record of the transaction, including the following information:

- An order number.
- What was ordered.
- Who ordered it.
- Where it will be shipped.
- Total amount of the sale including all shipping and handling costs.

- Customer service contact information in case the customer has a question about the order.

Yahoo! store automatically sends an email with all the information cited here except for the customer service contact information. This has to be added by you and you also have the option of additional text in the email confirmation. Another email message should be sent confirming that the product ordered is in stock and when it will be shipped. A third email message should be sent after the product is actually shipped, containing the name and tracking number of the shipping company that was used. Finally, send an email to your customers after they have received their orders asking them for feedback and even offering them a discount on their next purchase if they buy within the next few weeks. For merchants that use UPS Shipping tools to ship orders in the Yahoo! store Order Manager, an email is sent after processing the order with UPS. The email includes the tracking number, which saves the merchant time cutting and pasting tracking numbers.

Yahoo! store again helps you out here. Yahoo! allows you to create coupons and or discount codes to send to customers if you use their Merchant Standard and Merchant Professional packages.

Provide Multiple Means of Contact

Always provide a number of different ways that a customer can contact your customer service department. There are several ways to do this.

Return Policies: Tip

One of the best ways to gain customer confidence is to offer them a money-back satisfaction guarantee. As an eBusiness, you should offer a money back guarantee with your products and clearly state your guarantee policy on your website.

List your customer service email address on your website and include in it all email correspondence with your customer. In addition, tell people where you are located. Include your company's address, telephone number, and fax number on your website.

List a telephone number for customer service. Let customers know when a live person will answer the telephone. If you use an answering machine, be sure you leave a message that tells the caller when they can expect their call to be returned.

Invest in a toll-free telephone number and list it on your site. Not only is a toll-free number relatively inexpensive, it goes a long way toward building a level of consumer confidence in your business. Remember that shoppers don't like surprises. Be sure they understand the terms of their purchase before they click the Buy Now button.

Tell the shopper under what conditions he or she can return a product. How many days or weeks do they have to decide to return it? Will they get a refund or a credit? Who shows how to use your product or service and gives troubleshooting tips in case customers run into trouble after hours? Be clear and specific and list all details about your return policy on your website.

Remember that it pays to keep all line of communications open with your customers and to provide a quick response to customer emails.

Convenience: Are You Easy to Do Business With?

When a shopper comes to your web store, he's got his credit card in hand and he is ready to buy. So don't let your website get in his way. A web store with a poorly designed navigation structure will frustrate a shopper. Even though you have a great offer, if the shopper can't easily find it and buy it, he'll click off to your competitor and probably will not come back.

A lot of thought must be given to how a shopper can search for products on your site. If you offer a shopper multiple navigation options, it will help her find what she is looking for fast. Have the capability on your site for shoppers to search by

- Product name
- Price
- Product category
- Manufacturer

The more site tools shoppers have to search with, the faster they can get to the products they're looking for, and the faster you'll make a sale.

Offer Live Customer Support-Without the Expense

Want to give live customer support on your site to shoppers? Don't want to spend the money for programming? Shoppers can download the free desktop application and communicate with you in real-time if they have a question. But, you have to be there for it to work.

But finding a product to buy is only the beginning. Just as important as price selection and service is convenience. How easy is it to navigate through your site? Getting lost in a site is discouraging and will send the shopper away fast if he can't easily find his way through your web store. Good site navigation entails telling your visitor where he is, how he got there, how he can get back, and where he can go next.

If your site navigation is done properly, your shoppers should be able to get to where they want to go in just three mouse clicks (Three Click Rule). Be careful when designing the navigation bar on your site. Graphic links to the different sections of your site are nice and give a professional look to your web store. But also include text links that duplicate your graphic navigation at the bottom of your pages in case your site loads too slowly through a shopper's browser.

Remember that your website should be intuitive to navigate. Your site pages should provide a visual map of how to get from one place to another that says, "Here's where I am. This is what I clicked on to get here. If I click on that, I'll go there next."

Security: How Trustworthy Is Your Site?

Good websites establish trust. Online shoppers can be a very skeptical bunch. They've been trained by the media to expect all kinds of online scams that are waiting to pick their pockets. If up to now you've given them a reason to buy from you, now they have to trust you enough to plunk down their money. Shoppers are looking for proof that your site is trustworthy to deal with. A good way to do this is join eTrust or the Better Business Bureau (BBB). You build trust in your website in two ways:

- The customer knows his or her credit card number is secure when placing an order on your site. Tell shoppers to your site that their credit card orders are secure. Put that testament right on your home page and on every product page.
- The customer knows that the private personal information he or she gives you is kept personal and private. A good, well written, non-legalese privacy policy should be easily accessible by visitors to your website.

Shoppers are very concerned about using their credit cards to make purchases online. When you build your store on Yahoo!, all credit card transactions are secured on their server. Still, some shoppers just will not place an order online with their credit card, no matter how secure it is. For these types of customers, provide a toll-free telephone number to call in their order to you. Also provide an order form on your site that they can print, fill out, and fax to you.

Privacy Policies

The Internet is a great medium of commerce. With it, you can create new marketing methods, tap new markets, and target potential customers with electronic ease. And it also can get you sued by millions of consumers for violating their privacy!

If you thought spamming consumers with unwanted email was a blight on your company's reputation, consumers are even more upset over the incessant abuse of their personal privacy, not to mention the government investigating the business practices of e-businesses. But companies need to gather a certain amount of information to personalize and better serve their customers.

After all, how can you connect with a customer if you know little or nothing about her? There has to be some kind of balance between protecting a consumer's privacy and the need for your business to target and personalize your offers to your customers. Consumers are sensitive to what's done with their personal information, but it doesn't mean they're against giving it if the circumstances change, including getting something back for the information.

Yahoo! store provides a default Privacy Policy page for your online store, so you are covered there, but you need to read and modify the statement to create your own privacy policy. Finally, make your privacy policy accessible right from your home page.

Appendix C provides a worksheet that will help you choose and integrate the different elements of a USP to create a unique selling position for your company. The object of this worksheet is to look at each of the elements and decide which of them, and which parts of them, will help define your USP then integrate them into an effective USP.

Your Unique Selling Position

Most business people have heard the term Unique Selling Position (USP) bandied about, often when the subject of sales or marketing comes up. Very few understand what it really is, what its significance is on your ability to sell, and most important, how to create one. It's tricky and not something you learn overnight, but it is critical to the success of your business.

Start talking about differentiation and you can't help but think of the ideas written about extensively: position your company in a way that makes you different from the competition in the mind of the prospect and customer.

It's all about how they perceive your message. Here' s another exceptional way to look at it that may help you. Ask yourself, what is my offer?

What are you giving in return for this prospect's time and money? Is the offer compelling enough to interest someone in spending their hard-earned dollars and even more precious moments? If your offer isn't strong and something they perceive themselves to need, they won't buy.

That might sound somewhat simplistic, but it's true-with the caveat that the higher the price of your product or service is, the more unique you have to be. And, you have to communicate it repeatedly throughout the sales process.

Mission

Do you remember the ah-ha moment when you decided you could start a business of your own or rejuvenate an existing one? At this point, you probably began to develop a strategy. Chances are reviewing that moment will give you insights into your USP.

- What is the purpose of your company?
- What products and/or services do you provide and to whom?
- Why are you the best company to provide these products and services?
- What made you think you could do it better than anyone else?
- What need in your industry is not being filled and how does your company offer a creative solution?

Frame It

Here's one of the best ways to make yourself different from the competition and achieve more sales: frame your message so your prospects are eager to hear what you have to say. How do you do that? Know who they are and what their specific needs are, and then present your solution in a way that clearly answers all of their questions and makes them jump at the chance to buy from you.

Framing means to paint a clear picture of what you want them to think and visualize while you are talking about your offer. It should be so irresistible that people are begging to buy from you or work with you when you're done.

There are probably only a few reasons why you won't make a sale:

1. They don't really need what you are selling. This should be an easy one to avoid if you are doing your market research and targeting the correct demographics.
2. They are price sensitive or just can't afford what you are selling. If you are selling a low-ticket item, move on because there's plenty more prospects. If what you're

selling involves a huge budget and long cycle of fulfillment, you can't afford to haggle much with price. Many studies have proven that highly desirable products cannot be given away, but as soon as you attach a price to them that allows the prospect to perceive value in the product and provider, you'll make a lot more sales.

3. They don't trust you. It's all about relationships from day one.

Relationship Building

One of the most powerful tools that companies often do not use at all, or use too late in the process, is a testimonial. In your print promotions as well as on your web site, one of the first things prospects should see is a glowing testimonial with the option to read more of them. The headline should be something like "Just look at what our satisfied customers have to say about us." Nothing sells like a good recommendation and you can't have too many of them.

Why should your prospects believe you when they are skeptical of so many others? The answer lies in the relationship you build from the initial contact. When you bond with someone and show that you understand what their problem is, they begin to feel like they have been "heard." This is a powerful psychological advantage. You continue by explaining how you have the exact solution they need, and they begin to warm up to you and a mutual, win-win relationship forms. It's also your job to sustain it.

Common USP Pitfalls

The same mistakes are often made when defining your unique selling position. Most play it too safe and try to please everyone and end up selling to no one. Successful business owners are innovators and they take risks. Experiment, evaluate and evolve into something even more unique on an ongoing basis.

Another mistake is that your marketing communications fail to reflect your uniqueness. Companies will try to emulate other successful branding campaigns. There is nothing unique about that. Don't stop looking at what your competition is doing, just don't copy it. Remember, unique is what you're going for.

Do your advertising vehicles sound the same as everyone else's? Your ad copy messaging must also reflect your USP. Even if you don't have the millions of dollars large corporations can afford to spend, you can still carve a niche for your firm that resonates with your target audience and makes them feel good about doing business with you.

Does your sales process cover all the steps from initial contact through close with your USP reflected throughout? Draw up a plan of what a typical sales cycle should look like, what marketing tools should be used at what levels, and be sure to leave room for flexibility and creativity on the part of your sales rep. Don't forget to use the darn thing.

An accomplished unique selling position is what builds your brand. Branding is what marketers use to capture the mind share of their target audience. It's what helps people think of your company and call you when they realize they need your product or services. Remember the last time you drank "the real thing?"

To paraphrase a great slogan, "Build your USP and they will come.

5

New Advertising Means in India

In recent years various big and notable changes have been witnessed in the field of communication and media. Many new concepts popped up and new media advertising is one of them. India is pretty new to new media advertising but this concept has been around for quiet a long time now. Going by the latest trend you will come to know that new media advertising is the emerging and hottest medium of advertisement.

New media advertising is synonym of online advertising and has taken web media with a stride. Now people instead of going for traditional advertising tend to give more weightage to online advertising. This is mainly due to the fact that it is more targeted maximum exposure. According to various media gurus' new media advertising has got a bright future and they also predict that within few years new media advertising will experience a boom in India and around the world.

The biggest advantage of new media advertising is that many other medium too fall in same bracket and the latest to join the bandwagon is cellular phones. Cellular phones have recently entered into the scope of new media advertising and are predicted to flourish in the coming time. New media advertising's main highlight is that it can be done via various means such as banner ads, pop-up advertisements, and interstitial and even pop-under advertisements.

The biggest advantage of new media advertising is that it is relatively cheaper in comparison to other media and can also be done in an attractive manner. Moreover, various small and upcoming businesses can easily go for new media advertising. In other words, you can say that it is very attractive in nature and simultaneously entices customers too. Going for new media advertising is the wisest choices as it gives the surfer both visual and graphic treat.

Also you can use new media advertising in any local language and customized message. This means it will be attracting more customers and visitors and ultimately boosting the business. Anyone irrespective of the place he resides can access the Internet from any corner of the globe. However, you will be surprised to know that it has emerged as one of the most convenient ways to promote any brand or company

MEDIA RELATION SERVICES IN INDIA

Media and communication has come a long way and they are getting popular in India with each passing day. With phenomenal growth of media and technology involved media relation has became an important strategic entity. Now more and more people are hiring public relations and Media relation services. There was a time when people or companies either select advertising or public relations but now public relations is one of the important component of marketing.

The main aim of public relation services is to create a favorable and positive image about the company. According to few media experts, there is no distinction between public relation and advertising but its usage makes them look different. Public relation is a kind of science which is applied in a proper manner can not only build a brand but also sustain it for years.

Companies providing public relations services have come a long way and have comprehensively shattered the image of mere postman which is just used to deliver press releases to the consultants who are involved in the brand building process. In fact it has been reformed now and has also shown the potential to rise high. Moreover, now it is easily fitted into the mainstream arm of marketing instead of the peripheral role. Last few years witnessed a kind of recession in public relations services but now the time has changed and soon it will be rolling over to become the country's top agencies growing at a blistering pace of 30-50 per cent. There is also a speculation that various MNCs are gearing up to use the public relations services in a full-fledged manner. Also you can say that this is the waking up call to the power of a good PR campaign. The biggest advantage of hiring public relations services is that it adds the credibility factor with consumers. Moreover, public relation is also highly versatile. This is the reason why many companies go for hiring public relations services not only in the initial stages of image building on a strategic level but also on a more tactical level.

Many big companies and brands have recognized the power of public relations services and are easily cashing on to this highly communicative channel. In short you can easily say that now public relations services have become an integral constituent of any well-balanced and integrated marketing mix.

PUBLIC RELATION: BEST TOOL FOR TODAY'S MARKETING SCENARIO

Looking to build a favorable brand name for your organization amongst public? If your answer is yes, then public relation services are there for you. Public relation is the best and most effective concept which is successfully implemented by various media organizations, marketing and communication professionals and even brand managers. In recent times it has been seen that along with advertising people also go for effective public relations services. By this they not only easily communicate their message but can also generate a favorable response.

Communication field is very vast and in that public relation plays a vital role. Public relation's main aim is to have a direct relation with public that's why public relation has become one of the most significant parts of a communications strategy. At times people tend to confuse public relation with advertising. This is a wrong notion as public relation solves different purpose whereas advertising has some other goals.

Advertising is mainly product centric whereas public relation mainly emphasizes on public image. This is the reason public relation campaigns include various media events and functions. A company providing public relation services mainly act as a bridge between the public and organization. In fact they are the gateways to propagate any message to the general audience. It has been seen that with the help of public relation agency one can easily reach out to the masses and the clients and provide what they crave for. But achieving positive public relation isn't an easy deal and prior going for hiring public relations firm, it is very decisive to understand the activities involved within and around the media with an alert mind. According to the experts, public relation is a process of building better and effective relations for the growth of any business. In other words, the main aim of public relation is to provide various media services such as powerful advertising campaign, effective marketing strategy, concrete media planning and also expert marketing consultation. All these factors play a vital role in making any public relation campaign a success.

ADVERTISING & MARKETING SERVICES

Success is one of the most important objectives of a business. To attain success, it is important that the business gives due consideration to the advertising and marketing of the products. For effective advertising and marketing the company should choose the right means and people to do the job. exchange4media offers advertising and marketing services to companies looking for effective and result oriented services.

The overall success depends how well the communication message is passed on to the target audience. The objective of marketing is to understand the target customer's requirement and to develop a plan accordingly. The marketing plan should include acquiring customers and persuading them to buy new product or service. The marketing of the product involves a variety of methods and advertising is an important medium to do so. Advertising helps in developing a targeted message and delivering the message to the audience.

By impressing the audience with the message, the advertiser increases his customer base. Advertising thus helps in increasing brand awareness converting it to sales. To effectively market and advertise a product or service the advertiser should use customized advertising and marketing strategies.

INDIAN ADVERTISING INDUSTRY

The Indian advertising industry is talking business today. It has evolved from being a small-scale business to a full-fledged industry. It has emerged as one of the major industries and tertiary sectors and has broadened its horizons be it the creative aspect, the capital employed or the number of personnel involved. Indian advertising industry in very little time has carved a niche for itself and placed itself on the global map.

Indian advertising industry with an estimated value of es13, 200-crore has made jaws drop and set eyeballs gazing with some astonishing pieces of work that it has given in the recent past. The creative minds that the Indian advertising industry incorporates have come up with some mind-boggling concepts and work that can be termed as masterpieces in the field of advertising.

Advertising agencies in the country too have taken a leap. They have come a long way from being small and medium sized industries to becoming well known brands in the business. Mudra, Ogilvy and Mathew (O&M), Mccann Ericsonn, Rediffussion, Leo Burnett are some of the top agencies of the country.

Indian economy is on a boom and the market is on a continuous trail of expansion. With the market gaining grounds Indian advertising has every reason to celebrate. Businesses are looking up to advertising as a tool to cash in on lucrative business opportunities. Growth in business has lead to a consecutive boom in the advertising industry as well.

The Indian advertising today handles both national and international projects.

This is primarily because of the reason that the industry offers a host of functions to its clients that include everything from start to finish that include client servicing, media planning, media buying, creative conceptualization, pre and post campaign analysis, market research, marketing, branding, and public relation services. Keeping in mind the current pace at which the Indian advertising industry is moving the industry is expected to witness a major boom in the times ahead. If the experts are to be believed then the industry in the coming times will form a major contribution to the GDP. With al this there is definitely no looking back for the Indian advertising industry that is all set to win accolades from the world over.

ADVERTISING AGENCY INDIA-SHIFTING PARADIGM

India's economic prosperity and maturity has also helped to shape the world of advertising agencies in India, enabling the latter to reach global standards. Advertising has become serious and big business in India, with its worth being estimated at Rs. 13,200-crore, by those in the know. This can only mean one thing that apart from the quality of work, the volume of work too has gone up. A decade back it was still a fledgling industry, with a colonial hang up. Today it has transformed itself into a thoroughbred performer, doing great work both in India and abroad and winning accolades. A prominent globalization has been observed in the operation of the Indian advertising industry as it has learnt to speak in different languages, be it urban rural and even global.

The advertising industry in India has gone through a sea change with the inception of various divisions under it to boost its productivity and progress, such as creative department, media planning, direct marketing, public relations, and so on. With blooming markets and an ever-deepening pocket of the Indian consumer, revenues for ad-spends are touching new highs as advertising agencies in India continue their triumphant march towards creating new Indian sensibilities.

Technological advancements in the last decade or so have enabled the common man to consume the media of their choice at their convenience and time. This blurring of lines between TV, Internet, mobile phones and other devices has increased media fragmentation and has led to paradigm shifts within the industry. In this part-real-part-virtual world, Advertising And Marketing Services in India are trying to marry the age-old traditions of storytelling and brand experience to the new-age reality of consumer control. Agencies are creating, sharing and managing stories and brand experiences in a manner that involves and engages, rather than interrupts or alienates.

All most all Marketing And Advertising agencies in India believe in the concept of 360 degree branding. The services provided by most of these agencies include advertisement for TV, print ads, creating web sites, working on web banners, email marketing, direct marketing, telemarketing, radio promotions, outdoor promotions, tracking retail visibility and communications, designing inputs on packaging, rural communications and PR. It is safe to say that at present a single ad agency provides a host of services from content creation, developing the artwork to radio jingles to monitoring the effectiveness of the advertisements and even inventing new idioms and language to relate to consumers of all pocket shapes and sizes.

NEW MEDIA ADVERTISING-AN EFFECTIVE MARKETING TOOL

New media advertising is a powerful medium of advertising through the Internet. In today's highly competitive environment, new media advertising acts as a cost effective meduim with a wider reach, targetting a huge online audience. New media makes it possible to communicate with the audience using the benefits of technology on a interactive platform. Unlike traditional media, it is possible to track the audience usage and traffic by using new media as a marketing medium. Due to its unique features and benefits it has become popular among the users and advertisers alike.

ADVANTAGES OF NEW MEDIA/ INTERNET ADVERTISING

Online Media advertising helps in targetting a selected audience for conveying specific information. Millions of users log on to the Internet everyday which gives greater visibility to the online advertisers. Internet advertising is also useful to track information about the number of users who visit the website everyday. Marketing and advertising on the Internet also helps in lowering the costs incurred through traditional form of advertising. Internet advertising enables one to conduct transactions using an interactive meduim catering to a given audience based on their age, gender, background, demography,interests targetting specifc needs.

Internet advertising is done through advertising banners which is an interactive meduim to communicate with the users. Advertising banners have been used for online marketing since the 1990's and have become a popular marketing tool.Many advertisers use banner ads to give publlicity to their products or services.

Marketing and advertising companies use creative banner ads to generate curiosity among the users so that they click on the banner to see further information. This gives greater visibility to the advertiser with more audience reach and helps in branding.

Successful Campaigns in Rich Media

Rich media gives an extensive range of new technologies that could be used as a powerful advertising medium. These technological innovations have given tremendous scope to the advertisers which helps them target consumers with their products.

Advertising with High Definition Television

Every business needs to effectively promote their products and services for generating more sales and transactions and thereby to have more profit and growth. They chalk out various strategies for achieving the objective. They look for various mediums which are effective enough for the brand promotion campaign to reach their targeted clients and customers. And one such effective medium which has been used effectively by businesses in India and all over the globe is High Definition Television or HDTV, a digital television broadcasting system with a significantly higher resolution than traditional formats such as NTSC, SECAM and PAL.

High Definition Television advertising is one of the best ways to promote any products and services in front of millions of clients and customers. Because of its ability to provide the best of television viewing with superior picture quality and improved quality of sound, the number of people using HDTV is increasing by days. The high definition TV also has facilities for connection with computer systems. You can use net and watch movies with good quality visuals. So, advertising agencies are using HDTV as their medium for effective advertising campaign.

Today everyone has TV and advertising on TV is one the best options to promote your products. The ad coming on TV also put high impact on the customers. There will be more positive effects in building brands. Advertisers are innovating new ways for their campaigns on high definition televisions. India Advertising agencies are coming up with glitzy, smart and tailored type ads targeting the middle classes. Besides, a number Hindi India media news channels have been launched and they are reaching to the masses both in urban and rural parts of the country. Indian television news channels are now have become more effective as advertising agency.

And ad on High Definition television has given much in return to the advertisers and investors. It is effective and gives the desired results. It is one time cost but gives you higher returns on your investment. Your target customers will remember your product easily and you will have more sales and transactions. There will be more profit in your business thereby growth and more return in your investment.

Copyright Information

Research, Teaching, Private Study, General Interest User Information

The images and texts on this web site have been made available for use in research, teaching, and private study. For these purposes you may reproduce (print, make photocopies, or download) materials from this web site without prior permission, on the condition that you provide proper attribution of the source in all copies.

Under certain conditions specified in the law, libraries and archives are authorized to furnish a photocopy or other reproduction. One of these specified conditions is that the photocopy or reproduction is not to be "used for any purpose other than private study, scholarship, or research." If a user makes a request for, or later uses, a photocopy or reproduction for purposes in excess of "fair use," that user may be liable for copyright infringement. This institution reserves the right to refuse to accept a copying order if, in its judgment, fulfillment of the order would involve violation of copyright law.

Commercial, Broadcast, Mirroring, etc. User Information

Any other use that does not fall under the above requirements, including but not limited to commercial or scholarly reproductions, redistribution, publication or transmission, whether by electronic means or otherwise, without prior written permission of the Rare Book, Manuscript, and Special Collections Library is strictly prohibited. Users must contact the Library to request permission to use materials in any manner that does not meet the above requirements. Persons wishing to broadcast or publish this material must assume all responsibility for identifying and satisfying any claimants of copyright or other use restrictions.

How to Obtain Reproductions

Due to the varying nature of the items represented in the Emergence of Advertising in America: 1850-1920 project, there may be different copyright or other reproduction restrictions that apply to each collection. If you would like to reproduce materials from this site in a way that does not fall under fair use, please contact the Research Services Department of the Rare Book, Manuscripts, and Special Collections Library. Specify what advertising items you are interested in (by the database number). We will be able to inform you of any reproduction restrictions on a case-by-case basis. In some cases, we may be able to supply you with publication-quality slides or scanned images of the items you are requesting, so if you are interested in using materials in this format, please let us know.

Commercial, Broadcast, Mirroring, etc. User Information

For other uses of materials from this web site-i.e. commercial products, publication, broadcast, mirroring, and anything else that doesn't fall under "fair use" (explained below)- we require that:

1. Users must obtain permission from the current copyright holder.

   Individuals wishing to publish or broadcast any advertisement included on this website must assume all responsibility for identifying and satisfying any claimants of copyright, trademarks, or service marks. Included on this website is a partial list of companies for which we have contact information. This is not a complete list of all companies represented in Ad*Access but it will assist in making contact with some of the rights owners.

2. Users must also obtain permission from the John W. Hartman Center for Sales, Advertising & Marketing History to reproduce materials held in its archive that are featured on this website.

A letter granting permission from the current copyright holder must be submitted along with the request to the Hartman Center. Contact the company that owns the product(s) contained in the advertisements you would like to use. (A partial list of company contacts is below.) You must provide written permission from these companies before the Hartman Center can provide permission to use an advertisement for a purpose which does not fall under "fair use." Please read on for more information.

The Hartman Center charges fees to cover the cost of reproduction of items in its collections. Requests that require extensive research or preparation by Center staff may require an hourly charge, negotiated in advance. In addition, requests to publish, broadcast, or otherwise disseminate ads may be subject to a commercial use fee. Please contact the Hartman Center Reference Archivist for more information and a fee schedule.

The Fine Print

The John W. Hartman Center for Sales, Advertising & Marketing History can provide high quality reproductions of items from Ad*Access, with permission in advance from the copyright holder(s). We will make such copies for commercial uses, publication, broadcast, etc. uses only with prior permission.

Users may make a single copy in print or digital form of images or other material from the Ad*Access site. These copies may be used only for use in the research, teaching, or private study. They may not be made for or donated to other repositories. They may not be further reproduced without permission.

The recipient agrees to give proper acknowledgement to the Duke University Rare Book, Manuscript, and Special Collections Library, and further agrees to secure written permission in advance from the rights owner to publish or broadcast any item, in whole or in part, from the Ad*Access on-line collection. Persons wishing to broadcast or publish this material must assume all responsibility for identifying and satisfying any claimants of copyright, trademark or service marks. These print advertisements fall under the "work-for-hire" stipulations of copyright law; the company that owns the product or product name, not the advertising agency which created the advertisement, holds copyright.

The recipient agrees to indemnify and hold harmless Duke University, its officers, employees and agents from and against all suits, claims, actions and expenses arising out of the use of reproductions provided by the Rare Book, Manuscript, and Special Collections Library. Duke University claims no rights to the advertising images included in Ad*Access beyond ownership of the physical items.

United States Copyright Law

The copyright law of the United States (Title 17, United States Code) governs the making of photocopies or other reproductions of copyrighted material. As of April 1999, the law was amended from its 1976 status with the inclusion of the Digital Millennium Copyright Law and the Sonny Bono Term Extension Act. Under certain conditions specified in the law, libraries and archives are authorized to furnish a photocopy or other reproduction to researchers. One of these specified conditions is that the photocopy or reproduction is not to be "used for any purpose other than private study, scholarship, or research." If a user makes a request for, or later uses, a photocopy or reproduction for purposes in excess of "fair use," that user may be liable for copyright infringement. This institution reserves the right to refuse to accept a copying or reproduction order if, in its judgement, fulfillment of the order would involve violation of the copyright law.

Fair Use

According to the copyright law:

"In determining whether the use made of a work in any particular case is a fair use the factors to be considered include-the purpose and character of the use, including whether such use is of a commercial nature or is for nonprofit educational purposes;

The nature of the copyrighted work;

The amount and substantiality of the portion used in relation to the copyrighted work as a whole; and

The effect of the use upon the potential market for or value of the copyrighted work. The fact that a work is unpublished shall not itself bar a finding of fair use if such finding is made upon consideration of all the above factors."

For more information on fair use, see the Indiana University-Purdue University Indianapolis (IUPUI) web page on Fair Use.

For information about copyright law and how it applies to information found on the Internet, see the IUPUI Copyright Management Center page and the Copyright Considerations Page from UCSD. The United States Copyright Office of the Library of Congress and Stanford University's page on Copyright and Fair Use provide links to a wide variety of web sites addressing these issues.

How to obtain permission to reproduce materials from the Ad*Access Project

The Duke University Rare Book, Manuscript, and Special Collections Library does not hold copyright to the advertisements in the Ad*Access on-line project. If you would like to reproduce any of the advertisements in a way that does not fall under fair use, please follow the steps noted below:

1. Obtain permission from the current copyright holder. Individuals wishing to publish or broadcast any advertisement included on this website must assume all responsibility for identifying and satisfying any claimants of copyright, trademarks, or service marks. Included on this website is a partial list of companies for which we have contact information. This is not a complete list of all companies represented in Ad*Access.
2. Obtain permission also from the John W. Hartman Center for Sales, Advertising & Marketing History to reproduce materials held in its archive and featured on this website.

A letter granting permission from the current copyright holder must be submitted along with the request to the Hartman Center.

Contact the company that owns the product(s) contained in the advertisements you would like to use. You must provide written permission from these companies before the Hartman Center can provide permission to use an advertisement for a purpose which does not fall under "fair use." Please read on for more information.

The Hartman Center charges fees to cover the cost of reproduction of items in its collections. Requests that require extensive research or preparation by Center staff may require an hourly charge, negotiated in advance. In addition, requests to publish, broadcast, or otherwise disseminate ads may be subject to a commercial use fee. Please contact the Hartman Center Reference Archivist for more information and a fee schedule.

Attached is a list of companies and addresses for making contact. This is NOT a complete list. When a company is not included below, this does not mean that copyright, trademark, and service mark claims are not viable. It only reflects our staff's lack of success in attempts to make contact with an individual or company holding copyright for the product and/ or company in the advertisement.

Individuals wishing to publish or broadcast an advertisement from a company not listed below must assume all responsibility for identifying and satisfying any claimants of copyright, trademarks or service marks.

Company List

How to cite materials from the Ad*Access Project.

When using advertisements from the Ad*Access Project, please acknowledge their source by clearly stating the name of the project, the advertisement number, the collection name, and the name of the library. Also include the URL of the project page. An example is noted below:

Ad*Access On-Line Project-Ad #R0108

John W. Hartman Center for Sales, Advertising & Marketing History

Duke University Rare Book, Manuscript, and Special Collections Library

Certain advertisements have additional copyright citation information required by the copyright holder. This information is included on the individual advertisment pages directly under the image. In some cases, supplemental citation information is included in the "Copyright Notice" section at the bottom of the advertisement pages. The user is responsible for including this information in all citations for those advertisements.

Use and Reproduction Information for other collections in the Rare Book, Manuscript, and Special Collections Library

Promotions: Do They Have a Place

When your mechanic sends you a coupon for a discount on an oil change, or your local coffee shop rewards you with a free cup of coffee every tenth time you buy, you're seeing a promotional program at work.

A promotion is a planned strategy for increasing sales over a short period. A promotion adds value to the product or service offered. It stimulates sales for reasons other than the product's inherent benefits.

We call those reasons incentives. Sometimes the incentive is designed to specifically make a sale, as in "$2.00 off medium pizza with this coupon." Other times the incentive is planned simply to expose the customer to the product--to break down preliminary barriers that are roadblocks to a future sale.

With a promotional program, you can persuade people to try your product, to experiment with new beliefs about your service; you can shift buying habits so that light users find reasons to buy more.

Who uses promotions? There are business-to-business promotional programs, and there are consumer programs. We'll talk mainly about consumer programs. The concepts we'll discuss are really about the same for both. Remember, people do business with people. It's just a matter of what market you're trying to influence--end users or intermediaries.

Different businesses are drawn to different styles of promotion. The most frequent users of promotional programs are the retail services, like car care, hair care, and restaurants. Coupons are the most common promotion for these types of businesses; dry cleaners use coupons extensively, and so do groceries. It's the ability to track results, as well as their proven effectiveness, that makes coupon offers so popular.

In the business-to-business world, suppliers frequently engage in promotions by offering sale prices. You are less likely to see coupons here, because the patterns of purchasing are a little different. The person making the decision to buy may not be the same person who is writing the check, so requiring the physical coupon to be used would be an unnecessary barrier to the desired sale.

Promotions work because people like something for nothing. They respond to two-for-one offers, and they love a good deal or free extras with their purchases. Special promotions help lots of businesses achieve their marketing objectives, such as combating seasonal cycles or stealing attention from the competition.

MEDIA PLANS

The largest category in your advertising budget is likely to be your media costs--the dollars you spend for air time on radio or for ad space in newspapers, magazines, and more. Because of this, it makes sense to have a sound plan to manage that investment. You'll want to set goals. You'll want to describe strategies for achieving them. You'll have to organize the day-to-day tasks of carrying out the strategies. The tool you'll need to do this is a media plan that begins with an overview and works its way down to the details. It will help you with every phase of your advertising.

Here's how many businesses manage their media buying. The person in charge of the budget starts saying yes to the salespeople who call. Advertising appears here and there as a result. When the budget's gone, the person in charge starts saying no, and the ad campaign is over. It's a method, but you wouldn't call it a media plan. And if that approach sounds familiar, you can bet you're passing up opportunities to maximize your return on investment.

Media planning is the process of choosing a course of action. Media planners develop yearly plans that list each media outlet--print or broadcast. Planning then gives way to buying, as each separate contract is negotiated, then finalized.

The media plan is a document in sections. A ring binder notebook is a good way to keep a media plan, because it's easy to update and easy to refer to. Or if you prefer to work on computer, simply think in terms of folders and files. The sections in your notebook will be:

- Media outlets (newspapers, etc.). This section lists all of the media in which advertising will be placed.
- Goals. This section describes the goals of the advertising, and explains why and how this plan meets these goals.
- Audience. In this section, collect all the information you can about your target audience. You will want statistics by demographics or lifestyle; your professional association can help you find this information, as can trade journals or your banker. Look for any relevant

articles or information about your potential buyers. Pay attention to everything that helps you imagine an individual buyer who is typical of the whole.

- Strategy. You will write a statement of strategy backed up by a rationale. The action steps you describe here will guide a year's activity.
- Budget and calendar. Your media plan will outline what money is to be spent where, and when.

The document you've compiled in this notebook guides you in the execution of the plan throughout the year.

Over time, these plans provide a history of your advertising. If you make alterations to the schedule in the course of the year, be sure to record those decisions in your notebook. Ring binders make it easy to update your plan as it evolves.

When you've finished this section, you will have an overview and the tools you need to create a media plan for your business. Let's start with basic vocabulary.

The term you'll hear most often is CPM, or cost per thousand. CPM analysis is the method media buyers use to convert various rate and circulation options to relative terms. CPM represents the cost of reaching one thousand people via different types of media. To calculate CPM, you find the cost for an ad, then divide it by the total circulation the ad reaches (in thousands). By finding this information and calculating this cost for each of your options, you can give them a numerical ranking for comparison. CPM is a basic media concept.

Print advertising prices are based on the circulation of the publication in question. Publications will quote you a circulation figure based on paid subscribers. The audited circulation figures are verified by monitoring organizations.

The publications will try to convince you that actual circulation is higher by including the free copies they distribute and the pass-along readership they claim. Sometimes these claims of "bonus" circulation are valid--for example, magazines distributed on airlines get at least eight readers per copy. Still, you should be wary of inflated circulation figures.

Audience is the equivalent of circulation when you're talking about broadcast media. Audience size varies throughout the day as people tune in and tune out. Therefore, the price for advertising at different times of day will vary, based on the audience size that the day-part delivers.

Penetration is related to circulation. Penetration describes how much of the total market available you are reaching. If you are in a town with a demographic count of 200,000 households, and you buy an ad in a coupon book that states a circulation of 140,000, you're reaching 70 percent of the possible market--high penetration. If, instead, you bought an ad in the city magazine, which goes to only 17,000 subscribers (households), your penetration would be much less--8.5 percent. What degree of penetration is necessary for you depends on whether your strategy is to dominate the market or to reach a certain niche within that market.

Reach and frequency are key media terms used more in broadcast than in print. Reach is the total number of people exposed to a message at least once in a set time period, usually four weeks. (Reach is the broadcast equivalent of circulation, for print advertising.)

Frequency is the average number of times those people are exposed during that time period. To make reach go up, you buy a wider market area. To make frequency go up, you buy more ads during the time period. Usually, when reach goes up, you have to compromise and let frequency go down. You could spend a lot of money trying to achieve a high reach and a high frequency. The creative part of media planning comes in balancing reach, frequency, and budget constraints to find the best combination in view of your marketing goals.

In developing your media plan, you will:

- Review your marketing objectives through the "lens" of media planning.
- Review the options available.
- Evaluate them against your objectives.
- Set your minimum and maximum budget constraints.

- Create alternative scenarios until you uncover the strategy that accomplishes your objectives within those constraints.
- Develop a schedule describing ad appearances in each medium.
- Summarize your plan in the form of a calendar and a budget.
- Negotiate with media representatives to execute your plan.

Tips on Negotiating Rates

Prices for print advertising are fixed, as the print media can be flexible in matching supply with demand. They have expandable space; if they sell more advertising than usual, they can print more pages. Your negotiations with print media will revolve around what other services they can offer you, such as reader response cards, additional ads in a special issue, special position, free color, and so on. You will probably not be able to negotiate an actual discount off the rate card.

Prices for radio are negotiable, because the amount of inventory is fixed. There are only so many minutes between the programs themselves that can be sold. If there is competition for those minutes, the price goes up. The effect is really noticeable when there's a sudden surge in demand for commercials.

Spring is the beginning of the broadcast media buying season, since networks issue their fall schedules in May. Networks like to get money early, so to encourage you, they will usually offer attractive package deals at this time. This is the best time to negotiate for overall lowest cost.

Opportunities come up throughout the year as other advertisers change their plans. You can make good buys at any time, but the deal might be structured differently. If you got a call from a radio station tomorrow saying that it has a highly prized time slot available during the morning newscast, and it will cost only $22 per spot, but you've got to decide fast, would you have an answer ready? A good media plan can help keep you focused on how that deal fits into your overall strategy. If it delivers an audience you want, and if it's available at a price that fits your budget, you're in business. It helps to have a well-documented plan to assist in these fast-breaking decisions.

If you plan to use broadcast media heavily, I recommend that you work with an agency or media service. Those who know the territory thoroughly and are working on your behalf will be better able to find the best buys. If you are buying your media time and space yourself, here are some tips:

- Be sure your chosen medium delivers your target market. The media sales reps are expert at putting their offerings in the best light. Everybody can find something to claim "We're Number One" about. You don't care. Does the medium deliver the audience you want to reach? That's the key question.
- Beware of bringing your personal biases to your media decisions. Don't buy a certain radio station just because you listen to it--ask instead if your potential customers do. And it works the other way, too. Don't not advertise in a certain newspaper just because you hate one of its reporters.
- Look for verifiable information from your sales reps. Audience size, share, gross rating points--these calculations should be based on information from third-party ratings sources. Beware of any statistic described as "estimated"--ask about the source for that information.
- Representatives from the various media will call on you; no matter what the title on their business cards, they are salespeople. Do not allow them to make your decisions for you. High-pressure sales techniques are fairly common. Rely on these people for information, but do your own calculations, and make the decisions that are right for you.

Advertising Techniques-Do's, Don'ts

Internet Advertising Techniques

- Do understand the most powerful advertising technique on the Internet is showing up in organic search results (ideally first page, in the first three results).

- Do understand that Wordtracker.com is currently your best tool along with Pay Per Click suggestion tools (from Google, etc) to discover which search terms get the most search volume.
- Do understand that Pay Per Click search ads provide your next best set of Internet advertising techniques after organic search engine placement.
- Do understand that text links almost always outperform banner ads as advertising techniques because they look more like content and people are used to clicking on content (text links) far more than ads.
- Do understand that Internet display ads perform best with flash animation, motion, or video.
- Do understand the eye reads top left to bottom right and that impacts your click-through rate depending on where your text links or display ads are on the page.
- Do understand that the page upon which the consumer clicks is just as important than the ad or link that got them there.
- Do understand that improving or optimizing your own pages and your own site has more impact than optimizing your advertising techniques in text links or display ads.
- Don't underestimate the importance of this sentence above.
- Don't assume that just because you built a website people will visit it.
- Don't underestimate the power of words: You, your, asking a question, amazing, discover, now are all proven "power" words that produce far higher response. See more on this down below.

Direct Mail Advertising Techniques

- Do use a stamp vs. a bulk mail endicia-Open rate on envelopes with physical stamps is 13% higher.
- Do make your letter look like newsworthy content-Content gets read, not advertising.

- Do attach news articles blown up to fit on 8 ?" x 11" paper as an attachment to your direct mail piece.
- If you are using a card vs. letter, use 6" x 9' stock or larger.
- Do not use any "special offer inside" language on your envelope or "hey look at me" advertising techniques when using a letter envelope.
- Do not use an adhesive address label unless it's a label from Stamps.com or endicia.com.
- Do not use an 8.5 " x 11" letter in B2B direct mail, but do use A4 or executive sized stationary-higher read rate and higher response rate vs. full sheet letter.

Writing as Advertising Techniques

Note: this applies to anything to do with Direct marketing, Internet marketing, even memos to your boss.

- Do understand that the use of certain words are power words which produce results.
- Do use present tense-better response than past tense.
- Do use the word "you" or "your" far more than "I" "me" or "we."

  Do use words like these in your writing or advertising techniques which produce demonstrated higher response rates:

  - You
  - Your
  - Now
  - Discover
  - This
  - These
  - Amazing
- Do understand that asking a question with the word you in it is one of the best ever advertising techniques.
- Don't, however, ask a question where the answer can easily be "no, and I don't care."

TV Advertising Techniques

- Do use TV as a way to legitimize your brand, launch your brand, or reposition your brand. When used prudently and selectively, it can be one of the best advertising techniques depending on your situation.
- Do investigate buying "remnant" TV media and making opportunistic buys for a fraction of retail prices.
- Do make sure your TV spot looks like nothing else on TV (in order to stand out).
- Do make sure you have a compelling offer, and a compelling newsworthy announcement.
- Do pay special attention to audio in your TV spot...recall of ads with music in the ad (not background music) produces higher recall and captures more attention.
- If you have people in your TV spots, do make sure to have them with their eyes looking right in the camera...the stopping power and attention rates are higher with ads that have people looking at you directly in the eye.
- Do have a response medium (website, telephone number, SMS number, etc). If you don't, it could be one of your worst advertising techniques.
- Do understand that for response, early AM and late evening produce higher response rates (if someone is up at those hours, they often have nothing else going on and are paying more attention than normal).
- Do understand that the creative that you put into the costly media of TV makes all the difference in the world. A bad TV spot in good TV media can be one of the worst advertising techniques.
- So: do test your TV creative on the Internet before putting it on TV...or test at small levels before putting on untested TV creative in large media buys.
- Do understand one of the cardinal rules of TV creative: see and say. See the product when the words are said. P.S. don't forget to show the actual product. See and say

in TV is one of the most basic, but often forgotten TV advertising techniques.

- Do understand that likeability of ads (plus the offer) produces the highest correlation to sales.
- Do understand the basics of targeting, but index the cost per thousand impressions (CPM) with the index of propensity to buy your type of product/service (e.g. a TV show with an index of 180 for buying laptops @ $20 CPM is actually more expensive than a TV show with an 130 index @ $10 CPM).
- Don't always do what you like...let the numbers dictate.
- Don't accept mediocrity in your TV creative. Mediocre TV spots in costly TV media, is the most common blunder in all advertising techniques.

Public Relations as one of the "Earned" Advertising Techniques

Do understand that Public Relations is fundamentally different than advertising. PR is not necessarily in the genre of advertising techniques, but on average PR is 6X more powerful because people pay attention to content 6X more than advertising (that's starting at 500% higher ROI).

The four keys to PR are the following:

- *A great story*: see the chapter in my book for the five most frequently written news stories in America.
- *A great headline*: consumers read headlines 19X more than body copy and the same is true for reporters you are pitching. Also know that the first 8 characters in your headline are more important than ever because a reporter only sees the first 8 characters in their Blackberry. Headlines are 19X more powerful than body copy-you should spend 19X more time working on the headline. Headlines should be less than 11 words.
- *A great database*: contrary to popular belief, it's not who you know, but if you have a great story. Even if you know the editor of The Wall Street Journal, it means nothing if your story isn't newsworthy. You need a large

database blended between custom and a standard news reporter database. Reporters are everywhere today and so is the Internet. All reporters want great stories...you need a database not necessarily a chummy rolodex.

Luck: yes. Reporters have 4-7 stories in various stages of development. If you happen to land on their desk when they just finished a story, it's luck and the law of large numbers when sending/phoning a pitch. Luck is a factor.

Test your pitch much like you would test a direct mail piece using the advertising techniques learned here. Test small, see what responds, and what doesn't. Find out before you blast a big push which may not work. And my shameless self-promotion: everyone should know the five most frequently written news media stories in America. These five most frequently written news stories are in my book, Buzzmarketing.

Print Advertising Techniques (Newspaper, Magazine, etc)

- Do understand that a print ad which looks like an "ad" will fail unless you have an amazing offer (great discount, sale, limited time only). Without an offer, an ad that looks like an "ad" won't get read.
- Do make your ad look like content (use the same font style and layout as the publication) or make your ad look like no other ad in the pub (reference Infiniti print ads from 2005 and Pfizer's Celebrex print ads from 2007).
- Do understand that white space can stop people in their tracks, and produce a higher response rate. One of the greatest advertising techniques is white space.
- Do understand that a photograph of a person with their eyes looking directly at you produces a higher response than a photograph of a person with eyes looking elsewhere. Perhaps the most powerful of all advertising techniques in print, or even on the Internet.
- Do understand that a print ad with a "Drop Cap" gets read more than without one.

- Do understand that ads with lists and bullet points get read more than ads with paragraphs.
- Do understand that a photograph's caption is extremely important...a good photograph can be the first thing a reader sees, and the caption the second thing they read. If the caption fails, they skip the rest of your ad...if the caption works, your ad gets read. Smart captioning can be of the most effective print advertising techniques.
- Do understand that copy in quotations gets read 13% more than without quotations.
- Do understand that ads delivering news value get read more than anything else.
- Don't ever use a reverse print ad (black background with white font) it's hard to read and has proven repeated lower response rates...one of the worst advertising techniques.

Radio Advertising Techniques

- Do understand that radio advertising works best with high frequency and proper timing.
- Do understand that the first five seconds of your radio ad may be the most important...a cell phone and the radio preset button is a moment away from avoiding your ad.
- Do understand that you need to say your brand name a lot more often than you would ever imagine in a radio ad (people daydream in their car), and you need to drill your brand name often.
- Do understand that reads from DJ's get more attention because they seem like content from a familiar voice versus a stranger's voice.
- Do understand that one of your most powerful advertising techniques is to produce fresh radio creative every week versus running the same radio spot for more than a week.
- Do understand that if it sounds like content, people will listen...if it sounds like an ad...people won't.

Word-of-Mouth and Buzz as Advertising Techniques

Note that word-of-mouth or buzz is created with pull, not "bought" like print advertising.

Also note that this lost art which was practiced before the advent of Television is more powerful than any other set of advertising techniques (Euro RSCG Study found it 10X more effective than TV or Print advertising).

- Do understand that the root of all buzz is a seven-letter word: stories.
- The crux of buzzmarketing and word-of-mouth is to give people a great story to tell, which they, in turn, can tell others...and by them telling the story it makes them interesting, fascinating, and newsworthy.
- Do not confuse buzz marketing with some other services which pay people to talk about products (still a push technique). Buzz marketing is about creating a pull. Creating a story which gives people social currency. Buzz marketing is about creating a story which pulls a brand along with the story (like my own renaming of Halfway, Oregon to Half.com, Oregon).

What creates a good story can be found in my book or in the free chapter download on this site's book page.

Buzz marketing happens when people start conversations that begin with "Hey did you hear..." or "Hey, you're never going to believe..." and then they tell a story which pulls your brand along with that story.

Hope these advertising techniques were helpful.

6

International Advertising Techniques

Generally speaking, advertising is the promotion of goods, services, companies and ideas, usually by an identified sponsor. Marketers see advertising as part of an overall promotional strategy. Other components of the promotional mix include publicity, public relations, personal selling and sales promotion.

HISTORY

In ancient times the most common form of advertising was 'word of mouth'. However, commercial messages and election campaign displays were found in the ruins of Pompeii. Egyptians used papyrus to create sales messages and wall posters. Lost-and-found advertising on papyrus was common in Greece and Rome. As printing developed in the 15th and 16th century, advertising expanded to include handbills. In the 17th century advertisements started to appear in weekly newspapers in England.

These early print ads were used mainly to promote books (which were increasingly affordable) and medicines (which were increasingly sought after as disease ravaged Europe and Britain). Quack ads became a problem, which ushered in regulation of advertising content.

As the economy was expanding during the 19th century, the need for advertising grew at the same pace. In America, the classified ad became popular, filling pages of newspapers with small print messages promoting all kinds of goods. The success of this advertising format led to the growth of mail-order advertising. In 1843 the first advertising agency was established by Volney Palmer in Philadelphia. At first the agencies were just brokers for ad space in newspapers, but by the 20th century, advertising agencies started to take over responsibility for the content as well.

The 1960's saw advertising transform into a modern, more scientific approach in which creativity was allowed to shine, producing unexpected messages that made advertisements interesting to read. Today, advertising is evolving even further, with "guerrilla" promotions that involve unusual approaches such as staged encounters in public places, giveaways of products such as cars that are covered with brand messages, and interactive advertising where the viewer can respond to become part of the advertising message.

MEDIA

One crude but effective advertising method is to pay someone to stand on a corner and wave a sign all day Commercial advertising media can include Chitra (outdoor advertising), street furniture components, printed flyers, radio, cinema and television ads, web banners, web popups, skywriting, bus stop benches, magazines, newspapers, town criers, sides of buses, taxicab doors and roof mounts, musical stage shows, subway platforms and trains, elastic bands on disposable diapers, stickers on apples in supermarkets, the opening section of streaming audio and video, and the backs of event tickets and supermarket receipts. Any place an "identified" sponsor pays to deliver their message through a medium is advertising.

The TV commercial is generally considered the most effective mass-market advertising format and this is reflected by the high prices TV networks charge for commercial airtime during popular TV events. The world cup of cricket is known as much for its commercial advertisements as for the game itself, and the average cost of a single thirty-second TV spot during this game has reached more charges.

Increasingly, other mediums such as those discussed below are overtaking television due to a shift towards consumer's usage of the Internet as well as devices such as TiVo. Advertising on the World Wide Web is a recent phenomenon. Prices of Web-based advertising space are dependent on the "relevance" of the surrounding web content and the traffic that the website receives.

E-mail advertising is another recent phenomenon. Unsolicited bulk E-mail advertising is known as "spam". A message is spam only when it is unsolicited and in bulk.

Some companies have proposed to place messages or corporate logos on the side of booster rockets and the International Space Station. Controversy exists on the effectiveness of subliminal advertising and the pervasiveness of mass messages

The most common method for measuring the impact of mass media advertising is the use of the rating point (rp) or the more accurate target rating point (trp). These two measures refer to the percentage of the universe of the existing base of audience members that can be reached by the use of each media outlet in a particular moment in time. The difference between the two is that the rating point refers to the percentage to the entire universe while the target rating point refers to the percentage to a particular segment or target. This becomes very useful when focusing advertising efforts on a particular group of people. For example, think of an advertising campaign targeting a female audience aged 25 to 45. While the overall rating of a TV show might be well over 10 rating points it might very well happen that the same show in the same moment of time is generating only 2.5 trps (being the target: women 25-45). This would mean that while the show has a large universe of viewers it is not necessarily reaching a large universe of women in the ages of 25 to 45 making it a less desirable location to place an ad for an advertiser looking for this particular demographic.

OBJECTIVES

Whereas marketing aims to identify markets that will purchase a product (business) or support an idea and then facilitate that purchase, advertising is the paid communication by which information about the product or idea is transmitted to potential consumers.

In general, advertising is used to convey availability of a "product" (which can be a physical product, a service, or an idea) and to provide information regarding the product. This can stimulate demand for the product, one of the main objectives of advertising.

More specifically, there are three generic objectives of advertisements: communicate information about a particular product, service, or brand (including announcing the existence of the product, where to purchase it, and how to use it), persuade people to buy the product, and keep the organization in the public eye (called institutional advertising). Most advertising blends elements of all three objectives. Typically new products are supported with informative and persuasive ads, while mature products use institutional and persuasive ads (sometimes called reminder ads). Advertising frequently uses persuasive appeals, both logical and emotional (that is, it is a form of propaganda), sometimes even to the exclusion of any product information. More specific objectives include increases in short or long term sales, market share, awareness, product trial, mind share, brand name recall, product use information, positioning or repositioning, and organizational image improvement.

Examples of the ideas, informative or otherwise, that advertising tries to communicate are product details, benefits and brand information. Advertising usually seeks to find a unique selling proposition (USP) of any product and communicate that to the user. This may take the form of a unique product feature or a perceived benefit. In the face of increased competition within the market due to growing numbers of substitutes there is more branding occurring in advertising. This branding attributes a certain personality or reputation to a brand, termed brand equity, which is distinctive from its competition. Generally, brand equity is a measure of the volume and homogeneity of, as well as positive and negative characteristics of, individual and cultural ideas associated with the product.

POLITICAL USES

The control of advertising translates into the control of money and power. Thus, it can and has been used for political purposes. The American culture wars between fundamentalist religious organizations on one hand, and organizations supporting the freedom of homosexual expression on the other, are one example. In spring of 2005, the American Family Association threatened a boycott of Ford products to protest Ford's perceived support of "the homosexual agenda and homosexual marriage."

Later in the year Ford announced it was curtailing ads in a number of major gay publications, an action it claimed to be determined not by cultural but by economic factors.

That statement was contradicted by the AFA, which claimed it had a "good faith agreement" that Ford would cease such ads. Soon afterwards, as a result of a strong upcry from the gay community, Ford backtracked and announced it would continue ads in gay publications, in response to which the AFA denounced Ford for backing out of the agreement and renewed threats of a boycott.Anti-Gay Group Renews Ford Boycott Threat.

IMPACT

The impact of advertising has been a matter of considerable debate and many different claims have been made in different contexts. During debates about the banning of cigarette adervertising, a common claim from cigarette manufacturers was that cigarette advertising does not encourage people to smoke who would not otherwise.

The (eventually successful) opponents of advertising, on the other hand, claim that advertising does in fact increase consumption. According to many sources, the past experience and state of mind of the person subjected to advertising may determine the impact that advertising has. Children under the age of four are may be unable to distinguish advertising from other television programs, whilst the ability to determine the truthfullness of the message may not be developed until the age of eight.

TECHNIQUES

Advertisers use several recognizable techniques in order to better convince the public to buy a product and shape the public's attitude towards their product. These may include:

Appeal to Emotion

Various techniques relating to manipulating emotion are used to get people to buy a product. Apart from artistic expression intended to provoke an emotional reaction (which are usually for associative purposes, or to relax or excite the viewer), three common argumentative appeals to emotion in product advertising are wishful thinking, appeal to flattery, and appeal to ridicule.

Appeals to pity are often used by charitable organizations and appeals to fear are often used in public service messages and products, such as alarm systems or anti-bacterial spray, which claim protection from an outside source.

Emotional appeals are becoming increasingly popular in the health industry, with large companies like 24 Hour Fitness becoming increasingly adept at utilizing a potential customers' fear to sell memberships; selling not necessarily the actual gym, but the dream of a new body.

Finally, appeals to spite are often used in advertising aimed at younger demographics.

Association: Advertisers often attempt to associate their product with desirable imagery to make it seem equally desirable. The use of attractive models, a practice known as sex in advertising, picturesque landscapes and other alluring images is common. Also used are "buzzwords" with desired associations. On a large scale, this is called branding.

Repetition: Some advertisers concentrate on making sure their product is widely recognized. To that end, they simply attempt to make the name remembered through repetition.

Advertising Slogans: These can employ a variety of techniques; even a short phrase can have extremely heavy-handed technique.

Controversy, as in the Benetton publicity campaign.

Bandwagon: By implying that the product is widely used, advertisers hope to convince potential buyers to "get on the bandwagon."

Guerrilla Advertising: Advertising by association. Done in such a way so the target audience does not know that they have been advertised to, but their impression of the product is increased (or decreased) if that is the intent of the advertiser. The focus is to promote the products or services in a way that revolves around ingenuity rather than finances in order to make a large impact, while spending as little money as possible.

Testimonials: Advertisers often attempt to promote the superior quality of their product through the testimony of ordinary users, experts, or both. "Three out of four dentists recommend..." This approach often involves an appeal to authority.

Pressure: By attempting to make people choose quickly and without long consideration, some advertisers hope to make rapid sales: "Buy now, before they're all gone!"

Subliminal Messages: It was feared that some advertisements would present hidden messages, for example through brief flashed messages or the soundtrack, that would have a hypnotic effect on viewers ('Must buy car. Must buy car.') The notion that techniques of hypnosis are used by advertisers is now generally discredited, though subliminal sexual messages are supposedly present in a variety of messages, ranging from car models with SX prefixes to suggestive positioning of objects in magazine ads and billboards.

Public Service Advertising

The same advertising techniques used to promote commercial goods and services can be used to inform, educate and motivate the public about non-commercial issues, such as AIDS, political ideology, energy conservation, religious recruitment, and deforestation.

Advertising, in its non-commercial guise, is a powerful educational tool capable of reaching and motivating large audiences. "Advertising justifies its existence when used in the public interest-it is much too powerful a tool to use solely for commercial purposes."-Attributed to Howard Gossage by David Ogilvy

Public service advertising, non-commercial advertising, public interest advertising, cause marketing, and social marketing are different terms for (or aspects of) the use of sophisticated advertising and marketing communications techniques (generally associated with commercial enterprise) on behalf of non-commercial, public interest issues and initiatives.

Critiques of the Medium

As advertising and marketing efforts become increasingly ubiquitous in modern Western societies, the industry has come under criticism of groups such as AdBusters via culture jamming which criticizes the media and consumerism using advertising's own techniques. The industry is accused of being one of the engines powering a convoluted economic mass production system which promotes consumption.

Some advertising campaigns have also been criticized as inadvertently or even intentionally promoting sexism, racism, and ageism.

Such criticisms have raised questions about whether this medium is creating or reflecting cultural trends. At very least, advertising often reinforces stereotypes by drawing on recognizable "types" in order to tell stories in a single image or 30 second time frame. Recognizing the social impact of advertising, MediaWatch, a non-profit women's organization, works to educate consumers about how they can register their concerns with advertisers and regulators.

Public interest groups and free thinkers are increasingly suggesting that access to the mental space targeted by advertisers should be taxed, in that at the present moment that space is being freely taken advantage of by advertisers with no compensation paid to the members of the public who are thus being intruded upon. This kind of tax would be a Pigovian tax in that it would act to reduce what is now increasingly seen as a public nuisance.

Public Perception of the Medium

Over the years, the public perception of advertising has become very negative. It is seen as a medium that inherently promotes a lie, based on the purpose of the advertisement-to encourage the target audience to submit to a cause or a belief, and act on it to the advertising party's benefit and consequently the target's disadvantage. They are either perceived as directly lying (stating opinions or untruths directly as facts), lying by omission (usually terms or conditions unfavorable to the customer) or portraying a product or service in a light that does not reflect reality. It is this increased awareness of the intention of advertising, as well as advertising regulations that have increased the challenges that marketers face.

Future

With the dawn of the Internet have come many new advertising opportunities. Popup, Flash, banner, and email advertisements (the last often being a form of spam) abound. Recently, the advertising community has attempted to make the adverts themselves desirable to the public. In one example, Cadillac chose to advertise in the movie 'The Matrix Reloaded', which as a result contained many scenes in which Cadillac cars were used.

Each year, greater sums are paid to obtain a commercial spot during the Super Bowl. Companies attempt to make these commercials sufficiently entertaining that members of the public will actually want to watch them.

Particularly since the rise of "entertaining" advertising, some people may like an advert enough that they wish to watch it later or show a friend. In general, the advertising community has not yet made this easy, although some have used the Internet to widely distribute their adverts to anyone wishing to see or hear them.

Effective Internet Marketing and Advertising Techniques

If your company is considering subcontracting to advertising agencies, SOHO Prospecting is a full-service graphic design and advertising agency committed to excellence in internet marketing and advertising techniques and strategy. We measure the success of our internet marketing and advertising campaigns by their ability to help our clients reach their objectives. We have years of experience handling a variety of clients, in a variety of industries, all across the country. Our proven advertising techniques-written and graphic-continue to help our clients grow their bottom line.

Effective internet marketing and advertising techniques include concept development, design, copywriting and media selection. The first step in any successful campaign is creating a concept that will cut through the clutter, reach your key audiences, and create more business. As a B2B advertising agency focused on obtaining measurable results for our clients, we analyze your objectives, strengths, points of differentiation and other critical factors before creating a positioning for your product or service. This analysis drives our internet marketing and advertising techniques. Subcontracting to Advertising Agencies allows companies to have access to design and copywriting resources not staffed in-house. A compelling design for your advertisement draws prospects into your message. Soho's designers create distinctive designs for your B2B advertising, regardless of the size or format. As an agency focused on results, SOHO never lets a design overshadow the key message or call to action-this is all a part of our advertising techniques.

Effective copy works hand-in-hand with good design to convince prospects that you offer the solutions they need and to spur them to take action. SOHO's writers, as a part of our internet marketing and advertising techniques, make sure your copy and artwork are integrated into a convincing B2B advertising message that prompts your customers to take action.

Subcontracting to Advertising Agencies

Subcontracting to Advertising Agencies is a growing trend. Businesses large and small alike are beginning to experience the value of outsourcing this service. SOHO Prospecting provides turn-key creative solutions, and innovative advertising techniques, and we take pride in providing the highest level of customer service. We also know that subcontracting to Advertising Agencies is a big step for some companies, which is why we treat all of our clients, no matter how big or small, as though they are our most important client. Every client has its own unique strengths, challenges, and personality-that's why each client's advertising techniques are unique and fresh.

Whatever your graphic design or advertising needs, SOHO Prospecting provides the knowledge, resources, advertising techniques, and experience to do the job right the first time.

Finally, subcontracting to advertising agencies allows companies to have access to experienced Media Planners. No matter how creative or compelling your B2B advertising is, it must reach the right audiences in order to be effective. As a full-service agency, committed to advertising techniques that get results, we develop advertising placement schedules that will give you the most impact for your money in the media that are seen by your customers and prospects.

If your company is considering subcontracting to advertising agencies and would like to receive the immediate and long-term benefits of working with an experienced, full-service B2B advertising techniques agency, call SOHO Prospecting.

PUBLIC RELATIONS AND ADVERTISING

Effective Uses of Public Relations

Soho Prospecting's Public Relations Campaign Management department measures its performance according to the impact that we have in driving your business forward. A strong Public Relations Action Plan is one of the most cost effective marketing activities available to growing companies or companies introducing new products or services.

Effective uses of Public Relations should generate revenue-enhancing results, and we measure our value accordingly. Soho's Public Relations Action Plan not only includes tracking media coverage and bylined articles, but also tracking our impact on such key business objectives as sales lead generation, inquiries, proposals written, revenues generated, etc.-objectives that directly tie our Public Relations Action Plan to your bottom line. That's what we mean when we say SOHO is committed to effective Public Relations Campaign Management. Good, effective Public Relations Campaign Management-unlike any other internet marketing and advertising endeavor-can support building value in a product or service. Effective use of Public Relations means a full page article with a photo in any magazine can garner greater and higher quality exposure than an advertisement in the same publication. A strong Public Relations Action Plan will incorporate articles written by third parties because these articles can build unparalleled credibility and value into the product. All of this can be achieved at a fraction of the cost of ad placement. That's effective Public Relations Campaign Management.

SOHO 's PR professionals understand effective uses of Public Relations and we know how to work with companies in all stages of growth. We know that a strong Public Relations Action Plan is critical to handling and promoting your product to the media, and we have an outstanding track record in Public Relations Campaign Management. We have an established editorial base and experience building new editor relationships from scratch. We are committed to delivering results that establish mind share, capture market share, and generate revenues!

Understanding Public Relations

Understanding effective uses of Public Relations is what makes SOHO's PR campaigns successful. It is not the goal of public relations to "sell" editors on your product. It is the goal to provide them with news and features that will interest their readers. How will your product change the marketplace? Who has used it effectively? Who will most benefit from it? When will it be widely available? Who will use it and how will it benefit that person's business or life? Providing answers to these questions in a well written article is part of effective uses of Public Relations

Soho Prospecting has built a strong reputation for our Public Relations Campaign Management and our ability to help companies achieve increased brand awareness and market penetration throughout the United States, Canada, and Europe. We help our clients gain greater name recognition for their products and services among media representatives, analysts, prospective customers, partners, and other target audiences through the implementation of a strong Public Relations Action Plan. Effective uses of Public Relations allow us to deliver measurable results to our clients, which range from small privately-owned start-up companies to larger, publicly-traded industry leaders. Our Public Relations Campaign management team specializes in delivering a broad spectrum of media and analyst relations support.

Whether you are launching a new product or service, introducing an entire product line, or repositioning an existing organization, Soho's Public Relations Campaign management team of highly qualified staff is committed to putting together an effective Public Relations Action Plan that can support your need to communicate your key messages.

7

Advertising and Government

The commission on Freedom of the press (1947) has listed most political and legal controls that have commonly been applied to the media. They include licensing in advance; censorship of offending material before publication; seizure of offending material; injunctions against publication of a newspaper or book or of specified content; requirement of surety bonds against libel or other offense; compulsory disclosure of ownership and authority; post publication criminal penalties for objectionable matter; post publication collection of damages in a civil action; post publication correction of libel and other misstatements; discrimination in granting access to news source and facilities; discrimination and denial in the use of communications facilities for distribution; taxes; discriminatory subsidies; and interference with buying, reading and listening.

STRUCTURAL TRANSFORMATION

Habermas believed that society becomes increasingly polarised into spheres of "public authority"-referring to the emergence of the state and associated political activity-and the "private"-the intimate domain of private relationships and the family.

Jürgen Habermas believed that the development of mass media was a crucial factor in the transition from an absolutist regime to liberal-democratic society. With the invention of the printing press and then the availability of newspapers and other forms of printed literature, Habermas claimed the emergence of an intermediate sphere which according to him is the bourgeois public sphere. This space will provide individuals with a chance to gather together to critically access, discuss and evaluate important contemporary issues of utmost importance for the people. He claimed that this will resemble the Greek agora. Habermas claims that this public use of reason not only acts as a regulatory mechanism over the state, which is now highly visible, but also as a catalyst for the replacement of the absolutist regime with a liberal democratic government.

Frankfurt School

The Frankfurt School came into existence in order to explain the success of Nazism in Weimar Germany. It sees the loss of individuality through decline of privacy as the main cause of dependence on great mass organisations. Habermas to a certain extent depends on some early critiques of the media from the 'Frankfurt School', such as that of Max Horkheimer, Theodor Adorno and Herbert Marcuse. For these three, media was a 'culture industry' which was creating an impact on passive individuals. These individuals merely absorb any information they are exposed to.

According to Thompson, the cause of this is the commodification of art and culture, which allows the possibility of "manipulation by demagogues". Emile Durkheim claimed that the interdependence of highly specialised individuals, or what is known as 'organic solidarity', is seen as being succeeded by a new and barbarous homogeneity. Due to this, only a 'mechanical' cohesion is possible, dependent on similarity and standardisation. Horkheimer thus argued that, paradoxically, individuality was impaired by the decline in the impulse for collective action. According to him, 'As the ordinary man withdraws from participating in political affairs, society tends to revert to the law of the jungle, which crushes all vestiges of individuality.' In this analysis the Frankfurt school saw totalitarianism emerging as a result of corrupt social institutions and the decline of liberal principles.

Thus Horkheimer claimed that: "Just as the slogans of rugged individualism are politically useful to large trusts in society seeking exemption from social control, so in mass culture the rhetoric of individuality, by imposing patterns for collective imitation, subverts the very principle to which it gives lip service." Adorno in The Jargon of Authenticity claimed that "mass media can create an aura which makes the spectator seem to experience a non-existent actuality". Thus a mass-produced, artificial culture replaces what went before.

MASS MEDIA AND MODERN SOCIETY

In political behaviour, opinion leading tends to correlate positively with status, whereas this is not the case in consumer behaviour. So for political behaviour, the general conclusion that the media merely fixes (confirms) people's opinion is not supported. Hovland, using experimental psychology, found significant effects of information on longer-term behaviour and attitudes, particularly in areas where most people have little direct experience (e.g. politics) and have a high degree of trust in the source (e.g. broadcasting). Since class has become a less reliable indicator of party (since the surveys of the 40s and 50s) the floating voter today is no longer the apathetic voter, but likely to be more well-informed than the consistent voter-and this mainly through the media.

There is also some very persuasive and empirical evidence suggesting that it is 'personal contact, not media persuasiveness' which counts. For example, Trenaman and McQuail (1961) found that 'don't knows' were less well informed than consistent voters, appearing uninterested, showing a general lack of information, and not just ignorance of particular policies or policies of one particular party. During the 1940 presidential election, a similar view was expressed by Katz and Lazarsfeld's theory of the two-step flow of communication, based on a study of electoral practices of the citizens of Erie County, Ohio. This examined the political propaganda prevalent in the media at the time during the campaign period to see whether it plays an integral role in influencing people's voting.

The results contradict this: Lazarsfeld et. al. (1944) find evidence for the Weberian theory of party, and identify certain factors, such as socio-economic circumstances, religious affiliation and area of residence, which together determine political orientation. The study claims that political propaganda serves to re-affirm the individual's pre-disposed orientation rather than to influence or change one's voting behaviour.

Thompson does not see 'mediated quasi-interaction' (the monological, mainly one-way communication of the mass media) as dominant, but rather as intermingling with traditional face-to-face interactions and mediated interactions (such as telephone conversations). Contrary to Habermas' pessimistic view, this allows both more information and discussion to come into the public domain (of mediated quasi-interaction) and more to be discussed within the private domain (since the media provides information individuals would not otherwise have access to).

FREE ENTERPRISE SOCIETY

Although a sizeable portion of mass media offerings-particularly news, commentaries, documentaries, and other informational programmes-deal with highly controversial subjects, the major portion of mass media offerings are designed to serve an entertainment function. These programmes tend to avoid controversial issues and reflect beliefs and values sanctified by mass audience. This course is followed by Television networks, whose investment and production costs are high. Jerry Mander's work has highlighted this particular outlook. According to him, the atomised individuals of mass society lose their souls to the phantom delights of the film, the soap opera, and the variety show.

They fall into a stupor; an apathetic hypnosis Lazarsfeld was to call the 'narcotizing dysfunction' of exposure to mass media. Individuals become 'irrational victims of false wants'-the wants which corporations have thrust upon them, and continue to thrust upon them, through both the advertising in the media (with its continual exhortation to consume) and through the individualist consumption culture it promulgates. Thus, according to the Frankfurt School, leisure has been industrialised. The production of culture had become standardised and dominated by the profit motive as in other industries. In a mass society leisure is constantly used to induce the appropriate values and motives in the public. The modern media train the young for consumption. 'Leisure had ceased to be the opposite of work, and had become a preparation for it.'

MASS MEDIA, MASS CULTURE AND ELITE

The relation of the mass media to contemporary popular culture is commonly conceived in terms of dissemination from the elite to the mass. There are periods when this process is reversed. During the 18th century it was the utmost chic for the aristocrats of the French Court to assume the guise of shepherds and peasants in their restive outings.

The long-term consequences of this are significant in conjunction with the continuing concentration of ownership and control of the media, leading to accusations of a 'media elite' having a form of 'cultural dictatorship'. Thus the continuing debate about the influence of 'media barons' such as Conrad Black and Rupert Murdoch. For example, the UK Observer reported the Murdoch-owned HarperCollins' refusal to publish Chris Patten's East and West, because of the former Hong Kong Governor's description of the Chinese leadership as "faceless Stalinists" possibly being damaging to Murdoch's Chinese broadcasting interests. In this case, the author was able to have the book accepted by another publisher, but this kind of censorship may point the way to the future. A related, but more insidious, form is that of self-censorship by members of the media in the interests of the owner, in the interests of their careers.

MODERN MASS MEDIA

During the recent years mass media has invaded the life of a common man in a big way. Upto seventies, mass media mainly remained confined to cinema, newspaper and radio. It was in the early eighties that audio-visual electronic medium in the form of television invaded the Indian scenario in a big way. The Government created huge infrastructure for spread of television network in the country. During this decade itself, advent of computers and Video Cassette Recorders (VCR) also supplemented the audio-visual media, putting well established medium of cinema to shade. During the early nineties, satellite television revolutionised the audio-visual media by reaching most of the households in the urban areas.

The latest invasion of audio-visual electronic media has suddenly increased the demand for professionals in journalism, technicians and other service individuals. These careers not only offer excellent opportunities, salaries, challenge and satisfaction of work, but also provide an opportunity for self-employment in various fields.

PRINT MEDIA

An old saying goes "pen is mightier than sword". The saying is not just a rhetoric. It reflects the power of print media. Being the most important media, print media pertains to broad activity of publication of newspapers, magazines and books and all persons connected with this activity have their contribution in successful running of this medium. While writing of books and contributing to magazines is largely a self-employment occupation, publication of newspapers and magazines involves a huge work force such as editors, technicians, printing technicians, composers, etc. In all these jobs the options of either working on desk or working in the field are available to the candidates. Reporters and correspondents generally operate in the field and submit their reports or stories on local, national or international issues pertaining to politics, trade, commerce, defence, sports, etc. One special category of reporters and correspondents operates in the field of investigative journalism.

This category of reporting pertains to investigation on the issues of public importance. This type of journalism and reporting attracts public attention instantaneously. Special attention in such reporting is required in the authenticity of information, selection of issues of public interest and succinct reporting in interesting and convincing language. In case of magazine reporting, many a times the reports, stories and features are contributed by free-lance reporters and part-time amateur writers. To pursue the career as a reporter one may attain bachelor's degree or post-graduate diploma in journalism.

Some of the universities offer post graduate diplomas of 9-month duration while others offer post-graduate one-year diploma in Public Relations or post graduate degree in mass-communication.

Latest trend in this regard is that big groups of newspapers advertise the posts of trainees in any of the above categories for which all graduates are eligible. After conducting the entrance examination, suitable graduate trainees, with flair for writing are selected and employed. In other words, now the formal academic qualification for being a reporter, copy writer or correspondent is not an essential qualification. Similarly, for writing features or analytical articles in magazines, one need not have any formal and professional academic qualification.

What is required is in-depth knowledge, command over the language concerned and outstanding analytical capability. Broadly speaking, anyone keen to pursue this career in any capacity must have outstanding general awareness, good perception, an eye for details and very keen observation. In turn, the career offers challenge, immense job satisfaction and fairly good compensation. For acquiring general awareness regular reading of newspapers, magazines and books on variety of topics is a must. Discussions on current topics also go a long way in widening the horizons of knowledge.

For the beginners, it is better to consult a good book on the background to current affairs so that further knowledge is strengthened after acquiring fundamental knowledge. Latest edition of "Current Affairs and Backgrounders" published by M/s Khanna Brothers (Publishers) Pvt Ltd is an ideal book for this purpose. Command over the concerned language is not a capability which can be acquired overnight. Regular and intensive reading as well as regular writing practice not only improves the command over the language, but also improves the flair for writing.

Candidates seriously pursuing this career should also go in for academic degree/diploma in Journalism/Public Relations/ Mass Communication from a good university or institute to have an edge over others.

AUDIO-VISUAL MEDIA

The requirement of personnel for the audio and audio-visual media is a little different than that for the print media. Traditionally, Radio has been the audio media having farthest reach. It was only with effect from the early eighties that Radio started getting replaced by Television. In most of the cases TV just supplemented the Radio. Despite the recent invasion by Doordarshan channels and Satellite and Cable TV, importance of Radio has not been undermined. The percentage of population covered by Radio is much more than the TV, mainly due to better technical infrastructure, longer range of short wave radio and cheaper cost and running cost of radio and transistors. Hence, Radio still remains very important medium.

Radio needs various types of personnel which includes announcers, news-readers, news-composers, writers, producers, commentators, and various categories of radio artists like singers, musicians, drama artists, narrators, etc. There is also a growing demand for good programmes and producers of such programmes. Audio-visual media is the strongest form of medium, but has limited reach. The earliest form of audio-visual medium was cinema which had very limited reach and people had to spend some money to have an access to it. Cinema, however, still enjoys the most glamorous place in the entire media. In this feature, Cinema as career in audio-visual media has been left out and will be covered later in a separate feature on careers.

Television, satellite and cable TV offer varied opportunities for career seekers. This medium offers excellent opportunities for newsreaders, composers, announcers, technicians, commentators, producers, models, actors, cameramen, script writers, etc. In addition to the Government-run Doordarshan, all other companies in the field of television, be it in production, direction, acting, cable operation and satellite TV operation, are handled by the individuals or private companies.

The choice of career is available in a variety of fields, not only with Doordarshan but with commercially-run media companies also. Candidates seeking any type of career in audio-visual electronic media must have characteristics like artistic inclination, expertise in own field of activity, pleasing personality, adaptability, general awareness, quick reflexes, flexibility and imagination. All these qualities must be coupled with the required technical and academic qualifications and professional competence. In case of announcers and newsreaders the qualities of good voice and presentable and photogenic face are additional requirements.

Good flow of spoken language and command over the language concerned are also pre-requisites in these cases. Capabilities to compare and compose become added qualifications. In addition to programmes and news, three other aspects of advertisement, engineering and management are also of paramount importance in TV and other electronic media. Technical and professional staff provide engineering services and act from behind the screen. These personnel are responsible for providing support services so essential for good quality of transmission, colour combinations, creation of support infrastructure for transmission, day-to-day management of video recording, time-management and other related aspects.

JOURNALISM

Journalism fascinates many young people who have a keen desire of seeing their name in print. Anyone who has written something for the college paper believes a career in journalism can be pursued. This feature points out that a career in journalism means more than merely writing well. As we receive a number of queries from our readers who want to become famous journalists and editors, we decided to describe in detail the requirements of newspapers and television channels today. This feature describes the skills required, as also the upside and the downside of the field. It also gives information about how one can become a journalist, the qualities that are required to be a successful one and addresses of some of the well known institutes. To an outsider, journalism is an exciting field in which fame and fortune can be achieved if one is able to write well. The names of some famous journalists come easily to mind. Khushwant Singh, who writes columns in several newspapers; M.J. Akbar, the editor of The Asian Age; and

Shobha De, former editor of Stardust and now a celebrated writer. Opportunities in the field have also multiplied with the boom in magazines and television channels.

Each of these requires people who can report and interpret events in a coherent and interesting manner. To assess whether you can be a famous journalist, you have to first know the skills that are required. The first is a good command over language. You must be able to express yourself well. A course in journalism will help sharpen these skills.

But this is not all. What is required is the ability to collect information and report events quickly. If you are in a television channel, it may mean going on camera as the event is happening, often a difficult task. In newspapers one has to write out the story before the deadline and it must contain all the correct information and the drama. Even a small error can destroy the credibility of the journalist. So journalism is just not about being able to write well alone.

The nature of a journalist's job is also changing. With news becoming competitive and personality-oriented, the job of a TV journalist often means waiting outside the offices or homes of politicians for hours and trying to catch a "sound byte" as the leader comes out.

The pursuit of truth does not extend beyond getting a small segment in the news programme. In this race, there is no room for being creative or following stories that one may like to. Threats of law-suits have made news channels and newspapers increasingly wary about publishing scoops and many of the investigative stories are just killed. There is little room for creativity in today's news organisations.

Increasing Scope

Once you accept these limitations, a career in journalism may be a good option. Some years back there was a boom in television channels which led to an increase in opportunities for aspiring journalists. Many print journalists shifted to television. Salaries had jumped. Today, there is a shakeout among the channels, which has led to the opportunities being reduced drastically. Newspapers and magazines continue to employ journalists, but with circulations and profitability under stress, three has been a decrease in opportunities somewhat. However, this situation may be linked to the economic slowdown and things may become better once the economy picks up. It may be mentioned that there are over 4,000 newspapers in 100 languages registered in India and the scope for employment will always exist, despite difficulties.

Avenues in journalism have multiplied because of unexpected growth in two new areas: (a) Niche publications; and (b) Web editing. We explain these below: Niche Publications: This means special purpose publications catering to particular industries, for example, travel and tourism, hotels, textiles or computers. Many such publications have been started in the past few years. These "niche" publications may not have the mass circulations of newspapers but are highly profitable. However, to work in them one needs to have journalistic skills as well as industry knowledge. Hence, MBAs are employed in business publications while computer experts find jobs in information technology magazines. The idea is to develop a specialisation and build on it. In the future, journalists with specialised skills in an industry may be more in demand than those with mere writing skills.

CULTURE AND DEMOCRACY

The Dominant Social Paradigm and Culture

A fruitful way to start the discussion of the significance of culture and its relationship to the mass media would be to define carefully our terms. This would help to avoid the confusion, which is not rare in discussions on the matter. Culture is frequently defined as the integrated pattern of human knowledge, belief, and behaviour.

This is a definition broad enough to include all major aspects of culture: language, ideas, beliefs, customs, taboos, codes, institutions, tools, techniques, works of art, rituals, ceremonies and so on. However, in what follows, I am not going to deal with all these aspects of culture unless they are related to what I call the dominant social paradigm. By this I mean the system of beliefs, ideas and the corresponding values which are dominant in a particular society at a particular moment of its history. It is clear that there is a significant degree of overlapping between these two terms although the meaning of culture is obviously broader than that of the social paradigm.

But, let us see first the elements shared by both terms. Both culture and the social paradigm are time-and space-dependent, i.e. they refer to a specific type of society at a specific time. Therefore, they both change from place to place and from one historical period to another. This implies that there can be no 'general theory' of History, which could determine the relationship between the cultural with the political or economic elements in society.

In other words, our starting point is the rejection not only of the crude economistic versions of Marxism (the economic base determines the cultural superstructure) but also of the more sophisticated versions of it (the economic base determines 'in the last instance' which element is to be dominant in each social formation).

In my view, which I expanded elsewhere, the dominant element in each social formation is not determined, for all time, by the economic base, or any other base. The dominant element is always determined by a creative act, i.e. it is the outcome of social praxis, of the activity of social individuals. Thus, the dominant element in theocratic societies was cultural, in the societies of 'actually existing socialism' political and so on.

Similarly, the dominant element in market economies is economic, as a result of the fact that the introduction of new systems of production during the Industrial Revolution in a commercial society, where the means of production were under private ownership and control, inevitably led to the transformation of the socially-controlled economies of the past (in which the market played a marginal role in the economic process) into the present market economies (defined as the self-regulating systems in which the fundamental economic problems—what, how, and for whom to produce—are solved 'automatically', through the price mechanism, rather than through conscious social decisions).

Still, the existence of a dominant element in a social formation does not mean that the relationship between this element and the other elements in it is one of heteronomy and dependence. Each element is autonomous and the relationship between the various elements is better described as one of interdependence. So, although it is the economic element which is the dominant one in the system of the market economy, this does not mean that culture is determined, even 'in the last instance' by this element. But, there are also some important differences between culture and the dominant social paradigm. Culture, exactly because of its greater scope, may express values and ideas, which are not necessarily consistent with the dominant institutions. In fact, this is usually the case characterising the arts and literature of a market economy, where, (unlike the case of 'actually existing socialism', or the case of feudal societies before), artists and writers have been given a significant degree of freedom to express their own views. But this is not the case with respect to the dominant social paradigm. In other words, the beliefs, ideas and the corresponding values which are dominant in a market economy and the corresponding market society have to be consistent with the economic element in it, i.e. with the economic institutions which, in turn, determine that the dominant elites in this society are the economic elites (those owning and controlling the means of production).

This has always been the case in History and will also be the case in the future. No particular type of society can reproduce itself unless the dominant beliefs, ideas and values are consistent with the existing institutional framework.

For instance, in the societies of 'actually existing socialism' the dominant social paradigm had to be consistent with the dominant element in them, (which was the political), and the corresponding political institutions, which determined that the dominant elites in this society were the political elites (party bureaucracy). Similarly, in the democratic society of the future, the dominant social paradigm had to be consistent with the dominant element in them, which would be the political, and the corresponding democratic institutions, which would secure that there would be no formal elites in this kind of society (although, of course, if democracy does not function properly the emergence of informal elites could not be ruled out).

So, culture and, in particular, the social dominant paradigm play a crucial role in the determination of individual and collective values. As long as individuals live in a society, they are not just individuals but social individuals, subject to a process, which socialises them and induces them to internalise the existing institutional framework as well as the dominant social paradigm. In this sense, people are not completely free to create their world but are conditioned by History, tradition and culture. Still, this socialisation process is broken, at almost all times-as far as a minority of the population is concerned-and in exceptional historical circumstances even with respect to the majority itself.

In the latter case, a process is set in motion that usually ends with a change of the institutional structure of society and of the corresponding social paradigm. Societies therefore are not just "collections of individuals" but consist of social individuals, who are both free to create their world, (in the sense that they can give birth to a new set of institutions and a corresponding social paradigm), and are created by the world, (in the sense that they have to break with the dominant social paradigm in order to recreate the world).

VALUES OF THE MARKET ECONOMY

As the dominant economic institutions in a market economy are those of markets and private ownership of the means of production, as well as the corresponding hierarchical structures, the dominant social paradigm promoted by the mainstream mass media and other cultural institutions, (e.g. universities) has to consist of ideas, beliefs and values which are consistent with them. Thus, the kind of social 'sciences' which are taught at universities and the kind of articles which fill academic journals, explicitly, or usually implicitly, take for granted the existing economic institutions.

Therefore, their search for 'truth' in the analysis of major economic or social problems is crucially conditioned by this fundamental characteristic. The causes of world-wide unemployment, for instance, or of massive inequality and concentration of economic power, will not be related to the system of the market economy itself; instead, the malfunctioning of the system or bad policies will be blamed, which supposedly can be tackled by the appropriate improvement of the system's functioning, or the 'right' economic policies.

In economics, in particular, the dominant theory/ideology since the emergence of the market economy has been economic liberalism, in its various versions: from the old classical and neo-classical schools up to the modern versions of it in the form of supply-side economics, new classical macro-economics etc. But, from Adam Smith to Milton Friedman, the values adopted are the same: competition and individualism, which, supposedly, are the only values that could secure freedom.

Thus, for Adam Smith, the individual pursuit of self-interest in a market economy will guarantee social harmony and, therefore, the main task of government is the defence of the rich against the poor. So, in Smith's system, as Canterbery puts it, 'individual self-interest is the motivating force, and the built-in regulator that keeps the economy from flying apart is competition'. Similarly, for Milton Friedman, the Nobel-prize winner in economics (note: the Nobel Prize in economics was never awarded to an economist who challenged the very system of the market economy) the capitalist market economy is identified with freedom:

> The kind of economic organisation that provides freedom directly, namely, competitive capitalism, also promotes political freedom because it separates economic power from political power and in this way enables the one to offset the other...The two ideas of human freedom and economic freedom working together came to their greatest fruition in the United States

It is obvious that in this ideology, which passes as the 'science' of economics, the values of individualism and competition are preferred over the values of collectivism and solidarity/co-operation, since freedom itself is identified with the former values as against the latter. But, it 'happens' also that the same values are the only ones, which could secure the production and reproduction of the market economy. No market economy can function properly unless those in control of it, (i.e., the economic elites), at least, and as many of the rest as possible, are motivated by individualism and competition.

This is because the dynamic of a market economy crucially depends on competition and individual greed. Furthermore, the fact that often the economic elites resort to state protection against foreign competition, if the latter threatens their own position, does not in the least negate the fact that competition is the fundamental organising principle of the market economy. It is therefore no historical accident that, as Polanyi has persuasively shown, the establishment of the market economy implied sweeping aside traditional cultures and values and replacing the values of solidarity, altruism, sharing and co-operation (which usually marked community life) with the values of individualism and competition as the dominant values. As Ray Canterbery stresses:

> The capitalistic ethic leans toward the extreme of selfishness (fierce individualism) rather than toward altruism. There is little room for collective decision making in an ethic that argues that every individual should go his or her own way. As we have seen, the idea that capitalism protects 'individual rights' would have been rejected during the early Middle Ages. 'Individual rights' were set in advance by the structure of feudalism, governed by the pull of tradition and the push of authority. Economics was based upon mutual needs and obligations.

A good example of the enthusiastic support for these values today is, again, the Nobel-prize winner in economics Milton Friedman. According to him:

> Few trends could so thoroughly undermine the very foundations of our free society as the acceptance by corporate officials of a social responsibility other than to make as much money for their stockholders as possible. This (social responsibility) is a fundamentally subversive doctrine.

Indeed, it is not Friedman who supports values which are inconsistent with the market economy system but the various social democrats and Green economists, who, taking for granted the market economy system, proceed to argue in favour of utopian economic institutions incorporating values which are inconsistent with this system (*e.g.*'stakeholding' capitalism, 'social investment' etc).

As I attempted to show elsewhere, the basic cause of the failure of both the 'actually existing socialism' in the East and social democracy in the West was exactly that they attempted to merge two fundamentally incompatible elements: the 'growth' element, (which implies the concentration of economic power and expresses the logic of the market economy), with the social justice element (which is inherently linked to equality and expresses socialist ethics).

Chomsky's Views

However, quite apart from social democrats and reformist Greens, there is an alternative view about the values of the market economy proposed by Noam Chomsky, which, however, ends up with similar conclusions about the feasibility and desirability of state action with respect to controlling today's market economy.

Thus, for Chomsky, the values which motivate today's elites in advanced capitalist countries are not individualism and competition; instead, these elites simply use such values as propaganda in their attempt to 'persuade' their own public and the countries in the periphery and semi-periphery to implement them whereas they themselves demand and enjoy the protection of their own states:

For the general public, individualism and competition are the prescribed values. Not for elites, however. They demand and obtain the protection of a powerful state, and insist on arrangements that safeguard them from unfettered competition or the destructive consequences of individualism. The process of corporatization is a standard illustration, as is the reliance in every economy—crucially, the US—on socialisation of risk and cost. The need to undermine the threat of competition constantly takes new forms: today, one major form, beyond corporatization, is the development of a rich network of "strategic alliances" among alleged competitors: IBM-Toshiba-Siemens, for example, or throughout the automotive industry.

This has reached such extremes that prominent analysts of the business world now speak of a new form of "alliance capitalism" that is replacing the managerial/corporate capitalism that had largely displaced proprietary capitalism a century ago in advanced sectors of the economy.

Chomsky has recently expanded on the same theme in a New Left Review article in which it is made clear that his views above about the values of the market economy are perfectly consistent with his views on the nature of today's capitalism. In this article he first states that the word 'capitalist' does not mean capitalist but rather it refers to state subsidised and protected private power centres, or 'collectivist legal entities,' which embody today's corporatization of the market economy. He then goes on to describe corporatization and the role of the state as follows:

The corporatization process was largely a reaction to great market failures of the late nineteenth century, and it was a shift from something you might call proprietary capitalism to the administration of markets by collectivist legal entities-mergers, cartels, corporate alliances-in association with powerful states...the primary task of the states-and bear in mind that, with all the talk about minimising the state, in the OECD countries the state continues to grow relative to GNP, notably in the 1980s and 1990s-is essentially to socialise risk and cost, and to privatise power and profit.

Furthermore, Chomsky's views about the market economy's values and the nature of present capitalism are, in turn, entirely consistent with his present views on the potential role of the state in controlling today's market economy. Thus, as Chomsky stresses in the aforementioned article: The long-term goal of such initiatives (like the Multilateral Agreement on Investment-MAI) is clear enough to anyone with open eyes; an international political economy which is organised by powerful states and secret bureaucracies whose primary function is to serve the concentrations of private power which administer markers through their own internal operations, through networks of corporate alliances, including the intra-firm transactions that are mislabelled 'trade'. They rely on the public for subsidy, research and development, for innovation and for bailouts when things go wrong. They rely on the powerful states for protection from dangerous 'democracy openings'. In such ways, they seek to ensure that the 'prime beneficiaries' of the world's wealth are the right people: the smug and prosperous 'Americans'; the 'domestic constituencies and their counterparts elsewhere. The scale of all of this is nowhere near as great or, for that matter, as novel as claimed; in many ways it's a return to the early twentieth century. And there's no reason to doubt that it can be controlled even within existing formal institutions of parliamentary democracy.

One, however, could object on several grounds this stand, as portrayed by the above extracts. First, the argument about the values of the economic elites, as I attempted to show above, is contestable; second, the nature of today's market economy could be seen in a very different analytical framework than the one suggested by Chomsky and, finally, it could be shown that the way out of the present multi-dimensional crisis and the related huge concentration of power can not be found in fragmented and usually 'monothematic' defensive battles with the elites. Such battles, even if sometimes victorious, are never going to win the war, as long as they are not an integral part of a new popular movement's fight against the system of the market economy itself, which is the ultimate cause of the concentration of economic power.

Shift from proprietary (or entrepreneurial) capitalism to the present internationalised market economy, where a few giant corporations control the world economy, did not happen, as Chomsky presents it, as the outcome of 'a reaction to great market failures of the late nineteenth century.' What Chomsky omits is that it was competition, which led from simple entrepreneurial firms to the present giant corporations.

The market failures he mentions are not a God-given calamity. Excepting the case of monopolies, almost all market failures in history have been directly or indirectly related to competition. It is competition, which creates the need for expansion, so that the best (from the profit of view of profits) technologies and methods of organising production (economies of scale etc) are used. It is the same competition, which has led to the present explosion of mergers and take-overs in the advanced capitalist countries, as well as the various 'strategic alliances'. For instance, the recently announced merger of giant oil companies, in a sense, is the result of a 'market failure' because of the fall in their profits. But, in a deeper sense, this merger, as well as the take-overs, strategic alliances etc going on at the moment, are simply the result of self-protective action taken by giant corporations, in order to survive the cut-throat competition launched by the present internationalisation of the market economy. Therefore, it is competition, which has led to the present corporate (or 'alliance') capitalism, not 'market failures' and/or the associated state activity, which just represent the effects of competition.

Similarly, the present internationalisation of the market economy is not just the result of state action to liberalise financial and commodity markets. In fact, the states were following the de facto internationalisation of the market economy, which was intensified by the activities of multi-nationals, when, (in the late seventies), under pressure from the latter, started the process of liberalising the financial markets and further deregulating the commodity markets (through the GATT rounds). Therefore, the present inter-nationalisation is in fact the outcome of the grow-or-die dynamics, which characterises the market economy, a dynamics that is initiated by competition, the crucial fact neglected by Chomsky.

It is also the same internationalisation of the market economy, which became incompatible with the degree of state control of the economy achieved by the mid seventies, that made necessary the present neoliberal consensus. The latter, therefore, is not just a policy change, as socialdemocrats and their fellow travellers suggest, but represents an important structural change. So, minimising the state is not just 'talk', as Chomsky assumes basing his argument on the assumption that 'the state continues to grow relative to GNP, notably in the 1980s and 1990s'. However, not only the fall in the growth rate of government spending in OECD countries was higher than that of the other parts of aggregate demand in the period 1980-93 but, in fact, the (weighted average) general government consumption of high income economies was lower in 1995, at 15% of GNP, than in 1980 (17%). All this, not taking into account the drastic reduction in the overall public sectors in the last twenty years, as a result of the massive privatisation of state industries. Therefore, minimising the state, far from being 'talk' is a basic element of the present neoliberal consensus.

Also, strategic alliances, mergers and take-overs do not represent a movement away from the market economy but a movement towards a new form of it. Away from a market economy, which was geared by the internal market and towards a market economy, which is geared by the world market. This means further and further concentration of economic power not only in terms of incomes and wealth but also in terms of concentration of the power to control world output, trade and investment in fewer and fewer hands. However, the oligopolisation of competition does not mean lack of competition.

Furthermore, it will be wrong to assume that the main characteristic of the present period is an 'assault against the markets', as the purist neoliberal argument goes, which Chomsky accepts. The present period of neoliberal consensus can be characterised instead, as an assault against social controls on markets, particularly those aiming at the protection of humans and nature against the effects of marketization, (the historical process that has transformed the socially controlled economies of the past into the market economy of the present). Such controls have been introduced as a result of social struggles undertaken by those who are adversely affected by the market economy's effects on them (social security legislation, welfare benefits, macro-economic controls to secure full employment etc).

What is still debated within the economic elites is the fate of what I call social controls in the broad sense, i.e. those primarily aiming at the protection of those controlling the market economy against foreign competition (tariffs, import controls, exchange controls—in the past, and non-tariff barriers, massive public subsidy for R&D, risk-protection (bailouts), administration of markets etc—at present). Thus, pure neoliberal economists, bankers, some politicians and others are against any kind of social controls over markets (in the narrow or broad sense above). On the other hand, the more pragmatic governments of the neoliberal consensus, from Reagan to Clinton and from Thatcher to Blair, under the pressure of the most vulnerable to competition sections of their own economic elites, have kept many social controls in the broad sense and sometimes even expanded them (not hesitating to go to war to secure their energy supplies) giving rise to the pure neoliberal argument (adopted by Chomsky) about an assault on markets.

In this context, one should not confuse liberalism/ neoliberalism with laissez-faire. As I tried to show elsewhere, it was the state itself that created the system of self-regulating markets. Furthermore, some form of state intervention has always been necessary for the smooth functioning of the market economy system.

The state, since the collapse of the socialdemocratic consensus, has seen a drastic reduction in its economic role as it is no longer involved in a process of directly intervening in the determination of income and employment through fiscal and monetary policies.

However, even today, the state still plays an important role in securing, through its monopoly of violence, the stability of the market economy framework and in maintaining the infrastructure for the smooth functioning of it.

It is within this role of maintaining the infrastructure that we may see the activities of the state in socialising risk and cost and in maintaining a safety net in place of the old welfare state. Furthermore, the state is called today to play a crucial role with respect to the supply-side of the economy and, in particular, to take measures to improve competitiveness and to train the working force to the requirements of the new technology, in supporting research and development and even in subsidising export industries wherever required. Therefore, the type of state intervention which is compatible with the marketization process not only is not discouraged but, instead, is actively promoted by most of the professional politicians of the neoliberal consensus.

It is true that the economic elites do not like the kind of competition which, as a result of the uneven development of the world market economy, threatens their own interests and this is why they have always attempted (and mostly succeeded) to protect themselves against it.

But, it is equally true that it was the force of competition which has always fuelled the expansion of the market economy and that it was the values of competition and self-interest which have always characterised the value system of the elites which control the market economy. Chomsky, however, sometimes gives the impression that, barring some 'accidents' like the market failures he mentions, as well as the aggressive state support that economic elites have always enjoyed, the 'corporatization' of the market economy might have been avoided.

But, of course, neither proprietary capitalism (or any other type of it) is desirable—since it cannot secure covering the basic needs of all people—nor can we deny all radical analysis of the past hundred and fifty years or so, from Marx to Bookchin, and all historical experience since then, which leads to one conclusion: the market economy is geared by a grow-or-die dynamic fuelled by competition, which is bound to lead to further and further concentration of economic power.

Therefore, the problem is not the corporatization of the market economy which, supposedly, represents 'an attack on markets and democracy', and which was unavoidable anyway within the dynamic of the market economy. In other words, the problem is not corporate market economy/capitalism, as if some other kind of market economy/capitalism was feasible or desirable, but the market economy/capitalism itself. Otherwise, one may easily end up blaming the elites for violating the rules of the game, rather than blaming the rotten game itself!

If the above analytical framework is valid then obviously it is not possible, within the existing institutional framework of parliamentary democracy and the market economy to check the process of increasing concentration of economic power. This is a process that is going since the emergence of the market economy system, some two centuries ago, and no social-democratic governments or grassroots movements were ever able to stop it, or even to retard it, apart from brief periods of time. In fact, even the grass root 'victory' hailed by Chomsky against the MAI proposals is doubtful whether it would have been achieved had there been no serious divisions among the economic elites about it.

Furthermore, the 'victory' itself has already started showing signs that it was hollow, as it is now clear that the MAI agreement was not, in fact, set aside, but it is simply implemented 'by installments', through the 'back door' of the IMF at present, and possibly the World Trade Organisation in the future. The basic reason why such battles are doomed is that they are not an integral part of a comprehensive political program to replace the institutional framework of the market economy itself and, as such, they can easily be marginalised or lead to simple (easily reversible) reforms.

The inevitable conclusion is that only the struggle for the building of a new massive movement aiming at fighting 'from without' for the creation of a new institutional framework, and the development of the corresponding culture and social paradigm, might have any chances to lead to a new society characterised by the equal distribution of power.

CULTURAL HOMOGENISATION

The establishment of the market economy implied sweeping aside traditional cultures and values. This process was accelerated in the twentieth century with the spreading all over the world of the market economy and its offspring the growth economy. As a result, today, there is an intensive process of culture homogenisation at work, which not only rules out any directionality towards more complexity, but in effect is making culture simpler, with cities becoming more and more alike, people all over the world listening to the same music, watching the same soap operas on TV, buying the same brands of consumer goods, etc.

The establishment of the neoliberal consensus in the last twenty years or so, following the collapse of the socialdemocratic consensus, has further enhanced this process of cultural homogenisation. This is the inevitable outcome of the liberalisation and de-regulation of markets and the consequent intensification of commercialisation of culture.

As a result, traditional communities and their cultures are disappearing all over the world and people are converted to consumers of a mass culture produced in the advanced capitalist countries and particularly the USA. In the film industry, for instance, even European countries with a strong cultural background and developed economies have to effectively give up their own film industries, unable to compete with the much more competitive US industry.

Thus, in the early 1990s, US films' share amounted to 73% of the European market. Also, indicative of the degree of concentration of cultural power in the hands of a few US corporations is the fact that, in 1991, a handful of US distributors controlled 66% of total cinema box office and 70% of the total number of video rentals in Britain.

Thus, the recent emergence of a sort of "cultural" nationalism in many parts of the world expresses a desperate attempt to keep a cultural identity in the face of market homogenisation. But, cultural nationalism is devoid of any real meaning in an electronic environment, where 75 percent of the international communications flow is controlled by a small number of multinationals. In other words, cultural imperialism today does not need, as in the past, a gunboat diplomacy to integrate and absorb diverse cultures.

The marketization of the communications flow has already established the preconditions for the downgrading of cultural diversity into a kind of superficial differentiation akin to a folklorist type. Furthermore, it is indicative that today's 'identity movements', like those in Western Europe (from the Flemish to the Lombard and from the Scots to the Catalans) which demand autonomy as the best way to preserve their cultural identity, in fact, express their demand for individual and social autonomy in a distorted way.

The distortion arises from the fact that the marketization of society has undermined the community values of reciprocity, solidarity and co-operation in favour of the market values of competition and individualism. As a result, the demand for cultural autonomy is not founded today on community values which enhance co-operation with other cultural communities but, instead, on market values which encourage tensions and conflicts with them. In this connection, the current neoracist explosion in Europe is directly relevant to the effectual undermining of community values by neoliberalism, as well as to the growing inequality and poverty following the rise of the neoliberal consensus.

Finally, one should not underestimate the political implications of the commercialisation and homogenisation of culture. The escapist role traditionally played by Hollywood films has now acquired a universal dimension, through the massive expansion of TV culture and its almost full monopolisation by Hollywood subculture.

Every single TV viewer in Nigeria, India, China or Russia now dreams of the American way of life, as seen on TV serials (which, being relatively inexpensive and glamorous, fill the TV programmes of most TV channels all over the world) and thinks in terms of the competitive values imbued by them. The collapse of existing socialism has perhaps more to do with this cultural phenomenon, as anecdotal evidence indicates, than one could imagine.

As various TV documentaries have shown, people in Eastern European countries, in particular, thought of themselves as some kind of 'abnormal' compared with what western TV has established as the 'normal'.

In fact, many of the people participating in the demonstrations to bring down those regimes frequently referred to this 'abnormality', as their main incentive for their political action. In this problematique, one may criticise the kind of cultural relativism supported by some in the Left, according to which almost all cultural preferences could be declared as rational (on the basis of some sort of rationality criteria), and therefore all cultural choices deserve respect, if not admiration, given the constraints under which they are made. But, obviously, the issue is not whether our cultural choices are rational or not. Nor the issue is to assess 'objectively' our cultural preferences as right or wrong. The real issue is how to make a choice of values which we think is compatible with the kind of society we wish to live in and then make the cultural choices which are compatible with these values.

This is because the transition to a future society based on alternative values presupposes that the effort to create an alternative culture should start now, in parallel with the effort to establish the new institutions compatible with the new values. On the basis of the criterion of consistency between our cultural choices and the values of a truly democratic society, one could delineate a way beyond post-modern relativism and distinguish between 'preferable' and 'non-preferable' cultural choices.

So, all those cultural choices involving films, videos, theatrical plays etc, which promote the values of the market economy and particularly competition for money, individualism, consumerist greed, as well as violence, racism, sexism etc should be shown to be non-preferable and people should be encouraged to avoid them. On the other hand, all those cultural choices, which involve the promotion of the community values of mutual aid, solidarity, sharing and equality for all (irrespective of race, sex, ethnicity) should be promoted as preferable.

ROLE OF MASS MEDIA TODAY

A basic issue in the discussion of the role of the mass media in today's society is whether they do reflect social reality in a broad sense, or whether, instead, the elites which control them filter out the view of reality which they see fit to be made public. To my mind, the answer to this question is that the media do both, depending on the way we define reality.

To take, first, political reality, mass media, in one sense, do not provide a faked view of it. Taking into account what is considered as politics today, i.e. the activity of professional politicians 'representing' the people, one may argue that it is politics itself, which is faked, and mass media simply reproduce this reality. In this sense, the issue is not whether the mass media manipulate democracy, since it is democracy itself, which is faked, and not its mass media picture, which simply reflects the reality of present 'democracy'.

But, at the same time, if we give a different definition to political reality, mass media do provide, in general, a distorted picture of it. In other words, if we define as real politics the political activity of people themselves (for instance, the collective struggles of various sectors of the population around political, economic or social issues) rather than that of professional politicians, then, the mass media do distort the picture they present about political reality. They do so, by minimising the significance of this type of activity, by distorting its meaning, by marginalising it, or by simply ignoring it completely.

Furthermore, mass media do provide a distorted picture of political reality when they come to report the causes of crises, or of the conflicts involving various sections of the elites. In such cases they faithfully reflect the picture that the sections of the elites controlling them wish to reproduce. The latest example of this was the way in which the Anglo-American media, in particular, distorted the real meaning of the criminal bombardment of the Iraqi people at the end of 1998. Thus, exactly, as in their reporting during the war in the Gulf, the real cause of the conflict, (i.e. who controls the world's oil, irrespective of where the oil stocks are located—the elites of the North versus those in the South), was distorted as a conflict between the peace loving regimes in the North versus the rogue regimes in the South, or, in more sophisticated versions supported by socialdemocrat intellectuals, as a conflict between the 'democracies' in the North versus the 'despotic regimes' in the South over the control of oil.

Under these circumstances, it is obvious that the mass media usually offer a true glimpse of reality only when the elites are divided with respect to their conception of a particular aspect of political reality. From this point of view, concentration in the mass media industry is significant and whether the media are owned by 100 or 10 owners does indeed matter in the struggle for social change. It is for instance such divisions among the European elites over the issue of joining the European

Monetary Union which have allowed a relatively wide media discussion on the true meaning of European integration, particularly in countries like Britain where the elites were split.

It was also similar divisions between the Anglo-American and the European elites over the latest war crime in the Gulf which made a bit clearer the directly criminal role of the former (support for the bombardments), as well as the indirectly criminal role of the latter (support for the embargo). It is not accidental that in the USA and UK, where the media played a particularly despicable role in distorting the truth and misinforming the public, the polls showed consistently vast majorities in favour of the criminal activities of their elites. Of course, this does not mean that decentralisation of power in the mass media industry (or anywhere else) represents by itself, even potentially, a radical social change leading to an authentic democracy. Still, the significance of decentralisation in the media industry with respect to raising consciousness should not be ignored.

THE ECONOMIC REALITY

As regards economic reality, mass media, in one sense again, do provide a relatively accurate picture of what counts as economic reality today. This is when the media, taking for granted the system of the market economy, end up with a partial picture of economic reality where what matters is not whether the basic needs of the population are covered adequately but whether prices (in commodity and stock markets), interest rates, exchange rates and consequently profit rates are going up or down. Still, in another sense, the very fact that mass media take for granted the system of the market economy means that they cannot 'see' the 'systemic' nature of most of the real economic problems (unemployment, poverty and so on) and therefore inevitably end up with a faked image of economic reality. This way of seeing economic reality is not imposed on the media by their owners, important as their influence may otherwise be, or by their internal hierarchical structure etc. The media simply reflect the views of orthodox economists, bankers, businessmen and professional politicians, i.e. of all those who express the dominant social paradigm.

But if the picture of political and economic reality offered by the media is mixed this is not the case with respect to ecological reality. As no meaningful reporting of the ecological crisis is possible unless it refers to the systemic causes of it, which by definition are excluded by the discourse in the mainstream media, the result is a complete misinformation, or just straightforward description of the symptoms of the crisis. The mass media are flooded by the 'realist' Greens who fill the various ecological parties and who blame technology, consumerist values, legislation etc—anything but the real cause of the crisis, i.e. the very system of the market economy.

Similarly, the reporting of the present social crisis never links the explosion of crime and drug abuse, for instance, with their root cause, i.e. the increasing concentration of political, economic and social power in the hands of various elites. Instead, the symptoms of the social crisis are distortedly reported as its causes and the media blame, following the advice of the establishment 'experts', the breaking of the traditional family, or of the school, as the causes of crime. Similarly, various 'progressive' intellectuals (like the lamentable ex 'revolutionary' and now well promoted by the mainstream media Euro-parliamentarian Con Bendit) blame the prohibitive legislation on drugs for the massive explosion of drug abuse!

However, there is another approach being promoted recently by system theorists, according to which mass media do not just either reflect or distort reality but also manufacture it. This is not said in the usual sense of manufacturing consent described by Chomsky and Herman or, alternatively, by Bourdieu, which is basically a one-way process whereby the elites controlling the mass media filter out the information, through various control mechanisms, in order to create consent around their agenda.

Instead, system theorists talk about a two-way process whereby social reality and mass media are seen as two interdependent levels, the one intruding into the other. This is based on the valid hypothesis that reality is not just something external to the way it is conceived. TV watching is a constituent moment of reality since our information about reality consists of conceptions that constitute reality itself. At the same time, the conception of reality is conditioned by the media functioning, which is differentiated in relation to the other social systems (political, economic etc).

In the systems analysis problematique, it is not the economic, or the political systems, which control the media functioning. What determines their functioning, as well as their communicative capability, is their ability to generate irritation-a fact that could go a long way to explain the high ratings of exciting or irritating TV programs.

The diversified functioning of mass media creates, in turn, the conditions for a social dynamic which, in a self-reflective and communicative way, reproduces, as well as institutes, society. Thus, whereas the early modern society is instituted through a transcendental subjectivity and a material mode of production, the present post-modern society's reproduction depends on the processes of communicative rationality. The mass media are an integral and functional part of the communicative processes of post-modern society.

However, one may point out here that although it is true that social reality and mass media are interacting, i.e. that our conception of TV news is a constituent element of reality and at the same time our conception of reality is conditioned by TV functioning, this does not imply that the diversified functioning of mass media creates the conditions for a social dynamic which acts for the institution of society, although it does play this role as far as its reproduction is concerned.

The meaning we assign to TV reporting is not determined exogenously but by our world view, our own paradigm, which in turn, as we have seen above, is the result of a process of socialisation that is conditioned by the dominant social paradigm.

Furthermore, TV functioning plays a crucial role in the reproduction of the dominant social paradigm and the socialisation process generally. So, the diversified functioning of TV does indeed create the conditions for a social dynamic leading to the reproduction of the status quo, but in no way could be considered as doing the same for instituting society.

AIMS AND ACHIEVEMENTS

The goals of the mass media are determined by those owning and controlling them, who, usually, are members of the economic elites that control the market economy itself. Given the crucial role that the media could play in the internalisation of the dominant social paradigm and therefore the reproduction of the institutional framework which secures the concentration of power in the hands of the elites, it is obvious that those owning and controlling the mass media have broader ideological goals than the usual goals pursued by those owning and controlling other economic institutions, i.e. profit maximising.

Therefore, an analysis that would attempt to draw conclusions on the nature and significance of media institutions on the basis of the profit dimension alone, (i.e. that they share a common goal and consequently a similar internal hierarchical structure with all other economic institutions and that they just sell a product, the only difference with other economic institutions being that the product is the audience,) is bound to be one-dimensional. Profit maximising is only one parameter, often not even the crucial one, which conditions the role of mass media in a market economy. In fact, one could mention several instances where capitalist owners chose even to incur significant losses (which they usually cover from other profitable activities) in order to maintain the social influence (and prestige), which ownership of an influential daily offers to them (Murdoch and The Times of London is an obvious recent example).

Given the ultimate ideological goal of mass media, the main ways in which they try to achieve it are:

- first, by assisting in the internalisation of the dominant social paradigm and,
- second, by marginalising, if not excluding altogether, conceptions of reality which do not conform with the dominant social paradigm.

But, what are the mechanisms through which the media can achieve their goals? To give an answer to this question we have to examine a series of mechanisms, most of them 'automatic' built-in mechanisms, which ensure effective achievement of these goals. It will be useful here to distinguish between 'internal' and 'external' control mechanisms, which function respectively as internal and external constraints on the freedom of media workers to reproduce reality.

Both internal and external mechanisms work mainly through competition which secures homogenisation with respect to the media's main goals. Competition is of course the fundamental organisational principle of a market economy; but, it plays a special role with respect to the media. As Bourdieu points out, competition 'rather than automatically generating originality and diversity tends to favour uniformity'. Still, competition is not the only force securing homogenisation. In a similar way as with the market economy itself, competition provides only the dynamic mechanism of homogenisation.

It is the fact that owners of mass media, as well as managers and the highest paid journalists, share the same interest in the reproduction of the existing institutional framework which constitutes the 'base', on which this competition is developed.

But, let us consider briefly the significance of the various control mechanisms. The main 'internal control' mechanisms are ownership and the internal hierarchical structure, which are, both, crucial in the creation of the conditions for internal competition among journalists, whereas the 'ratings' mechanism plays a similar role in the creation of the conditions for external competition among media.

Starting with ownership, it matters little, as regards the media's overall goals defined above, whether they are owned and controlled by the state and/or the state-controlled institutions or whether, instead, they are owned and controlled by private capital.

However, there are certain secondary differences arising from the different ownership structures which may be mentioned. These secondary differences have significant implications, particularly with respect to the structure of the elites controlling the media, their own organisational structure and their 'image' with respect to their supposedly 'objective' role in the presentation of information.

As regards the elite structure, whereas under a system of state ownership and control the mass media are under the direct control of the political elite and the indirect control of the economic elites, under a system of private ownership and control, the media are just under the direct control of the economic elites.

This fact, in turn, has some implications on whether filtering out of information takes place directly through state control, or indirectly through various economic mechanisms (e.g. ratings).As regards the media organisational structure, whereas state-owned media are characterised by bureaucratic rigidity and inefficiency, privately owned media are usually characterised by more flexibility and economic efficiency. Finally, the 'objective' image of mass media suffers less in case of private ownership compared to the case of state ownership. This is because in the latter case control of information is more direct and therefore more obvious than in the former.

Another important internal control mechanism is the hierarchical structure which characterises all media institutions (as it does all economic institutions in a market economy) and which implies that all-important decisions are taken by a small managerial group within them, who are usually directly responsible to the owners.

The hierarchical structure creates a constant internal competition among journalists as to who will be more agreeable to the managerial group (on which their career and salary prospects depend).

Similarly, people in the managerial group are in constant competition as to who will be more agreeable to the owners (on which their highly paid position depends). So, everybody in this hierarchical structure knows well (or soon learns) what is agreeable and what is not and acts accordingly. Therefore, the filtering of information works through self-censorship rather than through any kind of 'orders from above'. The effect of the internal hierarchical structure is to impose, through the internal competition that it creates, a kind of homogenisation in the journalists' performance.

But, does this exclude the possibility that some media workers may have incentives other those determined by career ambitions? Of course, not. But, such people, as Chomsky points out, will never find a place in the corridors of media power and, one way or another, will be marginalised:

They (journalists) say, quite correctly, "nobody ever tells me what to write. I write anything I like. All this business about pressures and constraints is nonsense because I'm never under any pressure." Which is completely true, but the point is that they wouldn't be there unless they had already demonstrated that nobody has to tell them what to write because they are going to say the right thing... it is not purposeful censorship. It is just that you don't make it to those positions. That includes the left (what is called the left), as well as the right. Unless you have been adequately socialised and trained so that there are some thoughts you just don't have, because if you did have them, you wouldn't be there.

But, how is it determined what is agreeable? Here it is where the 'external' control mechanisms come into play. It is competition among the various media organisations, which homogenises journalists' behaviour.

This competition takes the form of a struggle to improve ratings (as regards TV channels) or circulation (as regards newspapers, magazines etc). Ratings or circulation are important not per se but because the advertising income of privately owned mass media (which is the extra income determining their survival or death) depends on them. The result is, as Pierre Bourdieu points out that: Ratings have become the journalist's Last Judgement... Wherever you look, people are thinking in terms of market success.

Only thirty years ago, and since the middle of the nineteenth century—since Baudelaire and Flaubert and others in avant-garde milieux of writers' writers, writers acknowledged by other writers or even artists acknowledged by other artists—immediate market success was suspect. It was taken as a sign of compromise with the times, with money... Today, on the contrary, the market is accepted more and more as a legitimate means of Iegitimation.

The pressures created by the ratings mechanism, as Bourdieu points out, have nothing to do with the democratic expression of enlightened collective opinion or public rationality, despite what media ideologues assert. In fact, as the same author points out, the ratings mechanism is the sanction of the market and the economy, that is, of an external and purely market law.

I would only add to this that given how 'public opinion' is formed within the process of socialisation and internalisation of the dominant social paradigm, it is indeed preposterous to characterise the ratings mechanism as somehow expressing the democratic will of the people. Ratings, as well as polls generally, is the 'democracy of the uninformed'. They simply reflect the ignorance, the half-truths, or the straightforward distortions of the truth which have been assimilated by an uninformed public and which, through the ratings mechanism, reinforce the role of the mass media in the reproduction of the dominant social paradigm.

One may therefore conclude that the role of the media today is not to make the system more democratic. In fact, one basic function of the media is, as Chomsky stresses, to help in keeping the general population out of the public arena because 'if they get involved they will just make trouble.

Their job is to be "spectators," not "participants". Furthermore, the media can play a crucial role in offsetting the democratic rights and freedoms won after long struggles. This has almost always been the case when there was a clash between the elites and trade unions, or popular movements generally. Walter Lippmann, the revered American journalist was explicit about it, as Chomsky points out. For Lippmann, there is a new art in the method of democracy, called "manufacture of consent." By manufacturing consent, you can overcome the fact that formally a lot of people have the right to vote. We can make it irrelevant because we can manufacture consent and make sure that their choices and attitudes will be structured in such a way that they will always do what we tell them, even if they have a formal way to participate. So we'll have a real democracy. It will work properly. That's applying the lessons of the propaganda agency. Within this analytical framework we may explore fruitfully the particular ways through which the filtering of information is achieved, as, for instance, is described by Chomsky and Herman in their 'propaganda model'. Similarly Bourdieu shows in a graphic way how the filtering of information takes place in television, through the structuring of TV debates, the time limits, the methods of hiding by showing etc. Particularly important is the way in which the media, particularly television, control not just the information flow, but also the production of culture, by controlling the access of academics as well as of cultural producers, who in turn, as a result of being recognised a public figures, gain recognition in their own fields.

Thus, at the end, the journalistic field, which is structurally very strongly subordinated to market pressures and as such is a very heteronomous field, applies pressure, in turn, to all other fields. An illustrative application of the above analytical framework is the crucial contribution of the mass media in the creation of the subjective conditions for the neoliberal consensus. Thus, the mass media have played a double ideological role with respect to the neoliberal consensus. On the one hand, they have promoted directly the neoliberal agenda:

- by degrading the economic role of the state,
- by attacking the 'dependence' on the state which the welfare state supposedly creates,
- by identifying freedom with the freedom of choice, which is supposedly achieved through the liberation of markets etc. (talk radio and similar TV shows play a particularly significant role in this respect).

On the other hand, the media have also attempted to divert attention from the consequences of the neoliberal consensus (in terms of growing inequality and poverty, the explosion of crime and drug abuse and so on):

- by promoting irrational beliefs of all sorts (religion, mystical beliefs, astrology etc). The film and video explosion on the themes of exorcism, supernatural powers etc (induced mainly by Hollywood) has played a significant role in diverting attention from the evils of neoliberalism.
- by manufacturing irrelevant and/or insignificant 'news stories' (e.g. Monica Lewinsky affair), which are then taken over by opposition politicians who are eager to find fictitious ways (because of the lack of real political differences within the neoliberal consensus) to differentiate themselves from those in power.
- by creating a pseudo 'general interest' (for instance around a nationalist or chauvinist cause) in order to unite the population around a 'cause' and make it forget the utterly dividing aspects of neoliberalism.

At the same time, the creation of the neoliberal conditions at the institutional level had generated the objective conditions for the mass media to play the aforementioned role. This was because the deregulation and liberalisation of markets and the privatisation of state TV in many European countries had created the conditions for homogenisation through the internal and external competition, which I mentioned above. It is not accidental anyway that major media tycoons like Murdoch in the Anglo-Saxon world, Kirsch in Germany, or Berlusconi in Italy have also been among the main exponents of the neoliberal consensus agenda.

TELEVISION THE BEST MEDIUM OF ADVERTISEMENT IN INDIA

A huge industry by itself, the Indian silver screen has thousands of programmes in all the states of India. The small screen has produced numerous celebrities of their own kind some even attaining national fame. TV soaps are extremely popular with housewives as well as working women. Some small time actors have made it big in Bollywood.

Television first came to India (named as Doordarshan or DD) as the National Television Network of India. The first telecast started on September 15, 1959 in New Delhi. After a gap of about 13 years, second television station was established in Mumbai (Maharashtra) in 1972 and by 1975 there were five more television stations at Srinagar (Kashmir), Amritsar (Punjab), Calcutta (West Bengal), Madras (Tamil Nadu) and Lucknow (Uttar Pradesh). For many years the transmission was mainly in black & white. Television industry got the necessary boost in the eighties when Doordarshan introduced colour TV during the 1982 Asian Games.

1980s: Indian small screen programming started off in the early 1980s. At that time there was only one national channel Doordarshan, which was government owned. The Ramayana and Mahabharata was the first major television series produced. This serial notched up the world record in viewer ship numbers for a single program. By the late 1980s more and more people started to own television sets. Though there was a single channel, television programming had reached saturation. Hence the government opened up another channel which had part national programming and part regional. This channel was known as DD 2 later DD Metro. Both channels were broadcast terrestrially.

Post Liberalization Television: The central government launched a series of economic and social reforms in 1991 under Prime Minister Narasimha Rao. Under the new policies the government allowed private and foreign broadcasters to engage in limited operations in India. This process has been pursued consistently by all subsequent federal administrations. Foreign channels like CNN, Star TV and domestic channels such as Zee TV and Sun TV started satellite broadcasts. Starting with 41 sets in 1962 and one channel (Audience Research unit, 1991) at present TV in India covers more than 70 million homes giving a viewing population more than 400 million individuals through more than 100 channels. A large relatively untapped market, easy accessibility of relevant technology and a variety of programmes are the main reasons for rapid expansion of Television in India.

Cable Television: In 1992, the government liberated its markets, opening them up to cable television. Five new channels belonging to the Hong Kong based STAR TV gave Indians a fresh breath of life. MTV, STAR Plus, BBC, Prime Sports and STAR Chinese Channel were the 5 channels. Zee TV was the first private owned Indian channel to broadcast over cable. A few years later CNN, Discovery Channel, National Geographic Channel made its foray into India. Star expanded its bouquet introducing STAR World, STAR Sports, ESPN and STAR Gold. Regional channels flourished along with a multitude of Hindi channels and a few English channels. By 2001 HBO and History Channel were the other international channels to enter India. By 2001-2003, other international channels such as Nickelodeon, Cartoon Network, VH1, Disney and Toon Disney came into foray. In 2003 news channels started to boom.

THE SPECTATOR AS SPECTACLE

In April last year, a banner appeared on the terraces of the Newlands cricket ground in Cape Town, South Africa, during a one-day international. It was a blow-up of a dollar bill bearing a picture of the disgraced South African captain Hansie Cronje's face. The legend above the photo read: Rally Round the Green Machine.

The banner appeared a few days after Cronje had been sacked for lying about his involvement with an illegal Indian bookmaking ring, and it raised a few wry laughs. It reflected fairly accurately the public cynicism over the entire affair, soon nicknamed Hansiegate. But the banner had also hijacked one of cricket's most triumphal chants "Rally Round the West Indies" and turned it into a cruel dig at the state of the game itself. Back in the 1970s, the West Indies cricket team was close to unbeatable, playing cricket with a flair and a freedom that disguised its tactical heart and discipline. Everywhere they played, whenever a handful of their supporters turned up at grounds, the cry would go out, "Rally Round the West Indies!"

In the year 2000, as West Indies cricket struggles for survival and the credibility of cricket and some of its most celebrated names has been called to question, the banner at Newlands speaks of many truths. Not just about the current crisis, but about the distance that the sport has travelled from the era of "Rally Round The West Indies" to the present day, when cricket has turned into an entertainment industry. Particularly in South Asia, where its liaison with satellite television and big business has led to a financial boom, prompting an image make-over and now, in the light of the match-fixing scandal, something approaching overkill.

Banners like the one at Newlands may seem like the graffiti of the sport, a medium for off-the-cuff and irreverent comment. The individuals who think up and display such banners may even be considered a late 20th century version of the legendary barrackers who flocked to the cheap stands at grounds in England and Australia before the advent of television and passed deafening comment on the state of the game. Caribbean grounds still feature characters who try to puncture superstar egos and lighten the atmosphere, but these men have now shrunk to a handful; in the popular culture of modern cricket, it is the banner that rules over the banter.

The world has absorbed this change over 25 years. In India, it has taken place in less than ten and the stresses are still with us. Until the late 1980s, the slow pace of Test cricket was believed to be ideally suited to the Indian temperament (it was open-ended, and had a casual disregard for time), one scholar stating that it was an Indian game invented by the British. Yet today, that theory stands on shaky ground as the Indian temperament has become an addict to the culture of the insta-thrill one-day game, which is both a product of television and now a force driven by it. This spatial and territorial shift has not only changed the way Indians watch cricket, but also the way they see themselves as its spectators.

The country has staged two World Cups of Cricket, almost ten years apart: the first in 1987, organised with Pakistan, was hugely popular, a subcontinental financial success story. In 1987, spectators would pack into grounds, carrying food and drink and do as they always did: behave with sobriety and restraint in Bangalore and Madras, risk being lathi-charged in Delhi and take up chanting in Bombay. What astonished overseas visitors most was the fact that Australia played England in the final in front of a vociferous capacity crowd. In no other country in the world, it was said, would such an enthusiastic non-partisan reception have been possible. (Indeed, when India played Pakistan in the 1985 World Championship of Cricket final in Australia, the stadium was far from full, and a banner described the final thus: "Bus Drivers vs. Tram Conductors," a snide reference to the most common image of the Indian and Pakistani presence in Australia.

Nine years later, the second World Cup, organised by India, Pakistan and Sri Lanka in 1996, marked the zenith of the sport's popularity and marketability. But for the Indian team, it ended in a crowd riot at the Eden Gardens, caused by the knowledge that the national heroes were going to lose.

The period between these two World Cups is virtually a case study of the effect of television on a sport and on its fans. The end result? The growth of a very large, easily-manipulated spectator mass with a low tolerance for failure and a large appetite for jingoism. The elevation of cricket to a vehicle of National self-esteem, the sensitive index of urban morale.

A street performer tries to attract spectators for viewing a snake-mongoose fight, but with little success.

The chief catalyst in this process was the advent, in 1993, of satellite television: for the first time in a long and colourful history, there were banners, and the Indian flag made its appearance at cricket grounds.

At the same time, cricket on television began to resemble the slick, much-envied coverage on Australia's Channel 9 in the days when Doordarshan's best efforts were black and white blurs. The banners and face-painting were imported adaptations of what Indians saw Australians doing in Melbourne or Sydney (minus, of course, two cultural no-nos: streakers and sunbathers in bikinis). Shrewd Australian marketing men now pay $500 prizes for the wittiest banners picked out by the TV cameras at a match provided they include the logo of the company sponsoring the prize; it is a practice which will no doubt soon be latched on to by Indian sponsors.

The Indian flags, again imitative of fan behaviour overseas, have come to represent an angry and aggressive nationalism; the old, somewhat harmless practice of a century-maker being garlanded by someone jumping the fence at grounds is now abandoned for orgies of bottle-throwing. Indian cricket is no stranger to crowd disturbances, but the frequency and the venom have increased manifold.

Perhaps this has something to do with the fact that the pot of public sentiment is kept boiling by promotional ad campaigns in which Indian cricketers no longer bat or bowl in advertisements: they leap over burning tyres to make stops in the field, hurl balls of fire at opposition batsmen and bat against bowlers shooting machine guns. Westernised accents promote cricket series nicknamed Badla, Qayamat, and Sarfarosh. The imagery and vocabulary smoothly subvert Orwell's analogy of sport as war minus the shooting and justify themselves by the ominous reminder that only two things bring India together: cricket and war. Defeat, therefore, is not an option. This may sound like the hackneyed MTV Theory of Social Change: how traditional Indian values (here, institutions like cricket) are being corrupted by the impact of television. In most cases, blaming the media may be the easiest option, but in the case of sport it is perhaps the most valid one.

A soccer fan stabbing a supporter of a rival team.

Live sport cricket in India, football in Europe or basketball in the U.S. is the highest-revenue earner on television. The sale and purchase of TV "rights" is a multi-million dollar business, and sporting events are turned into "properties" sold for terrestrial and satellite television, radio and now the internet.

Such an exhaustive dissemination of sport spawns imitative but largely homogeneous behaviour over large swathes of the globe. It could spark off a trend in street fashion (e.g. the baggy shorts of NBA basketball superstars), teach Indian cricket spectators to do the Mexican wave and pass on to the athletes themselves, who turn any key moment on the field-a goal, a catch, a three-pointer-into an elaborate celebratory ritual.

The high-five, the chest-butt, the mass pile-up of bodies near the football goal-mouth... no matter what their tribalistic origins, where or why they were actually "invented" or first used, this elaborate sign language of sport is always "discovered" by the media, mostly television, and returned to the public as a legitimised, desirable code of behaviour.

This phenomenon of crowd participation, largely for the benefit of the all-seeing eyes of television in the form of celebrations, chanting, banners, has turned the spectator from a witness into an element of the spectacle itself. It is a self-perpetuating cycle, a mass of flag-waving, banners, Mexican waves, each gesture magnified time after time to catch the attention of the camera.

The Indian Board's drive to take cricket and its revenue-earning television cameras to all corners of the country, including smaller metros, has created and perpetuated the image (more like an orientalist caricature) of the Indian cricket crowd: large, "colourful" "passionate" "volatile"-words sprinkled all over television commentary from a group of distinguished English or Australian experts, who have turned into the eyes and mind of the crowd. It sees what they want it to see, it believes what they tell it. With little work for the powers of imagination or interpretation, it acts the way they would like it to act.

Television companies know that the tempo of a match, no matter how humdrum, can now be cranked up merely by turning a television camera on a section of the crowd. The temperature of a crowd can be raised by replaying a controversial umpiring decision over and over again on a giant screen. The whole production, its mechanics and its "look" is under control.

Mark Mascarenhas, chief of World Tel, which brought the 1996 World Cup live to television, told Sportstar that his company's television coverage changes from nation to nation, the Indian formula being ridiculously simple: "In India spend much more time on the crowd because they are so animated, so colourful. We spend more time on the VIPs because in India people like to be seen on television... If you try to do this Indian type of coverage in England it won't go over very well."

Such commodification and codification of public space has left little room for spontaneity or candour, which is really the heart of a spectator's response. During the Australian Open tennis tournament a few years ago, "fans" of French tennis player Mary Pierce showed up in the stands wearing all her trademark tennis dresses and naturally caught the cameras. They turned out to be employees of Nike, whose tennis clothing is endorsed by the statuesque Frenchwoman, planted in the stands to do precisely that.

Hansie Cronje's disgrace was made complete, again by "fans" who blackened his face on an advertising hoarding a few days after his admission of dishonesty. But the fans (in reality, members of the "youth" wing of a political party) made sure that they did so in the presence of television cameras. Cronje's descent from role model to persona non grata was formalised in footage. Other hoardings featuring Cronje and the South African team were pulled down; in the age of the media, removal from the public gaze is akin to punishment, humiliation and exile. In India, cricket's sign language may appear to become more varied, more elaborate, richer in colour and bolder in gesture. But its words today, as part of a pre-determined script written by someone else, come up empty.

A SNAPSHOT OF INDIAN TELEVISION HISTORY

Television in India has been in existence for nigh on four decades. For the first 17 years, it spread haltingly and transmission was mainly in black & white. The thinkers and policy makers of the country, which had just been liberated from centuries of colonial rule, frowned upon television, looking on at it as a luxury Indians could do without. In 1955 a Cabinet decision was taken disallowing any foreign investments in print media which has since been followed religiously for nearly 45 years. Sales of TV sets, as reflected by licences issued to buyers were just 676,615 until 1977.

Television has come to the forefront only in the past 21 years and more so in the past 13. There were initially two ignition points: the first in the eighties when colour TV was introduced by state-owned broadcaster Doordarshan (DD) timed with the 1982 Asian Games which India hosted. It then proceeded to install transmitters nationwide rapidly for terrestrial broadcasting. In this period no private enterprise was allowed to set up TV stations or to transmit TV signals.

The second spark came in the early nineties with the broadcast of satellite TV by foreign programmers like CNN followed by Star TV and a little later by domestic channels such as Zee TV and Sun TV into Indian homes. Prior to this, Indian viewers had to make do with DD's chosen fare which was dull, non-commercial in nature, directed towards only education and socio-economic development. Entertainment programmes were few and far between. And when the solitary few soaps like Hum Log (1984), and mythological dramas: Ramayana (1987-88) and Mahabharata (1988-89) were televised, millions of viewers stayed glued to their sets.

When, urban Indians learnt that it was possible to watch the Gulf War on television, they rushed out and bought dishes for their homes. Others turned entrepreneurs and started offering the signal to their neighbours by flinging cable over treetops and verandahs. From the large metros satellite TV delivered via cable moved into smaller towns, spurring the purchase of TV sets and even the upgradation from black & white to colour TVs.

DD responded to this satellite TV invasion by launching an entertainment and commercially driven channel and introduced entertainment programming on its terrestrial network. This again fuelled the purchase of sets in the hinterlands where cable TV was not available.

The initial success of the channels had a snowball effect: more foreign programmers and Indian entrepreneurs flagged off their own versions. From two channels prior to 1991, Indian viewers were exposed to more than 50 channels by 1996. Software producers emerged to cater to the programming boom almost overnight. Some talent came from the film industry, some from advertising and some from journalism.

More and more people set up networks until there was a time in 1995-96 when an estimated 60,000 cable operators were existing in the country. Some of them had subscriber bases as low as 50 to as high as in the thousands. Most of the networks could relay just 6 to 14 channels as higher channel relaying capacity required heavy investments, which cable operators were loathe to make. American and European cable networks evinced interest, as well as large Indian business groups, who set up sophisticated headends capable of delivering more than 30 channels.

These multi-system operators (MSOs) started buying up local networks or franchising cable TV feeds to the smaller operators for a fee. This phenomenon led to resistance from smaller cable operators who joined forces and started functioning as MSOs. The net outcome was that the number of cable operators in the country has fallen to 30,000.

The rash of players who rushed to set up satellite channels discovered that advertising revenue was not large enough to support them. This led to a shake-out. At least half a dozen either folded up or aborted the high-flying plans they had drawn up, and started operating in a restricted manner. Some of them converted their channels into basic subscription services charging cable operators a carriage fee.

Foreign cable TV MSOs discovered that the cable TV market was too disorganised for them to operate in and at least three of them decided to postpone their plans and got out of the market..

The government started taxing cable operators in a bid to generate revenue. The rates varied in the 26 states that go to form India and ranged from 35 per cent upwards. The authorities moved in to regulate the business and a Cable TV Act was passed in 1995. The apex court in the country, the Supreme Court, passed a judgement that the air waves are not the property of the Indian government and any Indian citizen wanting to use them should be allowed to do so. The government reacted by making efforts to get some regulation in place by setting up committees to suggest what the broadcasting law of India should be, as the sector was still being governed by laws which were passed in 19th century India. A broadcasting bill was drawn up in 1997 and introduced in parliament. But it was not passed into an Act. State-owned telecaster Doordarshan and radiocaster All India Radio were brought under a holding company called the Prasar Bharati under an act that had been gathering dust for seven years, the Prasar Bharati Act, 1990. The Act served to give autonomy to the broadcasters as their management was left to a supervisory board consisting of retired professionals and bureaucrats.

A committee headed by a senior Congress (I) politician Sharad Pawar and consisting of other politicians and industrialist was set up to review the contents of the Broadcasting Bill. It held discussions with industry, politicians, and consumers and a report was even drawn up. But the United Front government fell and since then the report and the Bill have been consigned to the dustbin. But before that it issued a ban on the sale of Ku-band dishes and on digital direct-to-home Ku-band broadcasting, which the Rupert Murdoch-owned News Television was threatening to start in India. ISkyB, the Murdoch DTH venture, has since been wallowing in quicksand and in recent times has even shed a lot of employees. But News Corp has been running a C-band DTH venture in the country which has around 20,000 subscribers.

CHANGING LIVES THROUGH TV PROGRAMMING

Nothing can be more devastating for a father than not being able to touch his own children. And that is exactly what happened to Panchu Bhol, a villager in the southeastern state of Orissa, India. Many men from this poverty-stricken hinterland of Puri district migrate seasonally to Gujarat in search of livelihood. Panchu had also embarked on this migration route, regularly sending money to his family, until he contracted HIV in Surat, the port city of Gujarat.

News of Panchu's HIV status spread like a wildfire. His family was excommunicated, and his village declared Panchu a curse. Even Panchu himself started to believe it. He lost the courage to pick up his daughter, fearing that he might infect her. Banned from the village life, Panchu cried at his fate, seeing death as the only way out.

But an extraordinary event in December 2005 turned his life around. Panchu still remembers the mild afternoon breeze on the day when the Kalyani team came to his hamlet. Kalyani-meaning the one who provides welfare-is a television health telecast on Doordarshan, the national television of India. Since

May of 2002 when it was launched, the program about building positive health behaviours has been reaching nearly 50% of India's population.

Doordarshan national television is the world's largest public broadcaster and a signatory to the Global AIDS Media Summit. Providing localized content, Doordarshan produces its key messages in consultation with the National AIDS Control Organisation and the Ministry of Health. Its telecasts feature short spots, folk songs, and informative segments with experts, in an attempt to tackle themes of HIV related stigma, discrimination and treatment. Kalyani program also provides follow up action through expert visits to rural areas to interact with the target audiences.

Actors playing Kalyani characters 'Sehri Didi and Chakulia Panda', along with the rest of the Kalyani team, reached Panchu's village. The team met an emaciated, bearded and confused Panchu. And as the villagers gathered to catch a glimpse of the movie stars, tears rolled out of Panchu's eyes. It was the first time that someone had visited him since he had been diagnosed with HIV.

Informed of Panchu's situation, Sehri Didi (the character portraying the sister's role in the programme) offered to become Panchu's "sister" in real life and tied him a raakhi, the traditional auspicious red thread. She also shared some sweets with him.

Sehri Didi challenged the villagers not to stigmatize her new "brother" Panchu. An elderly man from the crowd summed up the sentiments of the village: "You told us that HIV does not spread by touching people living with HIV or eating with them. Why should we hate Panchu? We are sorry we did not know this before."

Panchu was finally accepted. Having learned about means of HIV transmission, Panchu took his daughter into his arms for the first time. For Sehri Didi, accustomed to crying with glycerine on screen, it was difficult to control her tears.

When the Kalyani team visited Panchu's village three months later, they could hardly recognize him-now a clean shaven and confident young man championing HIV prevention.

The doctor treating Panchu thanked the Kalyani team for removing a major hurdle in Panchu's recovery-the social stigma. Kalyani program airs in the capital cities of eight highly populated Indian states and there now exist nearly 2,000 community level Kalyani Health Clubs, with close to half million members.

A CLIENT-CENTRED NETWORKING PROJECT IN RURAL INDIA

TV Firms Gear up for Rural Market: When Oscar Television made it to ORG-Gfk's list of 10 top-selling colour television brands earlier this year, there was one person who wasn't satisfied.

Arpita Khurana, Oscar's youthful director, insisted that the ORG-Gfk survey didn't tell half the story because it collected figures only in the metropolitan areas.

Oscar, she said, was flying off the shop-shelves in semi-urban and rural India. What's more, Khurana predicted that semi-urban and rural demand would zoom by around 80 per cent this year. That, say her rivals, may be an overestimate. But the other colour television and consumer electronics manufacturers aren't disagreeing loudly. In fact, they are also gearing for a buying spree in rural and semi-urban India.

The industry association too is bullish about sales this year. Cetma (the Consumer Electronics and TV Manufacturers Association) has projected sales of 10 million sets in 2004 compared to around 8 million to 8.25 million TVs likely to be sold this year. That's compared to 6.7 million sets sold in 2002.

- Cetma believes that between 8 million and 8.25 million TV sets will be sold this year compared to 6.7 million last year
- In 2002 63.1 per cent of sales came from cities and smaller regions with a population of less than 1 million
- Companies like LG and Philips are almost doubling distribution networks in the rural areas
- To attract rural buyers 14-inch televisions are being sold for as little as Rs 3,500

Most amazingly, about 70 per cent of this will come from the semi-urban and rural market. "This means the rural market will grow by as much as 25 per cent compared to 5 per cent growth in the urban markets," says an association executive.

What's fuelling the rural optimism? There's a growth in awareness, say the manufacturers. Also, they have boosted penetration in semi-urban and rural areas.

And this year there have been good monsoons followed by good harvests. Diwali sales have been robust and the feel-good factor in the economy is boosting buying.

It's important to keep one thing in mind. This isn't the first year when rural demand has climbed sharply. Market research firm Francis Kanoi recently said in a report (on consumer electronic market growth and projections) that the top seven metros contributed 24.1 per cent of total sales in 2002. That was followed by towns with a population of over 1 million where 12.0 per cent of the sets were bought. The remaining 63.1 per cent of sales in 2002 came from cities and smaller regions with a population of less than 1 million.

The tilt towards the smaller towns and rural areas is becoming more pronounced with each passing year. This year, for instance, it has been reckoned that buying in the top seven metros will contribute only 22.6 per cent a fall from last year. Smaller towns and regions will be 64.3 per cent of total sales.

"Barely five years ago, the contribution from semi-urban and rural markets for us was 20 per cent. Today we get 70 per cent of our volumes from these markets," says Chandramani Singh, product group head (consumer electronics) at LG Electronics India.

But another subtle change is taking place this year, according to industry analysts. Until now, the market transformation has happened primarily because owners of radios and B&W televisions were upgrading to colour televisions. As per Francis Kanoi data, the upgrades from B&W to the colour TV segment forms over 60 per cent of total CTV purchases.

But now the industry is talking of other factors, which will drive growth like the booming rural economy. Also, they feel consumers will be making up for lost time: the feel-good factor has been distinctly missing for the last two years so rural consumers have held back on big ticket purchases.

But there's an additional factor that's likely to fuel growth. Loans for products like televisions have become easier in the rural areas because the public sector banks are moving in with offers of easy credit.

Add to that the fact that prices of televisions have fallen steeply and companies are taking extra initiatives to promote sales.

"Rural consumption is linked with agricultural output and the availability of cash. Untill very recently, financing was available to the rural people at very high interest rates and that too, not made available by any financing agents or banks but by the village sahukars (money lender). Thus, the trend in the rural areas still is to make cash purchases, which links to good harvests and ready availability of cash," says Ravinder Zutshi, director (sales) of Samsung India Electronics Ltd.

Zutshi is convinced that buying will climb even more sharply in coming years because of cheap financing. Banks such as the State Bank of India are pushing their loan schemes in the rural areas and so are financing companies like Bajaj Finance.

"The manufacturers too are expanding both their penetration as well as the products for the rural markets, all of which should help boost rural sales," he says.

Says LG's Singh, "Electrification of villages and an increase in awareness among the people, a good harvest and a booming economy will help drive growth. The rural market should see a growth that is three to four times that in the urban markets."

"The potential is high as the penetration levels are low, and hence our efforts towards creating a bigger market here," adds Devender Saini, senior product manager (television), Philips India Ltd.

"If we look at the penetration levels in rural markets, it is less than 10 per cent. This is lower than the all-India average of 21 per cent and the urban markets which are at 35 per cent to 40 per cent." The increase in penetration levels in the rural markets has also shown the way to the Oscars and Belteks of the world, which are carving out a niche by positioning themselves as price warriors. And their cut-price tactics have forced LG, Samsung and Philips, among others, to launch products targeted only at these markets.

These products have fewer frills, and are hence, cheaper. As a result, the rural masses are being tempted by the lower prices offered by all manufacturers. The entry of the bigger players in these market segments has forced the smaller ones to squeeze margins and reduce prices further.

R K Caprihan, an old industry hand and the chief executive of The Kelon Corporation, claims he is selling 14-inch for as low as Rs 3,600 and a 20-inch for only Rs 5,500.

In fact, the success of the smaller brands and the entry of the bigger players have started a war on many fronts. It's not restricted to pricing, but it's also about visibility and value for money.

Oscar, for instance, which derives 40 per cent of its sales from the semi-urban and rural sectors, has launched a battery-operated television model in the 14" segment to cater to parts of Eastern UP and Bihar.

This has boosted the company's sales by 5 per cent to 7 per cent. It is planning to come out with a similar 21" model this month. Says Arpita Khurana: "Since electricity is a problem in these areas we felt the model would be a success."

LG is putting more emphasis on dealership network. The company had only one distributor in Jaipur. But it now has distributors in Jodhpur, Jaisalmer, Udaipur and several other places. Over the past year, the company's direct dealers have risen from 1,000 to 1,500 and the number of sub-dealers has climbed from 2,800 to 5,000.

The company, which is the market leader in the colour television segment, has focused on decentralising its operations to increase its rural penetration this year. It has increased its 'remote area offices', which function at district levels, from 27 earlier to 62 this year. Similarly, Philips is planning to double its retail presence. From an existing network of 6,000, the company plans to have 12,000 retailers. About 75 per cent of this increase will take place in the rural areas.

Companies are also spending on huge sums on advertising, especially in local vernacular newspapers. Philips has fallen back on some unconventional advertising media like wall-writing and radio advertising. Says D Shivakumar, vice-president, consumer electronics, Philips India: "We have a strong base of loyal consumers of transistor sets as well as B/W TVs who are now ready to upgrade. We will try and tap these consumers for our rural scheme."

Companies are also organising rural melas and haats and use mobile hoardings to reach potential customers in villages and semi-urban markets. And, if the rural customers are switching on in larger numbers the picture can only get brighter for all the companies.

SOCIOLINGUISTIC DISTINCTION OF TV

In sociolinguistics, a T-V distinction describes the situation wherein a language has second-person pronouns that distinguish varying levels of politeness, social distance, courtesy, familiarity, or insult toward the addressee.

History and Usage

The expressions T-form and V-form were introduced by Brown and Gilman (1960), with reference to the initial letters of these pronouns in Latin, tu and vos. In Latin, tu was originally the singular, and vos the plural, with no distinction for honorific or familiar. According to Brown and Gilman, usage of the plural to the Roman emperor began in the fourth century AD.

They mention the possibility that this was because there were two emperors at that time (in Constantinople and Rome), but also mention that "plurality is a very old and ubiquitous metaphor for power". This usage was extended to other powerful figures, such as Pope Gregory I (590-604). But Brown and Gilman note that it was only between the twelfth and fourteenth centuries that the norms for the use of T-and V-forms crystallized. Less commonly, the use of the plural may be extended to other persons, such as the "royal we" (pluralis majestatis) in English.

Brown and Gilman argued that the choice of form is governed by either relationships of 'power' and/or 'solidarity', depending on the culture of the speakers, showing that 'power' had been the dominant predictor of form in Europe until the twentieth century. Thus it was quite normal for a powerful person to use a T-form but expect a V-form in return. However in the twentieth century the dynamic shifted in favour of solidarity, so that people would use T-forms with those they knew, and V-forms in service encounters, with reciprocal usage being the norm in both cases.

Modern English has no T-V distinction. It can often be confusing for an English speaker learning a language with a T-V distinction to assimilate the rules surrounding when to call someone with the formal or the informal pronoun. Students are often advised to err on the side of caution by using the formal pronouns. However, this risks sounding snobbish or ridiculous. Though English has no syntactic T-V distinction, there are semantic analogies, such as whether to address someone by first name or last name (or using sir and ma'am).

However the boundaries between formal and informal language differ from language to language, and most languages use formal speech more frequently, and/or in different circumstances than English. In some circumstances it is not unusual to call other people by first name and the respectful form, or last name and familiar form. For example, German teachers use the former construct with upper-secondary students. The use of these forms calls for compensating translation of dialogue into English. For example, a character in a French film or novel saying "Tutoie-moi!" ("Use [the informal pronoun] tu when addressing me!") might be translated "Don't be so formal!"

Examples

In many languages, the formal singular pronoun derives from a plural form. Many Romance languages have familiar forms derived from the Latin singular tu and formal forms derived from Latin plural vos, sometimes via a circuitous route. Sometimes, singular V-form derives from a third person pronoun. Some languages have separate T and V forms for both singular and plural; others have the same form; others have a T-V distinction only in the singular.

Different languages distinguish pronoun uses in different ways. Even within languages, there are differences between groups (older people and people of higher status tending to both use and expect more formal language) and between various aspects of one language. For example, in Dutch, u is slowly falling into disuse in the plural, and thus one could sometimes address a group as jullie when one would address each member individually as u. In Latin American Spanish, the opposite change has occurred-having lost vosotros, Latin Americans address all groups as ustedes, even if the group is composed of friends whom they would call tú or vos (mostly in Argentina). In Standard Peninsular Spanish, however, vosotros is still regularly employed in familiar conversation. In some cases, V-forms are likely to be capitalized when written.

TRADITIONAL MEDIA

For generations, rural populations living in isolated villages without access to modern means of communication have relied on the spoken word and traditional forms of communication as a means of sharing knowledge and information and providing entertainment.

For illiterate rural women in particular, occasions for information exchange have consisted solely in local festivities, family gatherings, traditional and religious associations, interaction with itinerant merchants and encounters at marketplaces or water wells. However, women have made use of the oral tradition to ensure their own as well as their families' survival and, as a result, have developed a rich communication environment.

They have lived creative lives, transmitting culture, knowledge, customs and history through traditional forms of communication such as poetry, proverbs, songs, stories, dances and plays. Within their communities, women are active participants in social communication networks. They use indigenous communication methods for information exchange, knowledge sharing and the dissemination of strategies for mutual assistance and survival.

Culture and history play an important role in the social development of a community. The preservation of traditional forms of communication and social change are not mutually exclusive.

Traditional communication methods can be important channels for facilitating learning, behavioural change, people's participation and dialogue for development purposes. Indigenous media have been successfully adopted by change agents to promote rural development issues of relevance to women. They have been used, for instance, to influence attitudes towards family size, female genital mutilation, teenage pregnancies, unsettling lifestyles and HIV/AIDS.

They have also been applied in health care, environmental protection and women's literacy programmes as well as in teaching mothers about child nutrition and in introducing new agricultural practices. Traditional forms of communication can also be integrated with other media such as radio, television, video and audio cassettes.

Communication is a product of culture, and culture determines the code, structure, meaning and context of the communication that takes place.

The participation of local folk artists, storytellers and performers in the production and use of traditional media ensures respect for traditional values, symbols and realities and, at the same time, ensures that such media productions appeal to rural audiences.

By tapping the community's creative pool of traditional culture, expressions and formats, women can maintain their cultural identity while gaining social self-reliance. Women's use of local media and communication channels also increases the credibility of media programmes and thus their effectiveness and impact on the knowledge, attitudes and behaviour of other women.

Grassroots Artists for Population Communication in Malawi

Population communication teams working in the Comoros, Burundi, Rwanda, Kenya, Uganda and the Philippines have tapped a variety of artistic expressions: the beat of drums, the sound of three-string guitars, the rhythm of skiffle bands, women's dance groups, village clowns, storytellers, theatre groups and puppets.

Building on those experiences, a population communication project in Malawi invited grassroots artists (including women) from the project's target audience to a communication workshop. The participants then worked together to produce a coherent multimedia package of songs and dances, stories and plays, village clowneries and drum shows addressing a variety of population issues and lifestyles.

The productions were pretested and integrated into a multimedia campaign, which also used radio, visual materials, drama and print. Yet it was the talent, creativity and intuition of the artists that triggered a process of village participation in the rural areas of southern Malawi.

The emotional excitement created by the launching of village campaigns gave way to the spontaneous development of traditional songs, dances and popular plays by other village artists. The Malawi experience proves the potential that traditional forms of communication have to involve and reach women audiences.

MULTIMEDIA

Communication programmes should make use of all media infrastructures and channels available in a country, both modern and traditional, in an orchestrated and mutually reinforcing fashion.

The combination of several media approaches and tools with interpersonal channels multiplies the impact of communication campaigns, which are being used increasingly to support clearly defined development priorities. Some striking examples include a health campaign in the United Republic of

Tanzania; nutrition programmes in Nicaragua, the Philippines and Tunisia; a breast-feeding campaign in Trinidad and Tobago; family planning programmes in China, Colombia, Egypt, Honduras, Pakistan and Thailand; and a campaign against female genital mutilation in Ethiopia.

Multichannel communication approaches can also help in identifying appropriate agricultural technologies for women as well as in disseminating the required knowledge and skills.

A recent evaluation of the Soul City "edutainment" programme in South Africa has demonstrated the added value and effectiveness of using a multichannel approach. This communication campaign aimed at delivering health education messages to women over a three-month period. It included a series of 13 television drama programmes, broadcast at prime time on the country's most popular television channel.

It was accompanied by a series of 15-minute radio drama programmes, called Healing Hearts, broadcast daily on the country's three largest radio stations. In addition, Soul City used newspapers to provide more detailed information and to supplement the health messages conveyed by electronic media. A booklet, illustrated with characters from the television series, was serialized in the major newspapers and distributed through clinics and health service organizations.

Finally, educational packages combining audio and video-tape together with written materials were produced to facilitate learning processes in both formal and informal settings. A public relations campaign strengthened the messages further by placing the issues on the public agenda by using editorial space, competitions and a range of actuality programmes in the various media.

The entire campaign was preceded by formative research to identify appropriate channels and messages. Messages were designed in consultation with the target audience and experts in the field, and materials and programmes were pretested with groups of women and men.

An evaluation analysed gender-desegregated data to assess the impact of the various channels and materials on knowledge, attitudes and behaviour. The results showed that the multimedia approach in this case was effective in reaching female audiences.

Audiovisual materials such as slides and video can assist extension workers. Women trainees, even if they are illiterate, can see and discuss innovations before putting them into practice.

Improving Extension and Training Programmes

Investing in the sharing of knowledge and learning for rural women through extension and training can be an effective means of reducing poverty and promoting food security and sustainable development. However, studies on agricultural extension have highlighted a number of weaknesses in current efforts to reach rural women. There are very few women extensionists; moreover, the attitudes and behaviour of male extension personnel can be a major barrier between extension services and women.

Extension services have often ignored the specific information needs of women as well as the fact that they may require different agricultural technologies from those suited to men. They have underestimated women's indigenous knowledge and experience and have not taken the time to listen to and learn from women themselves.

A combination of traditional and modern communication methods can help extension workers to improve the quality and outreach of their programmes with women. Fieldworkers need to abandon top-down approaches in favour of participatory communication skills and methods and establish a climate of confidence and trust.

They need to learn how to promote dialogue among women farmers, help them identify their needs and strengthen their self-confidence. Participatory communication methods can improve the linkages among women farmers, extensionists, researchers, policy-makers and planners, thereby fostering the exchange of information and knowledge and ensuring that development activities correspond to the real needs of rural communities.

Audiovisual materials such as slides and video can assist extension workers with their training activities. Women trainees, even if they are illiterate, can see and discuss innovations before putting them into practice.

Audio-visuals can compress time and space. For example, in a single session, a training group can explore an entire agricultural cycle, from sowing to harvest. Through visual materials, women can travel to places that are too distant to visit.

The extensionists themselves also benefit from using communication materials. The technical information presented can be standardized and of high quality and the presentations made attractive and interesting. Audiovisual materials spark dialogue and debate and, overall, they allow trainers to be more confident and professional.

The use of mass media, such as rural radio, can reinforce and multiply the impact of extension messages and allow extensionists to reach rural people in isolated areas. Radio and television can be used to conduct distance education programmes for rural women who are unable to attend formal education and training programmes.

Developing Agricultural Technologies

Rural women play an important role in Jamaican agriculture: as farmers in their own right, in partnership with men on household farms and as the main cultivators of kitchen gardens. A challenge to extension in Jamaica has been finding creative and cost-effective ways to communicate with rural women. A pilot project, supported by the Governments of Jamaica and Canada, used various participatory communication approaches to deliver appropriately designed soil nutrient technologies to rural women.

In order to develop appropriate agricultural and soil fertility technologies for rural women, a participatory communication methodology was used that incorporated both indigenous and scientific knowledge. The project demonstrated that women have specific information needs, and a set of participatory techniques for a gender approach to agricultural activities was developed. It also demonstrated how extension workers could select from a variety of traditional and modern communication methods according to the needs of rural women. The approaches and media applied, and the products generated, by the project included:

- a series of community video screenings, followed by discussion, showing agricultural practices in Jamaica;
- video tapes of community demonstration plots, comparing the effects of various soil nutrient applications;
- a visual baseline survey, with respondents interviewed either on video or on audiotape;
- a drama performance-for which rural women were hired as actors-to improve understanding of how gender relationships affect agricultural decision-making (the performance was used to verify the baseline survey findings);
- oral history testimonies about each community, (these emerged from interviews and were published in local newsletters);
- a quarterly newsletter, produced to inform project participants and other audiences about soil fertility and other agricultural issues;
- participatory video training carried out in each of the communities, resulting in a series of short, humorous programmes related to agriculture and soil fertility.

Based on findings from nine months of field testing as well as on the results of the video baseline survey and a mid-term evaluation, the technology package was redesigned and a final video was produced to present soil nutrient and soil conservation recommendations.

8

Role of Advertising in Social Change

As innumerable media corporations execute decisions made in boardrooms (where "globalization" and "deregulation" are the mantras), the challenges facing international communication scholars become veritable riddles of the Sphinx. They watch in bewilderment as transborder commercial satellites pulverize the protective, monopolistic, state-controlled broadcasting regimes of erstwhile colonies of South Asia. They ponder as the antediluvian legislation pertaining to airwaves prevalent in these nations fails in its attempts to cope with what Ithiel de Sola Pool called the new "technologies of freedom." Imagine their plight when they see the comprador bourgeoisie collaborate, nay, fraternize with the "invaders," waving market-friendly banners which spell out "joint venture."

This paper is an essay in empathy, the beneficiary being the aforementioned scholars of global media. Focusing on the Indian subcontinent, the author discusses the complex set of events leading up to the current conjuncture (the term used here in its fullest Althusserian import) in the nation's mediascape. The paper draws on literature in the field of global communication; print-media reports from the last six years; and a series of interviews with broadcast entrepreneurs, analysts, and consultants, conducted by the author in India.

It argues that the promise of global interconnectivity through new technology can fast become "technological" and "cultural imperialism" unless guided by a well-grounded understanding of global difference, national philosophies regarding the role of electronic mass media, and above all, the perils of leapfrogging developing societies into media ecologies borrowed heavily from the industrialized West. Finally, it underscores the importance of localizing the debate on globalization, allowing the concerned communities to develop and articulate broadcasting architectures most appropriate to their new role in the "global village."

The "Wonderland" of Communication Satellites

The Gulf War of 1990-91 did more than just convey images of SCUD missiles punching their targets. It also showcased to a captive worldwide audience, the technology that made this possible. Big city hotels with rooftop dish antennas were able to relay CNN's live reports to an aspiring, upwardly-mobile class of Indians. A class that would soon feature in India's own war of the airwaves.

Communication satellites are not new to India. In tune with the developmental communication rhetoric of the 1960s-1970s India conducted the world's largest techno-social experiment using a NASA satellite. The SITE project (Satellite Instructional Technology Experiment) of 1975-76 represented India's communication philosophy: a categorical rejection of the entertainment component of electronic mass media and a commitment to realizing their potential as agencies of social change. The models developed by Daniel Lerner and Wilbur Schramm served as guidelines for many of these experiments.

While television broadcasting under Doordarshan (from Sanskrit "distant vision") had already begun in 1959 as experimental programs to villages around Delhi, the SITE experiment unfolded the "national" reach of the medium for the first time. Indian broadcasting entered the satellite age with the launching of the first Indian satellite, INSAT-1A (Indian National Satellite) in April, 1982.

The viewers of CNN's live broadcast of the Gulf War in 1991 had lived through a decade of huge domestic growth in broadcasting led by a monopolistic, state-controlled Doordarshan. Plan outlays, coupled with the nation's aggressive space research program, had assured incremental coverage of

India's remotest regions. From a mere 26% of the population in 1982, Doordarshan's reach grew to approximately 80% by 1991 (Audience Research Unit 1996). Interestingly, the avowed non-commercial objectives had given way to the immense revenue-earning possibilities of the medium. Doordarshan's commercial revenue through program sponsorships on its single national network grew from a meager Rs 159 million in 1982 to a whopping Rs 3 billion in 1992 (Audience Research Unit 1996).

According to Kiran Karnik (1997), Managing Director of Discovery Communications in India, commercialism "completely overtook" the professed developmental communication objectives. "At the end of the year," he adds, "they would not say what great programs they did, what changes they brought, what social programs they did--but this was the profit that was made, this was the ad revenue earned."

In inverse proportion, Doordarshan's credibility as an impartial information medium had plummeted. Successive governments abused the "visibility" potential of the medium, hijacking news and public affairs programming and turning them into "a-day-in-the-life-of-your-prime minister" style coverage. Pendakur (1990) charges Indian television policy of the period with serving "its own propaganda needs as well as the demands of indigenous and transnational capitalists, along with the entertainment prerogatives of the middle/upper middle classes." Urbanites cringed at its insincere attempts at developmental programming, while ruralites "wondered why items alien to their world...be repeated through loud and annoying jingles."

However, lest this criticism be construed as a dismissal of all the achievements of television in India in the eighties, it is important to highlight what Doordarshan was up against. India's prolific film-industry had created a preeminent entertainment format comprising formulaic story-lines bundled with a heavy dose of hybridized song, dance, and music. It goes entirely to Doordarshan's credit that it made sincere attempts at delivering made-for-TV fare such as pro-social soap-operas in a climate loaded with escapist entertainment formats.

THE GROWTH OF SATELLITE-FED CABLE

Three months after CNN's historic broadcast, Hong Kong-based entrepreneur Li Ka-shing launched the preview channel of his pan-Asian satellite network STAR (Satellite Television Asian Region). The company started as a 50-50 joint venture between Li and a Hong Kong conglomerate Hutchinson Whampoa. It was beaming from a communication satellite Asiasat-1, whose footprint covered 38 countries from Egypt to Japan and the Soviet Far East to Indonesia. Potential viewership of STAR was estimated to be 2.7 billion people living in the above-mentioned countries.

The five channels initially offered by STAR-Prime Sports, MTV Asia, the Chinese Channel, BBC World Service Television, and STAR Plus-were piped into urban homes in India by underground, illegal cable operators. "It came so fast," says Pronnoy Roy (1997) of India's premier news and current affairs producer New Delhi Television. "It spread all over the country through small entrepreneurial cable operators in a disorganized fashion, which was the best way it could have happened."

Amid cries of "alien invasion" and large-scale policy-paralysis, fly-by-night cable operators were capitalizing on the "hotbird" frenzy. By June 1992, a mere twelve or so months after its launch, viewership in India had gone from zero to 1.28 million households. In July 1993, News Corp's Rupert Murdoch acquired 64% stake in STAR-TV, affirming the keen interest of global media companies in India's broadcasting future.

The chaotic growth of cable is a telling comment on India's rudimentary regulatory framework. The only Act governing "wireless communication" dated back a century to the colonial government's Wireless Telegraphy Act of 1885 which prohibited "both the transmission and reception of all forms of wireless signals on Indian soil without the consent of the Government of India" (Swami 1997). Clearly lacking the political will and the administrative machinery to arrest the errant "cablewallahs," the government offered them legitimacy in the form of The Cable Television Networks (Regulation) Act of 1995. The act was narrow in its scope, requiring cable operators to register and assume responsibility for providing content under the guidelines of the "program code" and "advertising code" included in the act. Also embedded in the act was a must-carry provision, asking cable operators to "retransmit at least two Doordarshan satellite channels of his choice" (emphasis mine).

As is evident from the "must-carry" provision, Doordarshan was not prepared to relegate itself to simply being the referee. It had responded to the alarms of "cultural invasion" by launching its own line of cable and satellite channels.

By 1995, it was offering a full-blown "Entertainment Channel" (the Metro or DD2), it had added a third "Infotainment Channel" (DD3) and beefed up its regional offerings with 13 regional language channels (India has 15 recognized languages). It had floated a Movie Channel and was also eyeing the Indian diaspora with a limited duration broadcast on DD-International Channel.

For a monolithic organization mired in red-tape bureaucracy, Doordarshan had responded remarkably well to competition. Its reach, as Pronnoy Roy (1997) of NDTV stated, was "at its peak...275 million people, while the best satellite channel can reach about 75 million...only one in every four TV households have satellite and cable." Given these figures, the image of a beleaguered state-broadcaster fighting off the foreign scare is difficult to conjure. A more serious challenge to its monopoly, according to the author, was represented by:

(a) the rapid growth of the domestic private broadcast industry in news and entertainment, and

(b) the increasing awareness among foreign broadcasters of the need to Indianize their program offerings.

Murdoch's investment in STAR was an endorsement of economic projections which placed Asia among the fastest growing economies of the world. Asian cities, wrote The Economist (1993), were "fast becoming a chain of sequentially exploding firecrackers of demand for one consumer good after another." It was difficult not to be lured by the promise of playing to an audience that would comprise 60% of the world's population by 2000. English was widely spoken in the area, and the number of television channels per home averaged 2.4. STAR burst onto the market with its American software libraries and became a household name in urban India.

"But will 3 billion Asians buy Homer Simpson?" queried a 1993 Time magazine article. India was answering with a decisive "no." When the foreign channels broke into the Indian household by offering an alternative to state-controlled monopoly, they also stirred up the imagination of a culture-industry that was sitting pretty atop a 750 movies-a-year production base. Within two years of its launch, as reported by the Far Eastern Economic Review, ratings for STAR's traditional attractions, Santa Barbara and The Bold and the Beautiful, were looking "pale compared with Hindi hits," a producer at United Television, summed up the situation succinctly: "Mahabharata has 60% of the Indian audience, (while) Santa Barbara is half a percent. Sometimes it reaches even 0 percent. I rest my case."

Says Siddharth Ray (1997) of SPA, referring to a half-hearted attempt to dub English programs into Indian languages: "...this audience was not prepared to watch a blonde with a scarf who speaks Hindi." A slew of Indian channels stole a leaf from Murdoch's book and undertook the challenge of beaming into their own country through the back door shown by STAR.

The latter part of the revolution was, thus, dominated by Indian channels and software houses, programming mainly in Indian languages. Zee, launched in October 1992, led the field with its unique line-up of Hindi soaps, dramas, game-shows, and made-for-TV movies.

By early-1994, Zee's prime-time audience share in three metropolitan cities was up to 37%, compared to 39% combined share of Doordarshan National Network and Metro Channel, and a meager 8% combined share of the STAR platform. SUN-TV (Tamil, one of the 15 recognized Indian languages) and Asianet (Malyalam, another recognized language) were making equally significant inroads into Doordarshan's Southern Indian stronghold. Others such as Sony Entertainment Television, ATN, Home-TV, and EL-TV completed the roster of domestic satellite players making STAR's opening market strategy unworkable. The response of international channels like STAR and MTV was predictable and swift. The new "foolproof formula," an Indian weekly reported, "was Indian concepts plus Indian execution equals neat Indian profits." By early 1997, STAR-TV, under the "home-grown expertise" of former Doordarshan chief Rathikant Basu, had started a daily "Hindi-band" on Star-Plus between 7 p.m. and 9 p.m., bookended by a news bulletin in Hindi and English (produced locally in India).

MTV Asia, re-entering the market after its 1994 breaking with STAR, decided to split its unified South Asian beam, creating MTV Mandarin and a dedicated Indian channel MTV India. Its biggest competitor was Channel V, STAR's hybridized music channel providing an eclectic mix of Indian film music, a fast-growing Indi-pop segment, and international hits. Speaking of a Channel V Indian top-ten show, Jules Fuller (1997), General Manager India, Channel V, said: "When we started out it was all international music, now we find at least half the chart, sometimes all the chart is Indian pop."

Between Channel V, MTV, and Music Asia (another Zee offering), the realigned objective was to cater to an indigenous market for music. Although traditionally dominated by Indian film music, the market for Indian pop was projected to rise from 6% in 1995 to 21% by 2000 due in no small part to the selling window provided by the three above-mentioned channels.

In an article written for the 1996 NATAS International Council Almanac, the author had argued against the "oversimplistic characterization of transborder satellite programming as 'cultural invasion.'" The active "local" cultural production in India, he stated, is more than likely to survive the initial onslaught of foreign programming.

Taking that argument further, not only has the local production base been revitalized, but international programmers have also been forced to approach the Indian viewer on different terms. Murdoch's 50% stake in the most popular Indian satellite channel ZEE, an 80-20 tie-up between United Television (a Mumbai-based private production house) and 20th Century Fox, are only a few examples of the recognition of the talent-base and creative potential within India. As Shashank Ghosh, creative director at Channel V, succinctly stated: "I refer to the global players as technology, and to Channel V as appropriate technology."

AMBIVALENCE IN THE NEW UNIVERSE OF CHOICE

The 250 million strong Indian middle class voted with its zappers" to signal approval of the new age of information choices. Clearly, satellite technology had rendered domestic strategies of delinking or cultural disassociation from global capitalist media an unviable option.

However, as the dust settled in the wake of the welcome-wagon, many were left wondering: is there really much to choose from in this new universe of choice? Was satellite television merely replacing state control with market control? Media advocacy groups, critiquing the homogenous content of the multi-channel universe, were raising serious concerns about the ability of a market-driven media culture to represent the "milieu of the complex social classes" that constitute India. In the following paragraphs, the author will discuss the various divisions in the ongoing debate over the democratization of the airwaves in India.

India's policy-makers are struggling with formulating a media-policy in a climate dominated by reactive, damage-control measures. In an article titled "Cultural onslaught: mass media, globalization and the state," Sashi Kumar, president of Asianet Communication, raises a cautionary voice against the prevailing ambivalence towards the haphazard growth of the electronic media in India. Information technology, he says, travels almost instantaneously from the industrialized West to the developing world. However, "as we demur and remain tentative and reactive in our response to technology...the liberating potential of the information technology goes unrealized by default."

The term "reactive" largely summarizes the state's response to non-government satellite broadcasting. The "Statement of Objects and Reasons" accompanying the Cable Television Networks (Regulation) Bill stated that the availability of foreign television signals has been perceived as "cultural invasion" in many quarters since their programs are "predominantly Western and totally alien to our culture." This stance has served successive coalition-based governments to cloak the official strategy vis-a-vis satellite television.

Ironically, the Indian government used the "culture" of the marketplace to dispel the "cultural invader." Media terminology such as "TRPs" (Television Rating Points), "profit centers," "SEC (socio-economic categories) Groupings," "DART" (Doordarshan Audience Research Television) has become the mainstay of the market-driven directors in Mandi House (home of Doordarshan). The state's response has been no less ambivalent than the stark contradictions between its official proclamations and actual practices. The following extract from the Press Information Bureau's annual publication pays lip-service to the electronic media: "It plays a vital role in creating awareness among the masses about policies and programs for development and helps in motivating them to be active partners in the nation building endeavour..."

The domestic broadcast industry has largely been positive in its view. Respondent after respondent interviewed by the author hailed the information revolution set off by satellite technology. The creation of new opportunities for Indian talent; the market-intelligence brought in by the foreign players; the introduction of higher technical standards; creation of a free-information society; the prospect of starting a reverse flow of Indian programming towards overseas markets-these were some benefits that the industry feels have clearly sprung from the satellite fountainhead.

Some, like Kiran Karnik of Discovery Communications, think it is a mixed-blessing. According to Karnik, satellite television has accelerated a kind of "consumerist... 'me-first' hedonistic kind of culture" which actually began with the turn-of-the-decade policy of economic liberalization. A by-product of this, he adds, and perhaps the "strongest input that has come to us from abroad," is an "immediate gratification type of culture" which has important consequence in terms of "the future orientation of India itself."

The new opportunities have resulted in a shifting cultural focus too. Amrita Shah (1997), editor of Elle Magazine India, feels that the advent of youth-targeted channels has altered how the young are perceived in society. "I think in India," she says, "we did not take young people very seriously for many years. We've always worshipped the old, the traditional. Thanks to MTV, thanks to Channel V, there is definitely...a platform given to young people."

Akhila Sivadas, coordinator of the New Delhi-based Media Advocacy Group, sees a discernible change in the representation of women on satellite channels. Targeting an urban, upwardly mobile market segment, these channels "were not only able to show women as being equals, they were also able to adopt the language of hegemony...that women could even dominate the situation." However, these images, rooted as they are "in the everyday experiences of the upper classes" are unable to deepen "insights about the process of exploitation" to a cross-section of women.

Other fora, like the New Delhi-based Forum for Independent Film and Video, seek "an alternative structure of broadcasting" which can exist outside "the point of view of the state on the one hand, and a purely commercial logic on the other." Referring to similar models of Public Broadcast Service, the forum cites three essential values for the proposed broadcasting system: Autonomy, Access, and Plurality.

Who shall be the Umpire?

In a landmark judgment (Union of India vs. Cricket Association of Bengal, 1995) echoing the 1934 Communication Act in the United States, Supreme Court judges ruled that "airwaves constitute public property and must be utilized for advancing public good." A ringing endorsement of the "rights of the listeners and the viewers," the judgment threw open the gates for a larger debate on the democratization of electronic media.

The Indian Supreme Court categorically stated that "diversity of opinions, views, ideas and ideologies...cannot be provided by a medium controlled by a monopoly...whether the monopoly is of the state or any other individual, group or organization."

Further, it stated that the "broadcasting media should be under the control of the public as distinct from the government" (emphasis mine). In one stroke, the judgment called for autonomy for India's state-controlled media, and the setting up of an independent referee to regulate all broadcasters.

The Indian judiciary had set the stage for the legislative arm to put the country's broadcasting industry within a broad philosophical framework pertaining to free speech and diversity of views. Instead, the Union cabinet chose to continue along its reactive vein, obsessed with regulating technology. Out of the laborious deliberations of the parliamentary subcommittee emerged a draft document dominated by issues such as "mandatory uplinking," "foreign equity," "prohibition of exclusive rights for live broadcasting," "DTH licensing," and "cross-media restrictions."

The Broadcast Bill, currently in the stage of its legislative passage, proposes sweeping restrictions on foreign players. One of its foremost aims is to set up a Broadcasting Authority of India and make it the apex regulatory body in the country. The BAI, it is proposed, would issue licenses only to companies in which foreign equity did not exceed 49%. Licenses would be given for terrestrial and satellite radio and TV, DTH (direct-to-home) TV, and cable.

The foreign equity cap meant that channels like STAR, Sony, MTV, Discovery and other channels with dominant foreign holdings had to find Indian partners and "hand over majority control (51%) to them." Foreign satellite broadcasting could continue unlicensed so long as it (a) remained free-to-air (b) carried limited-duration advertising or (c) carried sports or international news and current affairs programming only.

Further, with the bill becoming an act in its proposed form, all licensed channels would have to uplink from India. Given the fact that the legislation came in the sixth year of satellite broadcasting, companies that had locked themselves into arrangements with nearby countries like Hong Kong and Singapore would now have to invest in brand-new uplinking facilities from India. Remarked Kiran Karnik (1997) of Discovery Communication: "this is an economic issue really, it's not a matter of great policy or philosophy." Siddharth Ray (1997) offering a dissenting view, opined that "in the long term, if you are going to make money out of this market, the market has a right to demand some investment...." An upside of the proposal is the possibility of live-event coverage and live news broadcasts for satellite channels.

Severe restrictions have been proposed in the granting of inter-category broadcasting licenses, rendering STAR's DTH plans redundant, as it could no longer be a free-to-air satellite provider and a DTH player. There are cross-media curbs proposed, barring newspapers with more than 20% interest in a broadcasting concern from applying for a license.

While the attempt to arrive at some form of regulation has been lauded by most, widespread criticism has greeted the Broadcast Bill in its proposed form. Raging debate over key provisions relating to limits on foreign equity, uplinking requirements and inter-category limitations have clouded the larger issues set forth in the Supreme Court judgment. According to Raghav Behl (1997), managing director of the leading production house TV-18: "The Broadcast Bill is a document which has been much maligned. It is a document that has gotten lost in agendas that have very little to do with broadcasting."

Others have questioned the locus standi of the Indian government in the regulatory process. "At the moment," says Karnik of Discovery Communications, "the government or the Ministry of Information and Broadcasting is both referee and player, which is quite crazy." Ideally, he adds, the government should have legislated itself out of the refereeing process by issuing broad guidelines, setting up the Broadcast Authority of India, and letting it shape the regulatory framework independent of the government.

Along with prompting the formulation of the Broadcast Bill, the Supreme Court judgment had also forced the government to resurrect a 1990 act relating to autonomy for state-controlled electronic media (Doordarshan and All India Radio). Through the efforts of a liberal Information and Broadcasting minister the act was finally notified in the Gazette (all acts of the parliament must be notified in the Gazette before attaining full stature as acts) on June 22, 1997, seven years after it was passed by the Parliament. The act would place the erstwhile government-controlled TV and radio under a Broadcasting Corporation of India to be governed by an independent board. Together, the Broadcast Bill and the Prasar Bharati Act constitute India's response to the growing demands for regulation and autonomy. In order to understand the anomalies within this response, it is important to understand the fractured political alliances within the Indian government. Since the last mid-term elections held in 1995, in which no party emerged with a clear majority to form the government, a pragmatic coalition of left and centrist parties has governed India. Certain sections of the coalition have expressed grudging to unconditional support for private broadcasting (whether domestic or foreign). However, the Left has held that "public good...would be scarcely served by private broadcasting (which) would be bound to be motivated by profit." The "Murdochites," charges Sashi Kumar, "cleverly confuse globalization with economic liberalization," often disguising their support for the latter as "advocacy of a free information regime."

The Dream of the "Global Village"

India stands at the crossroads of choice-making in the new universe of technologies. Having erupted from a single-channel, government-controlled monopoly of the airwaves into a thirty-channel cornucopia over a two-year period, it must now become a savvy regulator of its spectrum. From among the hordes of opinion-wielders, lobbyists, and power-brokers it must discern the ones most appropriate for its unique and complex citizenry.

The task is no easy one for a young democracy with an unstable political centre. Objectives are defined, redefined, and finally rendered unrecognizable by successive changes of government, shifting coalitions, or confusing diktats from the powers-that-be. All this while, the expanding global powers lobby for loosening controls and opening the market, practicing advocacy-by-proxy for the choice-deprived Indian consumer.

What are the cultural imperatives unique to the understanding and shaping of India's broadcasting future? For one, according to the author, a contextual assessment of the peculiar "information needs" and "information sensibilities" should moderate all pronouncements favouring a "consumer-take-all" approach. The critique of the proposed "global information society" can only benefit from a ground-up approach which favours the information "user" as opposed to the "provider."

Media conglomerates are putting their versions of "audience research" in place, as is evidenced by the setting up of a joint-venture between Indian Market Research Bureau and A C Nielsen for a "people meter based rating system.". To what extent this unquestioned transposition of quantitative measurement systems will be able to assess the "information" vacuum in the Indian home remains to be seen.

In discussions of a burgeoning urban middle-class of 250 million, the profile of a nation with 48% illiteracy; three-quarters of the population living in rural areas; and agriculture providing the main mode of sustenance for 65% of the population is neglected. The selective use of statistics to drive the agenda for an "information revolution" serves the purposes of the global merchant. The challenge before the international communication scholar is to enrich the understanding of the culturally, linguistically, and economically diverse information industry in countries like India.

The electronic media in countries like the United States have fulfilled market functions from their very inception. While progressive deregulation has now placed the broadcasting industry at the confluence of traditionally discrete spheres of telecommunication and computer-aided communication, there has been a concomitant deepening of concern for the user. Witness the creation of the V-chip, the new ratings system for networks and cable, and the plethora of filtering software to aid parents in shielding the young from pornography and other inappropriate content available on the World Wide Web. The enrichment of the individual user's information resources enabling him/her to identify "usable," "unusable," or "useless" information has evolved alongside the industry responsible for providing that content.

Addressing the Pre-Conference Symposium on Southern Country Interests organized by the International Institute of Communication, David Nostbakken (1994), executive director of WETV, offered a skeptical prognosis: "So before we accept that technologies of information and communication will bring positive change, we need to consider the social, cultural, and political context into which the technologies are being introduced. Then, we must determine the kinds of actions that help to translate the improvements in communicative capacities and facilities into actual improvements in living conditions."

"When the delivery systems of the future are constructed and bandwidth becomes a commodity," wrote an analyst of European television, "power will shift to those who can create enticing things to fill it." In the preceding pages the author has described the creation of just such a delivery system in India.

As legislators, global conglomerates, and domestic media entrepreneurs struggle with evolving a regulatory framework which will allow a new democracy of the airwaves, the communication scholar must address the challenge of localizing the search for the user of information. As the profile of this user is defined and refined, so shall the power of meaningful content in the new information age become decisive. After all, as Thoreau pointed out in Walden, the consequences of doing otherwise are appalling: "We are in great haste to construct a magnetic telegraph from Maine to Texas; but Maine and Texas, it may be, have nothing important to communicate.

We are eager to tunnel under the Atlantic and bring the old world some weeks nearer to the new, but perchance the first news that will leak through into the broad, flapping American ear will be that Princess Adelaide has the whooping cough."

THE IMPACT OF FOREIGN TELEVISION ON INDIA

Increased competition and shrinking budgets have forced public service broadcasters around the world to reconsider their role. Doordarshan, India's public service television network, shares the problems faced by its counterparts in more developed countries. Although it continues to enjoy the luxury of being the only television network broadcasting its programs from within national boundaries, it has had to change its policies and programming to compete with foreign television channels including Murdoch's Star TV.

However, it is the Indian audience that has benefited most from this competition from the skies in the form of improved quality and quantity of programs. This discussion talks about an audience survey carried out in India earlier this year to gauge television viewers' perception of these benefits. The paper also gives background on the developments in the television industry in India.

The visibility of television as a mass medium and its perceived impact on audience always generates passionate debate about the role of public service broadcasting in any country. Whether it is the Public Broadcasting Service (PBS) in the USA, BBC in the UK, ABC in Australia, the Television Republik Indonesia (TVRI) in Indonesia or Doordarshan in India, these public service broadcasters have an important role to play in their respective countries. As with PBS's mission and the ABC's charter, Doordarshan has its own set of social objectives to live up to. In the United States, the PBS has to present programs that "educate and entertain, inform and inspire." In Australia, the ABC has to broadcast programs that "contribute to a sense of national identity and inform and entertain, and reflect the cultural diversity of the Australian community."

Similarly, Doordarshan's social objectives include that it has to:

(a) act as a catalyst for social change;

(b) promote national integration;

(c) stimulate a scientific temper in the minds of the people;

(d) disseminate the message of family planning as a means of population control and family welfare;

(e) provide essential information and knowledge in order to stimulate greater agricultural production; and

(f) promote and help preserve environment and ecological balance.

Like many public service broadcasters, over the past four decades Doordarshan has been criticised for not meeting its objectives. However, this criticism has been harsher from its viewers as Doordarshan was the only source of television in India from its beginning in 1959 until 1990.

Apart from a handful of Hindi soap operas which Indian viewers devoured, as they did not have a choice to switch channels, viewers have had to tolerate uninspiring programming for almost three decades. One of the reasons for the dismal performance by Doordarshan was lack of competition. Successive Indian governments legislated All India Radio (AIR) and Doordarshan as a duopoly. The AIR network was established in 1947. Doordarshan which was part of AIR since its inception in 1959, was separated from AIR in 1976 as the second public service broadcaster in the country.

However, in the past six to seven years Doordarshan has had to change its policies and programs to maintain its share of viewership and advertising revenue. In early 1990s following advancements in satellite technology and inadequacies in broadcast legislation in India, a number of broadcasters began telecasting their programs directly into Indian homes from foreign locations.

These broadcasters use satellite transponders to send their signals into the country, while enterprising cable operators receive these signals via dish antennas and distribute them to individual households for a small fee. As a result, Doordarshan has been forced to respond to this increased competition by increasing the number of channels and programs it broadcasts; improving the quality of its programs and trying to gain credibility for its news programs by offering prime time slots to outside producers. It has also reduced its advertising rates and launched a number of purely entertainment channels to satisfy audience demand.

Today Indian audiences have a wide variety of programs to choose from on both Doordarshan channels and other channels. They can watch numerous news and current affairs programs. Therefore, to find out how television viewers in

India perceive Doordarshan's current performance. The survey included questions about the television industry as a whole: Are viewers satisfied with television programming in India at present? Are they satisfied with Doordarshan's performance at present? If television as a medium as a whole gained people's confidence as a source of credible news and information sorely lacking before 1991?

The survey also asked whether news and current affairs programs improved sufficiently to provide in-depth information "to those who may not have a formal education" due to this competition in the television industry in India. This discussion looks at the survey results and discusses the impact of foreign competition on general programming, on public service broadcasting and, particularly news and current affairs programs in India.

DOORDARSHAN-A CALL FOR CHANGE

After the demise of British rule in the Indian sub-continent, Indian politicians and people whole-heartedly embraced ideals of socialism. Hence, after independence in 1947 most of the basic industries were set up as public sectors. Since the country already had a flourishing print media that was working on the principle of "free speech and free expression for all," no need was felt to develop broadcast media at the time. Therefore, it was almost by accident rather than through planning that television was introduced in India in September 1959.

The multinational company-Philips-had been exhibiting some television equipment at an industrial expo in New Delhi. The company gifted the closed-circuit television equipment to the government at the end of the exhibition. This is when the Indian government decided to experiment with the new technology.

From these beginnings the pattern was set for the growth of television in India, which was for almost two decades dependent on equipment gifted by either foreign governments or international agencies. Since AIR engineers were deeply involved with the development of the country's first TV centre, television was perceived as an extension of radio until the

1970s when progress in space technology spurred the Indian government to experiment with television as a development communication tool.

In the 1970s and 1980s, although Doordarshan continued to expand its coverage across the country, the public service broadcaster remained torn between its role as a catalyst for social change and as a tool for government publicity. The Satellite Instructional Television Experiment (SITE) in development communication was launched in 1975. Whereas on the political front, the imposition of a State of Emergency by then Prime Minister Indira Gandhi placed Doordarshan at government's disposal.

Indira Gandhi's government suspended many democratic rights and started using both AIR and Doordarshan to publicise government policies. As the print media largely decided to black out government propaganda, Doordarshan was used to churn out dozens of programs in support of the government's 20-point development program. Meanwhile, the SITE project which involved broadcast of development oriented programs to 2400 villages in six far-flung states, lasted for a year instead of 10 years as planned. Analysts are divided about the success of the project, some contending that the project was envisaged as an experiment in satellite broadcasting rather than educational or development communication.

However, realising the potential power of television as a communication tool, the government began to adopt policies to popularise television viewing in India. This skewed Doordarshan's focus from development to commercialisation. In 1976 Doordarshan started broadcasting imported programs and accepting advertisements to support the purchase of these programs. Again, in 1982-a significant year in the history of television in India-the government allowed thousands of colour TV sets to be imported into the country to coincide with the broadcast of Asian Games in New Delhi. There were also sponsored entertainment programs such as Hum Log and Buniyaad that added to its efforts to attract viewers in mid-1980s. Later serials based on Indian epics Ramayana and Mahabharta had a very successful run. But on the news front, viewers did not trust Doordarshan. To boost the state broadcaster's credibility, the Information and Broadcasting Ministry of India has over the past four decades appointed a number of committees to look into its status and performance.

But these committees' recommendations have never been effectively implemented. One such international body was the Media Foundation of the Non-Aligned. The Ministry appointed the specialist organisation to convoke the broad range of public opinion about television prevailing in the country at the time. In 1986 in its report, which was based on five "feedback" seminars and a national colloquium, NAMEDIA criticised Indian television (Doordarshan) for failing in its main objective of inducing development. A contributing factor was that television remained accessible only to urban, middle and high-income groups.

The NAMEDIA report concluded:

> *The primary purpose of television in India is development through education, information and enlightenment, to improve the quality of life of the largest masses of the people; to bring communities and societies, regions and the states together as one nation through mutual awareness and sympathy while preserving, consolidating and enriching their unique ways of life, cultures, customs and traditions. The secondary purpose is entertainment per se or show-business.*

The report also stated that "news" could not be used to promote those in power. It urged a variety of programs based on issues and current affairs, rather than just half-hour news programs, to facilitate better understanding for those without formal education. On the issue of credibility the report advocated that television in India needed an "openness" to gain credibility:

Such openness, it was considered, would not put either the government, or the ruling party or the nation in jeopardy. Squarely and properly placed in intelligent and honest context it would promote understanding and confidence and lead to greater and discriminative appreciation of issues by the people. In the longrun, it would strengthen the nation.

The NAMEDIA report stated that Doordarshan needed to establish a separate autonomous operation for producing television news:

It should have freedom of appraising news values and judgement, news selection and content, emphasis in presentation, and freedom of choice in summarising physical and human resources in making up a news programme. It should have a clear independent professional chain of command free from bureaucratic, political or other outside intervention and interference.

One of the themes which came across very clearly from the public forums organised by NAMEDIA was that television (in this case Doordarshan) in India should be free of all government control. Over the years Doordarshan, though established with high social objectives, has failed to satisfy the intellectuals as well as the common people in India.

Asok Mitra, former secretary of the Ministry of Information and Broadcasting from 1966 to 1969, in his submission to NAMEDIA recalled that in the 1960s television was considered "essential for accelerating development, modernisation and social change." He expressed his disappointment with the fact that India had followed a path similar to other Third World countries which first introduced television in the capital city and other metro cities, subserving the interests of the ruling class.

In the process of making television more attractive to the audience, government allowed more and more commercially sponsored, privately produced programs to be aired; though always retaining the final say about what was suitable for the Indian audience. Critics examining the development of Indian television say that as television grew, developmentalist alternatives were steadily eschewed, and "over the years hardware expansion was undertaken with no evidence of planning for software."

Television viewers, too, were not happy. Until 1990, most Indian viewers did not have a choice but to watch one national and one regional Doordarshan channel. In a survey in 1987,

Singhal found that 90 per cent of the respondents preferred Hindi-film-based entertainment programs, whereas 60 per cent appreciated educational and development programs.

The survey of 1170 respondents showed that although 76 per cent were in favour of commercial advertising on television, 60 per cent of the low-income households, 75 per cent of viewers in lower castes and 60 per cent of non-Hindi speaking viewers felt that the "problems and difficulties of their daily life were not adequately projected" by Doordarshan. Similarly, 92 per cent of them felt that political opposition's views were not sufficiently represented, whereas 85 per cent said that Doordarshan adequately covered government policies and programs.

The fact that Doordarshan's performance did not receive many accolades was compounded by the reality that the people of India could not switch channels. Either due to its charter or due to political and bureaucratic interference, Doordarshan's performance remained unsatisfactory and it was often referred to as "the government channel" and as being "dull and boring".

Competition from the Skies and Cable Network

The impact of foreign television in India has been two-fold: viewers-at least those living in urban areas-can watch more than 40 channels and the quality of television programs has improved. People subscribing to a cable service can now choose anywhere between 40 to 50 channels to watch. As an alternative to three half-hour news programs in three different languages, they can choose between the two 24-hour news channels (BBC & CNN) and up to 20 news and current affairs programs on various cable and foreign television channels everyday. Since the 1991-92 invasion from the skies by foreign television networks, Doordarshan too has expanded its service from 2 to 18 channels with a claimed viewership of 448 million at the end of 1997.

The first competition for Doordarshan came in the form of illegal distribution of television signal by cable and foreign television channels in late 1980s and early 1990s. With the introduction of VCRs in India, some dynamic entrepreneurs in Bombay in 1984 launched cable network. Instead of people watching programs on their VCRs at home by buying or borrowing videocassettes, the cable operator in the area/block connected their television set to a community network for a small fee. This way all those connected to the local cable network could watch one or two movies, sitcoms in a regional language and perhaps a pirated foreign program everyday. According to a survey cited by Rahim, there were about 3500 cable TV networks in India in May 1990. Another advertising group estimated that more than 330,000 households in four metros of Bombay, Delhi, Calcutta and Madras had cable connections with a total audience of 1.6 million.

Legally, there is no prohibition on receiving a TV signal in India.

Therefore, other television channels and networks owned by Indians or foreigners have been able to beam their programs into the country from the skies using satellite technology without violating any Indian law or regulation. However, there is legal uncertainty over its distribution. Until 1995, the Indian Telegraph Act 1885 governed the laying of cables on public property. It required the cable operator to apply for a licence to do so.

The success of cable operation was due to a number of reasons: on one hand the urban middle class had spare time and resources to seek more entertainment; on the other, "the government channel" remained slow in satisfying that demand. Being hooked up to a cable network became fashionable among the hotels that catered to tourists' needs. In fact, cable networks spread across smaller Indian cities during and after the Persian Gulf crisis in February 1991, when everybody was nervous about the war. One of the US television networks did offer the Indian government broadcast rights to its service at the time. Doordarshan declined the offer. Nevertheless, dish antennas picking up CNN and other satellite broadcast service signals sprouted everywhere, defeating the Indian government's attempt to protect the politically stifled public service broadcaster.

In the Far Eastern Economic Review, Hamish McDonald wrote that Doordarshan's credibility was undermined by its Gulf War coverage which was noted for its "state news, lack of visuals, use of ancient library footage and poor audio quality.". Although the war ended within weeks, people's desire for foreign programs had been aroused and they wanted more. Entrepreneurs took advantage of this market opportunity and started installing their cable networks in every block of big cities where people were willing to pay between Rs 50 and Rs 150 (Aus$2-6) a month for the connection. In May 1991, the Satellite Television for the Asian Region (STAR) TV launched its operation from Hong Kong beaming multi-channel television over a South Asian footprint via Asiasat.

The television scene in India or for that matter in Asia has not been the same again. By the end of 1991, experts in the communication field began speculating the effect satellite television, in this case STAR TV network which at the time included BBC news service, would have on television programming in Asian countries. Columnists Margaret Scott and Hamish McDonald in the Far Eastern Economic Review wrote that: Social, political and commercial surprises of immense proportions are bound to follow. For starters, using satellite for transborder television defies the tradition that national sovereignty includes state control over television within a nation's borders... Nowhere will the impact be more profound than in news coverage, for most of the countries under Palapa's and AsiaSat-I's footprint have spawned heavily regulated television industries, often government owned.

The small-time entrepreneurs who recognised the demand for more television in India spearheaded the massive, largely illegal proliferation of cable networks in India, rather than a single cultural imperialistic aggressor such as Rupert Murdoch. Cable operators began operating with two dishes-one pointed at Palapa for CNN and the other at AsiaSat for STAR TV (plus BBC)-and included them both in their menu of channels for sale. The scene described by commentators at the time (1991 year-end) was something like this: In crowded bazaars like Delhi's Lajpat Nagar or Bombay's Lemington Road, shops are busy taking orders for indigenously made satellite dishes. Rolls of cable are piled on pavements. All around Indian cities, private cable television operators are stringing coaxial cables along the road and up light poles. For a small monthly fee, people could watch 24-hours a day the U.S. open (live), Prime Sports (the wrestlers of the WWF), MTV (music videos), American soap operas such as Santa Barbara and The Bold and the Beautiful, morning cartoon shows and BBC's World News Service-all part of STAR TV network. Ninan says the impact of television in India in the 1990s has been accentuated by the rapid nuclearization of Indian middle class homes, the trend of the working mother, and the consequential rise in "latch-key children."

Television viewing in India had been on the rise since the introduction of Hindi soap operas in the late 1980s. However, the television scene changed sensationally after the advent of STAR TV and subsequently the launch of other foreign and local channels. TV homes have more than doubled in the last seven years from about 30.8 million in 1991 to 65 million by 1998. At the same time, according to the Indian readership survey, cable and satellite homes have grown from 1.28 million in June 1992, 9.30 million in June 1995, to 11 million in December 1996.

Doordarshan's Audience Research Unit puts the total number of cable and satellite homes at 14.2 million in December 1996; and Joshi estimates that there are about 15 million homes with cable connection.

An overwhelming number of viewers (90 per cent) in Hyderabad-a city in south of India-in July 1992 were thoroughly dissatisfied with programs and cited that as the reason for the switch-over to cable TV.

Abdur Rahim, who measured the impact of cable on television and VCR viewership, interviewed 250 people including 200 cable and satellite TV subscribers about a year after the launch of STAR TV. Many (62 per cent) felt that Doordarshan was wasting public money on "unimaginative", "absurd" and "silly" programs. The cable subscribers who participated in the study considered cable TV not as "more than television" but as "more of television." Viewers preferred cable TV channels to Doordarshan for both entertainment and news programs. Rahim found that BBC was the most popular channel because of the quality of its news programs.

RESEARCH METHOD

We carried out a survey in Bombay and New Delhi in January 1998 to explore people's response to the impact of foreign television and cable networks in the past five to seven years. The study was conducted in these two cities as the subscription to cable/foreign television channels remains an urban phenomenon. Self-administered questionnaires were delivered to 350 sample households and later collected in-person. In this way, the survey participants could seek clarification if they did not understand a question. This took into account the fact that English is a second or third language for Indians and even though they understand English, some of the complex questions can be confusing. This also prompted respondents to complete the questionnaire on time. A pilot survey was conducted in Bombay to fine-tune the questions, where 20 university students answered the questionnaire.

The stratified sampling method was used to ensure comparison between different groups of population. Three audience groups were chosen: 1. University students in Bombay, 2. Bombay residents and 3. New Delhi residents. The important variables included age, education and income levels, as these can influence the consumption habits among audiences. An effort was made to select different suburbs in Bombay to have approximately equal representation of various income groups in the survey. Questionnaires were given out in areas with low, middle and high-income groups in Bombay, which was the main location for the survey. No such distinction was made in New Delhi or when asking university students to answer the questionnaire.

The questionnaire included a combination of closed and open-ended questions. Besides asking audiences to indicate their level of satisfaction with television programs, they were given an option to comment on the reason/s for their satisfaction/

dissatisfaction. They were also asked of their perception of the quality of present day programs compared to those broadcast in 1991-92, and to name their favourite news programs and channels.

RESULTS

In all, 350 questionnaires were given out to households. Of these, 291 were completed (51 by university students, 205 residents in Bombay and 35 residents in New Delhi). Overall, 3 to 6 per cent did not answer one or the other question. There was a higher number (40.7 per cent) of respondents in the age group of 18-24 years. However, this group includes most of the university students. The over representation of younger people in the audience sampling was not planned, but can be explained by the fact that when a questionnaire was given to a household, it was generally answered by the younger member of the family. Reasons for this could be their better knowledge of English and interest in television programs.

Table: Distribution of respondents by age

Audience/age groups	*Bombay residents %*	*University students %*	*New Delhi residents %*	*All groups %*
Under 18 years	23.5	13.7	20.6	21.4
18-24 years	35	72.5	26.5	40.7
25-34 years	20.5	11.8	5.9	17.2
35-44 years	13	2	20.6	11.9
45-54 years	6	0	11.8	5.6
55 years & over	2	0	14.7	3.2

As many as 99.3 per cent of the respondents watch television, whereas 97.9 per cent watch television at home, indicating a very high level of television adoption among the urban population in India. Most people (80.6 per cent) said they watched television every-day of the week. More than 82 per cent watch television from one to four hours a day. It is significant to note that about 80 per cent of the cable subscribers watch television for one to four hours a day. Overall, about 68 per cent subscribe to one or more cable services. Those who do not subscribe to a cable service gave a range of reasons from "parents do not allow," "it distracts from studies" to "not interested".

Table: Distribution of respondents by income

Annual household income in rupees	*Bombay residents*	*University students*	*New Delhi residents*	*All groups*
More than 110,000	23.3	18.6	59.4	26.9
109,999-80,000	13	30.2	25	17.2
79,999-51,000	32.1	23.3	9.4	28
50,999-26,000	20.7	16.3	6.3	18.3
25,999 or less	10.9	11.6	0	9.7

Table: Distribution of respondents by education

Education level	*Bombay residents*	*University students*	*New Delhi residents*	*All groups*
University graduate	55.6	77.6	61.8	60.1
Secondary	34.3	17.6	20.6	29.9
Primary School	6.1	2	8.8	5.7
None of the above	4	2	8.8	4.3

Table: Average number of television viewing hours per day

Audience	*All areas (in %)*	*Cable Subscribers %*
1 hour	20.8	21.2
2 hours	29.6	26.4
3 hours	18.3	18.1
4 hours	13.7	14
5 hours	6.3	8.3
6 hours	4.9	6.2
7 hours	1.8	1.6
8 hours	1.4	1
10 hours	1.8	2.1
12 hours	0.7	0.5
15 hours	0.4	0
19 hours	0.4	0.5
Total =	100	100

In response to the question about "how many Doordarshan channels and 'channels other than Doordarshan' can you watch daily?", the response is so spread out that it is almost unquantifiable. Responses ranged between 1 to 100 channels. However, most of the television viewers watch either 1-3 channels (42.8 per cent) or 4-10 channels (47 per cent) regularly.

An overwhelming number of respondents have one or more favourite television programs. The 10 most-favourite programs are Hindi soap operas (known as serials in India), viz., (in order of preference): Amanat, Hum Paanch, Aahat, Just Mohabbat, Hasratein, Banegi Apni Baat, Boogie Woogie, Teacher, Thoda Hai Thode Ki Zaroorat Hai and Dastaan. The (English) News and Aaj Tak (a Hindi news & current affairs program) on Doordarshan channels are the 12th and 13th most-favourite programs respectively. This indicates that the television audience in India still prefers Hindi-entertainment programs to other programs. Similarly, the most favourite television channel is Zee TV-Star's Hindi channel 8; then in order of popularity Sony TV, Star Plus, Discovery, Star Movie, ESPN, Star Sports, DD2, DD1 and BBC.

Table: Number of channels regularly watched

Audience	*All areas (in %)*	*Cable Subscribers %*
1-3 channels	42.8	36.5
4-10 channels	47	51.8
11-20 channels	7.7	9.1
21-30 channels	1.1	1
More than 30	1.4	1.5

An impressive 78.7 per cent of the respondents regularly watch news and current affairs programs on television.

The most viewed news and current affairs programs are: Aaj Tak (a Hindi news & current affairs program on Doordarshan channel DD2) followed by The (English) News (on Doordarshan channel DD1), Zee News (A mix of Hindi and English news and current affairs program on Zee TV), Star News and the English news channel-BBC World service.

More than two-thirds of the respondents rely on television and newspaper for their daily news updates. However, the newspaper still remains as the source of news on which most people depend, followed by television.

Table: Source of news

Audience/Sources of news	*Bombay Residents %*	*University students %*	*New Delhi residents %*	*All areas %*
Television	74.1	86.3	85.7	77.7
Radio	9.3	17.6	5.7	10.3
Newspaper	80	86.3	94.3	82.8
Magazine	19	27.5	14.3	19.9
Internet	2.4	2	0	2.1

Relatively higher numbers of respondents are satisfied with programs on "channels other than Doordarshan" for their technical quality, entertainment value, credibility of information and overall performance. For overall performance, 91.1 per cent said they were satisfied with "channels other than Doordarshan", whereas 67.6 per cent were satisfied with Doordarshan channels. A striking majority (84-85 per cent) of the respondents said that Doordarshan programs had improved over the past five to seven years.

Table: Source of news on which people most depend

	Sources of news/Age Under 18	*18-24*	*25-34*	*35-44*	*45-54*	*above 54*	*Overall %*
Television	34.6	50	40	43.3	62.5	33.3	44.8
Radio	0	0	3.3	3.3	0	0	0.4
Newspaper	65.4	49.1	57.1	53.3	37.5	66.7	54
Magazine	0	0.9	2.9	0	0	0	0.8
Internet	0	0	0	0	0	0	0

A similar number of respondents wanted Doordarshan to improve further. Opinion varied about how Doordarshan programs should change from "needs to broadcast more entertainment programs" to "improve technical quality" and "show more educational and meaningful programs."

Table: How should Doordarshan programs be different?

How different should DD programs be?	% of response
More entertainment programs	24.4
Improve technical quality	20.3
Improve news and current affairs	11.6
More educational & meaningful	10.9
More variety, less repeats	7.2

Hindi entertainment channels such as Zee TV and Sony TV are among the most popular cable/foreign channels. However, BBC still gets the highest score for credibility of news and information. More than 70 per cent of the respondents feel that Doordarshan covers local, regional and national issues better than international issues; whereas an almost equal number feel that channels other than Doordarshan cover all these categories of issues well.

About 90 per cent of the respondents state that channels other than Doordarshan cover national and international issues better than Doordarshan. Once again, Zee TV is considered the best cable/foreign channel to cover local, regional and national issues, whereas BBC remains the best channel for covering international issues.

An impressive number of respondents feel that programs on Doordarshan channels represent Indian cultural values, whereas only about half of those feel that programs broadcast by "channels other than Doordarshan" represent Indian culture. As can be observed from the responses, younger generation is more satisfied with Doordarshan for representing Indian cultural values in their programs. However, more than two-thirds of respondents also think that foreign programs are good for the country as they are "informative and cover global issues".

Opinion is divided over the question of government censorship of programs. Most people are concerned about the broadcast of "vulgar programs" and "the need to preserve Indian culture"; however they "do not want the government to censor programs for political reasons". A majority of people said that programs are "not biased" on television. However, more viewers feel that programs are "not biased" on "channels other than Doordarshan", compared with Doordarshan. Most of the respondents commented that Doordarshan programs were still "government oriented", whereas "other channels" provided "more variety and entertainment".

Significantly higher number of people are satisfied with the quality of news in January 1998 (93 per cent) than before cable and foreign television channels became popular in 1992 (64.1 per cent). Cable subscribers are marginally more satisfied with the quality of news today than before. However, an overwhelming majority of respondents feel that news program have improved in technical quality, entertainment value, credibility and coverage of current affair issues.

Discussion

The survey results support the research hypothesis that increased competition in the television industry in India has immensely benefited the audience by providing them with better quality and quantity of programs and channels. Although the primary focus of programming provided by all channels has been entertainment, news and current affairs have not been far behind. Today, audiences have an option to switch between channels and watch a wide range of programs, and they do exercise this choice as is evident from the survey results.

The profile of an Indian television viewer is one who watches one to three hours of television daily and three to four channels regularly. Although the typical Indian viewer still prefers Hindi-entertainment programs, he or she watches a number of news and current affairs programs on anywhere between two to 10 different channels every week.

The survey shows that respondents are very discerning in comparing the quality of programs offered by all channels. Although they are satisfied with the programs on offer as of today on all channels including Doordarshan, Indian viewers still want Doordarshan to further improve as they perceive that Indian cultural values are better represented by an Indian television network.

This is one of the reasons why "other channels", which began their broadcast by showing re-runs of Western soap operas from yester-years, have been Indianising their menu of programs. Not surprisingly, Star network's Hindi channel-Zee TV-which essentially broadcasts Hindi-entertainment programs is the most popular among Indian audiences. Other channels including Doordarshan have tried to adopt Zee's success formula to achieve the same result.

One of the focus areas of the survey was to find out if viewers can rely on television as their source of news. With the addition of two 24-hour news channels and a vast range of news and in-depth current affairs programs, Indians are relishing the visual feast of watching live telecast of news events around the world. The respondents in Bombay and Delhi overwhelmingly indicate that they are keen to watch news and current affairs programs on television, and choose a combination of Hindi and English news and current affairs programs from both Doordarshan and "other channels".

A new language called Hinglish – a mixture of Hindi and English is becoming popular in India. Joshi refers to this language as the Bombay Hindi language. Channels such as Zee TV present news programs in this new language where a news story is told in both Hindi and English: sometimes even a sentence can have both Hindi and English words so that everybody can understand it.

This relaxing of standards to reach a mass audience is one of the surprising outcomes of the recent expansion of television industry in India. Yet Indian viewers still want to watch more of local or regional language news and current affairs programs. This is evident from the fact that channels covering local issues in local languages such as Sun TV in Tamil Nadu and Eenadu TV in Andhra Pradesh have achieved some degree of success against other more popular national channels such as Zee TV and Sony TV. Indian viewers are beginning to trust television as a source of news along with newspapers, which still remains popular.

One of the areas of dissatisfaction with the television industry had always been the technical quality of the programs telecast by the public service broadcaster. Although India has not lagged behind in venturing into satellite technology, during the first three decades of development of television, a number of factors from the quality of equipment used to produce programs to the quality of television sets at the receiving end diminished the entertainment value of television programs. However, with the advent of Star TV channels in 1991 and falling prices of television sets, Indian audiences today enjoy technically superior programming.

In the survey, the audience indicate that though they are satisfied with the improvements in Doordarshan's technical and entertainment quality of programming, they still consider "other channels" to be better. Overall, urban Indian viewers are more satisfied with television programming at present than five to seven years ago. However, a future potential study could be to gauge the impact of foreign television on the rural population of the country. Because of time and resource constraints, this audience survey had to be restricted to two cities.

But the study does allude to the improvements in programming for all viewers as competition from foreign and other cable channels has caused Doordarshan to improve its reach and programming. It could be deduced that as a result, today the Indian rural population is better off than before as they can view better Doordarshan programs. Cable networking has already spread to smaller cities and towns of India, and will soon reach the rural population.

There is no doubt that Doordarshan has a significant role to play in India, particularly in providing information and entertainment to the masses and, representing Indian cultural values. The network has to satisfy other social objectives such as disseminating the message of family planning and national integrity.

Television audiences across the world not only want to receive important information from their television sets, but also want to be entertained. Indian audiences in that respect are no different. They also want their television to be a window to the world via a variety of news and current affairs programs–

local, regional, national and international. In the case of India, it is the other channels including both owned by foreign or Indian private businesses which have provided them with that opportunity. As a result, the national public service broadcaster has improved its performance. On the other hand, the presence of Doordarshan has made other channels Indianise their programs rather than feed the starving Indian audience old Western sitcoms.

TV AND SOCIAL CHANGE IN RURAL INDIA

The wave of ICT innovation, that started in the United States of America in the eighties, hitting Japan and Europe rather soon in the nineties, has found new territory to flood.

India and China are preparing themselves to surf the waves, so many people and magazines tell us.

The Europe based Doors of Perception Conference, has been asking questions in the middle of these tumultuous movements "What is this stuff for?" By doing so, debates were triggered, many best practices shown, a powerful network evolved.

A network in which business, design and underground meet, all being there not to miss the next ripple in the waters, all there to show and benchmark their own work, find new people and/or companies to work with. It has been driven by a social agenda, an agenda in which the ameliorating quality of life was in the centre of attention. Always seeking the high ground in which public and commercial domain meets, in which design and serendipity exchange.

In December 2003 the Doors of Perception Conference organized for the second time its Indian edition, Doors East 2003 in Bangalore. Starting with a two day workshop in which over 40 people participated (25 from India, 15 from USA and EU) and resulting in a conference with 30 speakers and over 350 people participating.

The workshops and conference took place in the National Institute for Fashion and Technology (NIFT), partner of the Dutch Amsterdam Fashion Institute (AMFI).

In Confrontation with Indian Reality

India has 18 formal languages, and many more are spoken. The complexity of Indian society with its rich 6000 years of history, many religions, many geographical distinct areas and very fast entrance into the 21st century is very hard to grasp in such short time. The sensory experience of India with its colours, its smells, its tastes is impressive and changes perception of the world.

Bangalore, the India's Silicon Valley where the conference was held, is heavily polluted. CEO's of big companies run the city, up to the point that parks in town are taken care of by large companies. In return they can work by the law that says that if you can prove you need a certain piece of land for the development of industry, with or without houses on it or parks for example, it can be taken.

Bangalore is polluted, but even more so is Delhi. When the pollution of Delhi reached the unbearable point, all public utility vehicles (buses, taxis, rickshaws) were obliged to start running on gas. This sort of happened overnight, and the way gas is distributed is so dangerous that people leave the bus or rickshaw outside the gas station when it is time to fill up. And still, one can't see the sun in Delhi because of the smog, although it is improving people assure me. One third of India lives below the poverty line. According to Ravi Sundaram, urbanist at the school of architecture in Delhi, per year 60.000 new poor people move into Delhi, the city expands exponentially.

Next to huge office buildings you will find people living in tents. They have to find ways of livelihood, somehow, to survive. It is raw capitalism in its worst form.

Women's participation in public life is everywhere, but hardly in power. Shree Venkatram (journalist) wrote a report on women's presence in media in India over the last 50 years. She analysed 18 English and Hindi newspapers and found this presence has been ameliorating with 1,3% per year. Today women's presence is 13%, mostly in the adds though, Indira Gandhi being the only woman who made it to the front page till today.

Bangalore, India's Silicon Valley

Bangalore in the South, has a very pleasant climate. It is the booming city of ICT. Many small and large companies are all present. You find yuppie life with trendy cafes and nightclubs, next to Bollywood cinemas and little old fashioned food places everywhere. Of course, there are poor neighbourhoods with very poor people, but the city as a whole drives on industry and you can feel it everywhere.

The Door East Conference

Focus of the Doors East conference was 'Mobility, Geography and Access'. The overall evolving theme for me though, was the realization and the endeavour to understand the development of service design and service economy. Service design, as we understood it, has different meanings in different areas of application. To develop content is different from developing technological infrastructure, to sell goods is different from selling services.

In USA and EU the development of content is a constant area of concern. E-learning, my field, has many initiatives to make it flourish. But we yet have to find the workable service model that will be sustainable in the structural development of content as well as in the development of infrastructure that will deal with authorship and privacy in a convincing way.

Presentations of the western participants dealt a lot with how to move the private, public and commercial domains forward in cohesion: how to develop strategy, how to create support, how to design innovation in schools and design new schools. It were all questions we are familiar with over here.

Nevertheless it is interesting to hear how other people and institutions go about things. I realized again that the way we deal with things at the Hogeschool van Amsterdam is pretty impressive. I enjoyed presentations of some of the new interaction designers exploring for example, the body as interface for information, fluid time interfaces to monitor the going bad of milk-instead of just a date that is never correct anyway, elaborate time banking and car sharing designs as a service for mobile phone companies. My presentation raised questions derived from the experience of the 10 year innovation of the Hogeschool van Amsterdam and the experience of being part of the Digital University of the Netherlands.

The Indian presentations did not talk strategy, they talked business, but on issues we usually talk strategy. The given complexity of Indian society demands from any initiative to be extremely simple to be able to survive. What really cracked my brain was that I found in India, that a service economy is very much in place (one does not iron ones own clothes, it gives someone the opportunity to earn some money, etc).

Also, the development of content and integration of ICT is realized in apparently economically sustainable service models. Since Indian society is a complex one, simplicity of the ideas is actually very impressive and attractive. The buzzwords of the conference were corporate citizenship and social entrepreneurship.

Corporate Citizenship

In the workshop a variety of new Indian best practices was presented. Being a European participant, it struck me the very first day how socially driven projects were financed and organized in commercial ways. And in the conference this insight became even deeper when the Indian labs of the 4 of the big companies (Philips, Siemens, Nokia and Hewlett Packard) presented details on how they have been doing deep research into the lifestyles the poorest sections of society.

They did not only talk about their research but also about their difficulties in communicating with the mother companies about the results they find and designs they develop.

This trend started about two years ago. Realizing that the markets of the wealthy parts of this world are more and more saturated with technological devices, facing the burst of the ICT bubble and facing world recession, companies have become aware that the majority of the people on our planet are poor. And this is a huge potential, provided one changes the models of doing business. Poor people do not have the money to purchase tech-gadgets. Nevertheless, the services that are facilitated via those gadgets can be sold for millions time a few rupi's. This will make a huge market in the end, so the companies argue.

The business models that they are exploring are inspired by a new Indian tradition of innovation that have been first heard of in the Doors of Perception conference 4 in 1996 when Sam Pitroda (well known Indian businessman) talked about his plan to make sure a public phone system would be available in every village all over India. Pitroda gathered over 300 students one summer and made a complete roll out plan for putting wires in the ground to make sure every village would have this public phone.

He assumed that once there was a public phone in every village, all villages would have a chance to participate much better in the market place (making deals, finding out about market prices, communicate about transport and huge amount of personal communication that also helps to develop rural areas in unforeseen ways). He also assumed this huge scheme would be profitable, since in every village one person would be the service deliverer of this public phone service.

This person will find a living and the people from the village only have to pay a few rupees for the call they make. STD (Standard Trunk Dial) as it is called today, is indeed found all over India, in rural areas and also all the cities. It is a model that builds upon the already existing service infrastructure that is part of communities.

It took some years, but then in the Indian models of innovation it is remarkable that one does calculate at least 5 to 6 years before profit will happen. A very different time-frame than the figures that were shouted at the time of the hype in ICT in USA and EU, where investors and banks were going down to 6 months time to market and another 6 to make sure you were successful. Even Nokia, well known for its really short time-to-market which their modular building nearly developed into an art form, is now looking for ways to connect to this new scheme of innovation. You do not sell your goods, you design a framework in which other people will deliver services, the goods being the carrier of the service to be delivered.

We are used to the fact by now here in the west, that when we order a hamburger it will consist of meat from Argentina, pineapple from Israel, flour made of wheat from Russia, sauces made in Italy and wrapped in paper produced in China. We also know the coca cola model, the Amazon model of internet business, and the American callcenters based in India. We have not seen these service networks evolving on a scale like the present. Strangely enough, they have a social agenda we only knew from NGO's and charitable bodies. Now the social reality is the driver of new economic models, since in India everybody is convinced of the fact that sustainability in social terms can only be achieved when it is based on solid economic business structures. In education for example the innovation is financed with venture capital and the government hardly participates.

Off the record in the conference a lot of stories were shared about changes in companies from within. How do boards change opinion, how can one be effective, how and when to seek confrontation. It gave me a feeling of hope that maybe we are entering a new paradigm in doing business, when so many people are actually concerned and want to make a difference and are willing to work hard to find new forms.

Social Entrepreneurship

As a result of this new market strategy of the big companies providing technological service infrastructure, smaller initiatives are evolving, calling themselves social entrepreneurs. Jiva and N-Logue, two Delhi based companies, were part of the workshop. They have attracted serious venture capital to develop e-learning and e-health services to poor people mostly living in rural areas. Jiva 8 years old now was founded by Indian expatriates who came home to make a difference in their country. Jiva does three things: health, learning and social entrepreneurship. In 1995, Jiva first started exploring the health market and they were making money rather soon with providing an ayurvedic (traditional Indian medical and lifestyle system) internet shop.

They then took it further with the ambition to provide cheap and effective health-care to rural villages. In December 2003 they won the World Summit Award (at the World summit on the Information Society held in Geneva 10-12 December 2003) with their 'Teledoc' project.

Teledoc provides a mobile phone interface for doctors and health workers to diagnose people who are ill and who are elsewhere. The doctor sits behind a computer anywhere, and the local health worker (the one who runs the service), talks to the patient and fills in standard forms that the doctor sees on his screen. If necessary a man on a scooter will bring medication to the village (creating another job..). First aid and simple advice can be delivered efficiently at low cost. Health workers are trained by Jiva, establishing a relationship of trust between villagers and the health worker, between the health worker and the doctor. Creating this trust is the most critical success factor in this service model. Having developed this model together with 10 villages and Nokia, they are now preparing to 'roll out', as one of Jiva's founders, told me.

Jiva created a similar long term innovation scenario with their schooling department. Inspired by the development life long learning and the rise of the information society, Jiva has developed a learning to learn methodology for India. In 1999 Jiva started a school in an outskirt of Delhi and with a team of 10 designers and copywriters all the time present in the school and working with the teachers for over 6 years. Today they publish books, have internet sites and train teachers (IRL and on-line).

Since one and a half year they are now rolling out: today 500 village schools work with this methodology and it takes 54 hours to train teachers to change from the old way of trespassing curriculum to the new learning to learn strategies of learning. They plan to intensify the rolling out. The design team will stay in place, only working harder to unfold new parts of the curriculum to transform. And also here, Jiva is starting to earn money with their publications and with the training of teachers, with the continuous back up service they provide for teachers.

While Jiva specializes in development of content services, N-Logue focuses on creating small entrepreneurs in villages who deliver internet services including web cam connections via the already existing STD telephone infrastructure. They roll out a standard technology set (PC, printer, web cam), including training for the service deliverer, for a fixed start up price for which they take the risk for success.

Their service includes agricultural college, online clinics, marketing data, financial services (incl. microcredits, banking) and travel services. Over 8500 villages have been connected in the last two years as was presented in the doors east conference. The person running the service knows how to operate the machine.

Creative Resource

The creative aspect of service design in India is very much dominated by pragmatism and standard procedures. Nevertheless there are many design schools in India, and some really good designers. Being very well educated theoretically and being aware of western and Indian traditions, most designers look for ways of integrating these old and new cultures. There is a tremendous respect for the Indian heritage and big concern that it will evaporate with the evolving media-society. The Bollywood industry has become a commercial culture that is appreciated highly. But for young musicians, writers, designers and artists, there is very little space to develop new work. Visiting the Sarai medialab in Delhi was therefore very interesting. Sarai is a medialab in Delhi that is connected to the Waag Society in Amsterdam. They do social research, innovate design practice, publish, organize events and concerts and run a medialab. Two years ago they started two other medialabs in some poor neighbourhoods of Delhi, to foster creative resources. The medialabs in these localities are called Cybermohallah's. In these creative spaces young people between 15 and 20 years old, spend 3 to 6 hours a day.

These media labs are not a school, not a computer training, nor a job creation facility. They provide a creative space where young people write and visualize and critic each others work and discuss the notions and perceptions that underlie their work. In one Cybermohallah 15 young people will participate.

People from Sarai-being the 'motherlab'-will visit once a week to have conversation, and take time for this conversation, as well as to tackle technical or design issues. As Jeebesh Bagchi (one of Sarai and Cybermohallah's founders) formulated it: paper, pencil, conversation and duration will make creativity flourish. And that is what we need.

In another two years Sarai intends to start another 5 Cybermohallah's, creating in this way a new youth culture and influence the way people inside and outside the localities perceive of life in these localities. Building a creative resource and knowledge base eventually.

Two books have been published that are very impressive. Especially since the stories the young people write examine in detail experiences of day to day life in a very revealing way. The human experience in walking down the street, in realizing time passes by, in describing the fight-known-all-over-the-planet in a family negotiating what television program to watch.

The focus on creative resources is rather courageous in a country with so many people living below poverty lines. Why not make schools or jobs for those young people? Sarai takes the perspective that culture has always been this driving force in change and crisis, culture is an expression of wealth as it is of poverty. It is an expression of the human condition. Whether one is rich or poor, stories and songs and drawings will help to transcend the day to day life.

The raw capitalism in India does not take this into account, being very conservative. To see the results and the success of the Cybermohallah's, to read the work and meet young people, gave me great inspiration. And the realization that creative resource always needs fostering and space for self organization at the same time. The trust that Sarai puts in these young people, that no one considers to be good for anything else than work force, is more than worthwhile and already does and will pay off in the future in unforeseen ways today.

Conclusion

The confrontation with raw capitalism is intense for everyone coming from social democracies in the west. To see though that out of this raw capitalism now has evolved a social agenda in unforeseen ways till now, was very provoking. We are aware of the big difference big companies like Shell can make in peacemaking process like in South Africa. This new trend though where big companies look for poor people markets is very worthwhile following.

Local resonance and transparency of models appears to be a requirement though. Local resonance being the basis for trust for any one person to be able to express and act upon this. Transparency requiring simplicity and at the same time facilitating different forms in different places. The local has to resonate in the global.

Talking to the Jiva people they emphasized how the building of a trust relation is crucial for their success. The issue of trust has been on the ICT agenda because of e-cash and electronic banking.

But mostly it is a non issue in today's world. Trust is a two way thing, one can not build trust without listening. To create business models that actually take into account this local resonance's in the context of establishing trust relations was one of my deep insights in India.

We do develop learning to learn methodologies, talk about question-based design of curricula, but we always define how other people will act. Taking the scale of higher education institutions in the Netherlands into account, it would be a challenge to analyze and design learning environments from the perspective of trust relations and from the perspective of an infrastructure that allows local resonance's to be distinct.

Possibly this change of capitalism from within will actually make a huge difference in the decades to come. Social equality, creative development, eco-awareness and more still have to be put on this new market's economic agenda though.

And the question is whether this will be possible at all. But if this happens, India's wave of innovation will effect us all in ways we will inevitably learn to appreciate. Conferences like Doors East are the bridges that make this learning possible.

CHANGING RURAL SOCIETY: MYTH AND REALITY

Communication for social change is part of an evolution of communications methodology that can help accelerate global development. The process began in the first quarter of the 20th century with the use of publicity tools to bring attention to social problems such as hunger and disease.

It grew to a reliance on public relations as a means of identifying stakeholders and creating programs to fit the audience's interests. More recently, social marketing took centre stage-where sophisticated marketing and cause related advertising tools were applied to influence individual and societal behaviours-such as convincing couples in poor nations to use contraceptives.

This was followed by development communications and strategic communications, the latter which rightfully considers communication to be a process rather than as a series of products.

In the pages that follow, the two authors argue that communication for social change is a distinct way of doing communications-and one of the few approaches that can be sustained. Such sustainability is largely due to the fact that ownership of both the message and the medium-the content and the process-resides with the individuals or communities affected.

We believe that this approach can help make greater contributions to the pace of development. From this basic assumption we move to questioning "how" and "if" and "where" we might find interesting work and committed individuals to test the effectiveness of this approach.

In order to do this work, the Rockefeller Foundation has brought together a group of social activists, academics, filmmakers and journalists, funders, electronic communications experts, service providers and professional communicators. The ideas expressed in this position paper reflect discussions held at two conferences-one at the foundation's Bellagio Study and Conference Centre on Lake Como, in Italy, and the other in the fall of 1998 in Cape Town, South Africa.

In Bellagio we committed to a new agenda for global communications: communication that is empowering, many-to-many (horizontal versus top-down), communication that gives voice to the previously unheard, and that has a bias toward local content and ownership. The group's action steps, agreed upon at the end of the meeting, include a commitment to convince others of the value of this approach (broadening the debate), to publicize writings about the effectiveness of this work, and to continue to study the prospects in a global setting.

During the Cape Town gathering, we continued the inquiry with an expanded group of people. There we developed a concrete and comprehensive definition of communication for social change, put together an outline for the skills and attributes needed to do this work, began work on the skills/resources training "toolbox" or "practitioner's kit" or "knowledge transfer", reached agreement on measurements, and identified organizations and people that we'd like to engage in helping us do this work and to advocate for its effectiveness. What follows is further explanation of the value and benefits of the discipline of communication for social change.

AN ENVIRONMENT FOR NEW THINKING

This initiative is based on a simple premise: that recent developments--in communications technologies, in political and media systems, and in emerging development problems--suggest a greatly enhanced, radically different role for communication in development programming.

Communication programming has, very simplistically, tended to fulfill three roles in development thinking and practice:

First, its role has been to inform and persuade people to adopt certain behaviours and practices that are beneficial to them: for example, to inform people how to protect themselves from HIV and to persuade them to use a condom; to persuade them of the importance of vaccinating their child and to inform them when and where they can do so; to persuade them that simple sugar and salt solutions can cure diarrhoea and to inform them how to make them up; to persuade them to have fewer children and to inform them how to do so. Second, it has been used to enhance the image and profile of the work of organizations involved in development with a view to boosting the credibility of their work, raising more funding and generally improving public perceptions.

Third, it has been used on a more targeted level within communities to enable community consultation over specific initiatives.

The communication for social change initiative believes that all these roles are important and communication work in general remains underfunded and undervalued. We argue that these traditional approaches to communication are generally insufficient in addressing the reality of the development problems that exist, and they do not always reflect the complex changes in the communications environments taking place in many developing country societies.

We argue in this position paper that communication can play a much greater role in enabling people to take control over their own lives, in enabling people and societies to set their own agendas in relation to political, economic and social development; and in enabling, in particular, the voices of the economically and politically marginalized to be amplified and channelled to mainstream public and political debate.

We argue that the interaction between communication and the social well-being of people in developing countries will be radically redefined over the next few years. Global economic liberalization of communications, the deployment of the Internet, mobile telephony and other new technologies and the changing political environment in most developing countries are all coinciding to make the cusp of the new millennium a defining moment which will determine how successfully all countries, especially developing nations, adapt to and exploit these changes.

Information in society does not simply enable people to know what they should do or think.

Information is power--it enables people to make sense of their lives and it enables them to shape their aspirations. Ultimately it can enable them to take control of their lives. In many areas of the world, people have precious little access to information outside their community that enables them to make such "sense."

In other societies, despite a multitude of information outlets, people who are historically marginalized and excluded remain "voiceless" and "invisible" because those who control information channels refuse to share access equitably. Communication for social change principles focus on using direct, many-to-many communications which spring from the affected communities. The problems inherent in this work are those which have plagued communication practice for decades: how to assess impact beyond counting products produced or net impressions received; how to program communication for social change work on the micro community level and on the macro multinational level, often simultaneously; and how to transfer knowledge and skills to those most in need of "training" who often live and work in hard-to-reach areas. We also struggle with ways to capture the best learning-those cases that illustrate the power of communication for social change yet are not overly simplistic.

Language is also a challenge: the notion of how to explain this work in terms that can be readily accessible and used by grassroots activists as easily as by professional communicators. These are all issues that the groups assembled for the Rockefeller Foundation conferences grappled with. This paper reveals some preliminary thoughts on solutions. Others, such as site-based knowledge transfer, are in the early exploratory stages and will require more study, testing and applications, especially in developing nations with scarce human and financial resources.

Yet nothing in our questions should suggest lack of conviction nor should they prevent us from energetically embracing the potential of communication for social change to fulfill critical gaps in the development process.

What is Communication for Social Change?

The traditional understanding of the role of communication in development is one that seeks mainly to change individual behaviours. This behaviour change communication can be broadly defined as a process of understanding people's situations and influences, developing messages that respond to the concerns within those situations, and using communication processes and media to persuade people to increase their knowledge and change the behaviours and practices that place them at risk.

Communication for social change, on the other hand, is defined as a process of public and private dialogue through which people define who they are, what they want and how they can get it. Social change is defined as change in people's lives as they themselves define such change. This work seeks particularly to improve the lives of the politically and economically marginalized, and is informed by principles of tolerance, self-determination, equity, social justice and active participation for all.

This approach attempts to rebalance strategic approaches to communication and change by taking the overriding emphasis...

Away from people as the objects for change... and on to people and communities as the agents of their own change.

Away from designing, testing and delivering messages...and on to supporting dialogue and debate on the key issues of concern. Away from the conveying of information from technical experts... and on to sensitively placing that information into the dialogue and debate.

Away from a focus on individual behaviours...and on to social norms, policies, culture and a supportive environment.

Away from persuading people to do something ...and on to negotiating the best way forward in a partnership process.

Away from technical experts in "outside" agencies dominating and guiding the process...and on to the people most affected by the issues of concern playing a central role.

THE STARTING POINT

The starting point for this inquiry is the growing evidence that, as a generality, the "communications environment" in which most people on the planet live has changed radically over the last decade. It has changed both in relation to the information people have access to, and the opportunities people have to communicate their own perspectives on issues that concern them. This new communications environment is shaped by three main interlocking trends:

I. Media liberalization and deregulation

II. New information and communication technologies

III. The changing global political and economic context.

In general, and with important exceptions, these trends are tending to decentralize communications in developing countries, with a trend towards a more fragmented, more horizontal, people-to-people model of communication, and away from a highly centralized, vertical model.

In industrialized countries, media liberalization suggests more choice for consumers, which should, theoretically, mean increased access. Yet the way it plays out in countries like the United States is in encouraging the growth of huge media monopolies that result in far less community input to programming. With deregulation, public service programming has become just a fading memory, and station ownership has leaped beyond the realm of possibility for most community-based organizations or individuals of color.

This new communications environment has, we argue, important implications for development programming, an importance that is compounded by the emergence of new development problems--such as HIV/AIDS--that demand new approaches to communication. Our inquiry suggests that there are many opportunities to be seized, as well as real challenges to be faced in understanding and acting upon these changes.

Liberalization and Deregulation

Most people on this planet receive most of their information on issues beyond their immediate communities from the print and broadcast media. Fifteen years ago, much of humanity had one main source for this information--their governments. The means were stolid, formulaic broadcast and print media that had been established with the express purpose of telling people what they should know and think. Two general trends have changed this. First, following the end of the Cold War, a combination of internal pressure from their citizens and external pressure--often in the form of conditions set by donors--have led governments to relax censorship and freedom of speech laws. Second, this pressure for political liberalization has been combined with economic liberalization and deregulation of national media industries.

The result in many of those countries with tightly controlled media has been a blossoming of dynamic, generally populist and highly commercial newspapers, television and radio media in most developing countries, and flourishing of new community media in some. Meanwhile, old monopoly state-run media, particularly broadcasters, have tended to languish, losing their audiences to more dynamic competition. They also face declining government support and funding.

The implications of these changes for those involved in communication are challenging.

Monopoly broadcasters have presented a convenient way of communicating simple messages to huge audiences through one medium. In much more fragmented media environments, this opportunity no longer exists and reaching the same audience requires putting messages out through many different media, and adapting it to many different audiences.

Perhaps more importantly, the creation of these more complex and dynamic communications environments raises the deeper question of just what information do people have access to, and does it empower poor people and give them a greater voice--or does it move them further to the economic and social margins?

At their worse, new communications environments have done the latter. They have shifted from providing stodgy and dogmatic government propaganda to providing a uniform diet of often Western popular music. In some countries, state-controlled news has been replaced by no news, or information that is sensational, inaccurate or irrelevant to the daily lives of much of its audience, or news that is derived entirely from international sources. Often operating in anarchic regulatory environments, commercial and private stations have little obligation to provide anything other than entertainment. At its very worst, media have encouraged intolerance, sectionalism and tribalism, the most extreme example being the "hate" radio of RTML in Rwanda which played a key role in the massacres in that country.

At their best, however, commercial, community and, in some cases, newly invigorated state-run news and media organizations have managed to attract large audiences with compelling, popular and informative programming. In Kampala, Uganda, the FM station Capital Radio attracts some of its highest audiences for its Capital Doctor program, which provides advice and information on issues of sex, HIV/AIDS and other health issues. In South Africa, a form of "edutainment"-

"Soul City," set in a Johannesburg township--has become one of the most popular soap operas in the country, yet has succeeded in educating people about diarrhoea, HIV/AIDS and other issues.

Again in South Africa, deregulation has spurred the creation of more than 80 community radio stations broadcasting in 15 languages. Community stations have made serious inroads into the broadcast markets, often stealing audiences from the well-established public broadcasting stations. Community broadcasting provides communities with information that is relevant to their lives, as well as a voice through which people can make demands.

In Cape Town, the tiny community radio station, Radio Zibonele, drew on their audience's anger to play a key role in mediating and resolving the township's gang warfare surrounding the taxi business.

In fact, the success of community radio proves, in some small way, the ready market for communication for social change principles to be applied in diverse circumstances throughout the world. In addition to sub-Saharan African nations, community radio has succeeded where little else can from northwest Canada to southeast Asia.

The print media too is changing under similar pressure, with more entertaining, more populist and often more trenchant coverage of news issues. These changes have demonstrated how in the print media in particular, poor reporting undermines many other forms of social and political discourse; high quality reporting can play a major role in promoting and stimulating constructive public debate.

Well-informed, investigative reporting in particular can provide a key element of public accountability, both for national governments, for international institutions, and for NGOs and other civil society organizations.

Finally, the last decade has seen an explosion in satellite broadcasting. Take the South Asia region, home to one-fifth of the world's population which is today within the footprint of at least 50 broadcast satellites. In India, Pakistan and Bangladesh alone there are more than 70 million households with television sets, adding up to a total viewership of 300 million. By 2007, there will be 550 million television viewers in these countries. Half of them will be hooked up to cable-able to watch the 350 channels that will be available to them by then.

These changes do not apply to all people in all countries, but in one form or another they do affect the vast majority of people in the great majority of countries.

They present many problems; reaching lots of people with prepared messages is becoming more difficult and more expensive. They also present substantial opportunities: to work with communities to enable them to amplify their voices, to enable access to the information that can empower them, to help shape communication environments that can work for people, not against them.

New Information and Communication Technologies

The current revolution in information technologies represents probably the most profound set of technological developments human society has experienced since the industrial revolution.

The innovations of the Internet--and particularly e-mail--have transformed communications capacities in countries with often dilapidated telecommunications infrastructures; and have opened up access to much more information about global issues. The falling costs and increased access to telephony mean that an increasing number of people have the capacity to communicate rapidly beyond their immediate communities, thus opening up new economic opportunities and opportunities for social and political discourse.

For many participants in this communication for social change initiative these technologies represent a huge opportunity: Centralized control of information by governments or commercial interests becomes much more difficult. Increasingly, political systems can neither control the information their citizens receive nor monitor or constrain how they communicate with each other.

Technology is--for good and ill--increasing access to the kind of information that is uncensored and unfiltered. Technology is growing most rapidly in those areas where its demand is most clearly defined by the users.

The capacity of people to access information is substantially increased.The capacity of people to organize, advocate and lobby beyond physical boundaries is greatly enhanced.

The capacity for people and organizations in developing countries to communicate information--their aspirations, demands, experiences, analysis--becomes cheaper, more powerful and far more pervasive.

Nevertheless, we also recognize the limitations of these technologies. In particular, the "information gap" between rich and poor is stark. One of the least expensive of the information and communications technologies (ICTs)--the telephone--illustrates just how far apart the rich and poor worlds are in access to such technologies.

One quarter of the countries in the world still have fewer than one telephone line per 100 people. The majority of the population in developing countries--60% of the total--live in rural areas. Yet in these countries, more than 80% of main telephone lines are in urban areas. The distribution of new ICTs is no more equal.

Eighty four per cent of mobile cellular subscribers, 91% of all fax machines and 97% of Internet host computers are in developed countries.

Telecommunications is nevertheless becoming cheaper, more reliable and more accessible and will continue to do so.

Despite the constraints, it seems likely that we are seeing the emergence internationally of organizational structures that are increasingly based on networks, rather than hierarchies. It is this revolution which represents most powerfully the increase in horizontal, people-to-people communication, and which provides profound new opportunities for more inclusive public and policy debate.

A Changing Political and Economic Environment

The collapse of the Soviet Union and the end of the Cold War have had far reaching effects, a full exploration of which is beyond the remit of this paper. However, two key issues should be mentioned.

The first is the growing, though uneven, democratization and political liberalization that has swept much of the developing world over the last decade. Many of the highly centralized one-party states or dictatorships have given way to multi-party democracies, or at least to more open political systems.

This political liberalization has been matched by a still more pervasive economic liberalization and we have seen the rapid emergence of a new global economy. As Manuel Castells argues, "for the first time in human history the entire planet is capitalist, since even the few remaining command economies are surviving or developing through their linkages to global, capitalist markets."

As all governments are finding, including China's, maintaining strict and centralized control of information in a market economy (which, in turn, needs to rely on communications technologies) is both difficult and often inefficient.

The fragmentation and decentralization of information outlined above is potentially countered by the greater concentration of ownership in communications and media industries ushered in by globalization. According to UNESCO's World Communication Report 1997, "international [media] conglomerates are emerging with the purpose of controlling not only the transmission system (manufacturing, network, cable, satellite etc.) but also the programs they convey."

An increasing spate of mergers and acquisitions over recent years has seen the emergence of a handful of "world companies" who now dominate global media markets. Time Warner Inc., News International, Sony, Finivest and Bertelsman each have annual sales well in excess of $10 billion, an increasing percentage of which is generated outside the United States. This concentration is compounded by convergence of media and telecommunications industries leading to still greater concentration of ownership.

Such concentration may not matter and may be offset by the more horizontal and decentralized models of communications outlined above.

But both these trends--towards a decentralization of information production away from government, and a concentration of ownership of the means of communication in the hands of transnationals--should matter to anyone involved in communication. These trends are bound up intimately with questions of who controls the information that people receive.

Communication and emerging development problems These changes to communication environments come at the same time as important changes in how we think about development. Some of the most important emerging development challenges of the last decade have raised new questions.

Issues such as HIV/AIDS, reproductive health and reproductive rights, and others such as tobacco use have highlighted more intensely than ever how disease and poor health are linked not only to poverty and poor nutrition, but also to prejudice, to social, political and economic inequality, and to social dislocation. They have focused an especially strong spotlight on social and political environments where issues of sex and sexuality are habitually hidden or are difficult to debate in public.

Such complexities are forcing societies globally to change--to question long cherished, deeply rooted social, political, and religious mores and practices. A whole range of issues--from HIV to reproductive rights, from domestic violence to female genital mutilation--have crystallized the need for much wider social and political change. Such change is informed by what happens both within countries and by international debates, but if it is to be sustainable, change has to emerge from within societies.

The means of how societies change, and who drives such change is contentious and difficult. Part of such change will come from education about issues such as condom use--but much of the more deep seated changes that need to take place in societies, such as the improvement in the status of women, need to emerge from advocacy and vigorous public debate within and between societies.

Such debates depend fundamentally on communication: on communication within societies, within families, within communities, through political discourse; and on communication between societies, at the levels of the individual, of the community and of the global society. The capacity of people to communicate is intimately bound up with their capacity to effect change.

In short, a new model of communication could be emerging from a mixture of political, technological, economic and social change. It is decentralized, pluralistic and democratic; it seeks to empower rather than persuade people; it fosters debate among and between citizens, among and between communities, and between people and government. This model envisages increasingly horizontal communication allowing people to communicate with each other easily and inexpensively. It also involves the steady disintegration of traditional monolithic vertical lines of communication, where governments owned radio and television stations in order to control flows of information.

CREATING AN ENVIRONMENT FOR CHANGE

The Rockefeller Foundation has responded to a growing body of opinion and evidence that the role of communication in developing country societies is changing, and that the strategies of those working in development needed to change with it. The Foundation's inquiry is based on the premise that the changes that are taking place in communication and society may have profound implications for donor and development strategies, but that this premise remains poorly researched and articulated.

Communication for social change programming suggests a major shift in development. Above all it is about enabling publics and communities to articulate their own agendas for development--at the community, the provincial, the national and the international level. Programming in this area is about making connections--at these different levels and between them. It involves making connections between global trade policies and local communities, and it involves making connections between many different kinds of activities--between the issues themselves (such as HIV/AIDS, domestic violence) and the means that exist for debating and discussing them: community radio, women's radio listeners groups, an informed and responsive national media, quality media programming (e.g., Soul City), telecommunications.

It involves framing and phrasing debates in language and forms that are inclusive. It involves a responsibility of academics in particular, but those concerned with development in general, to communicate research and information not only to their peers, but to the wider public within developing countries. It involves "returning" research and analysis to where it originates. Perhaps, above all, it suggests that the key role for donor and development institutions is to create an environment for change. It suggests a role that sees these organizations continuing to inform and create development strategies, but also in creating the conditions where developing country societies can assess, challenge and adapt such strategies and begin to create strategies for themselves.

It provides new opportunities to open up development decisions and programming to public debate and dialogue, and to enable publics--and not just experts--to be more proactive in shaping debate on development issues.

THE PROCESS OF INQUIRY

The Rockefeller Foundation has been engaged aggressively in intellectual inquiry about the power of communications for nearly 60 years. In the late 1930s, program officer John Marshall formed the Rockefeller Communications Seminar whose goal was to promote a theoretical framework about the role of mass communications in American culture. Under Marshall's guidance, the foundation funded one of the country's first efforts to quantitatively document the effect of radio on listeners. The work expanded in the 1940s to include support for Paul Lazarsfeld, who began the new field of communication and attitude research. In this time-frame, the foundation also funded the creation of the first communications journal, Public Opinion Quarterly. It is from this historical base that the current communications efforts to promote an enhanced discipline known as communication for social change grows. The Rockefeller Foundation, like most other progressive U.S.-based foundations, is in the business of positive social change-change in attitudes, in behaviours, in utilization of technology, and of access to opportunities to enhance lives.

While a key player in the development arena, the foundation's focus remains predominantly on science-based knowledge. Yet at the core of much of the foundation's current portfolio is the need to affect individual and community norms and behaviours-the type of change that requires sophisticated, sustained communication.

Three years ago we began to ask the tough questions: how can we demonstrate that communication-planned and implemented strategically-can indeed bring about desired social change? Can we prove that such communication thinking and work is as systematic, scientific, sustained and measurable as other social sciences? And can we move beyond publicity and promotional activities to a new way of thinking and delivering communication that starts with the identified community or stakeholder's needs, engages the recipient of the communication in decision making and, most importantly, can be sustained and replicated. The answers are "yes", "maybe" and "watch us."

We began this inquiry the way much work starts at this foundation-with a group of people coming together at a Bellagio conference. While this may not have been a unique method, the process of discovery we used-search conference methodology-yielded encouraging results. We brought together disparate types with little in common except our belief that communication MUST be done differently. We, individually and collectively, knew that we were on the cusp of an evolutionary turn in the history of communication for development.

We felt that our work had to be bigger than embracing electronic technology or providing access to those in "unwired" parts of the world. We also believed, with some certainly, that the discipline of communication can be ill-defined, misunderstood, undervalued and often ignored for its contributions to the development process. What we're about today is, hopefully adding to the discourse rather than muddying it. In the process of figuring out what to do and where to start, we realized that the type of communication work that needs to be done is not often done-especially in poor areas of developing nations most in need.

It seems that a particular niche for this network will be in identifying needed skills, developing ways to transmit training and to reach those people and communities most likely to have scarce resources. Going forward we will work with such people and communities to bring communication for social change to them. We come to this work humbly confident that ultimately, development-in virtually any sector-cannot happen without innovative and sustained communication processes.

Where is Good Work Happening?

One question that we're asked frequently is "what does communication for social change look like? Who is practicing it, or where is the greatest potential?" In looking for examples of good work, it's important to keep in mind the key principles of communication for social change: it empowers individuals and communities, it engages people in making decisions that enhance their lives, it is many-to-many, it relies on democratic ideals, it allows previously unheard voices to be heard, and both the process of communications and the content of the messages are controlled by the receiving communities.

This can be heady stuff-at times bordering on the ideal rather than the practical. Yet even so, we've found examples of innovative social communications work in several locales. As we work in the United States, Africa and Asia, for example, it appears that the most likely practitioners of communication for social change are small struggling organizations with few resources.

Communication for social change in some respects becomes a means of survival. Without the benefit of large communications staffs or budgets, and facing media that are hesitant to cover social issues in substantive ways, some small NGOs and community-based organizations have figured out how to use the people most affected by their work to make the communications process work.

In Africa and Latin America, the community radio movement stands out. By definition, community radio stations cannot succeed without local control, citizen participation, local issues-based programming and open access. Yet radio remains essentially a top-down methodology; that is, someone decides what will be broadcast, it airs, and is received passively by listeners.

The better community radio stations, such as Cape Flats' (South Africa) Bush Radio, Radio Zibonele in the Khayelitsha community of Cape Town, South Africa, and Alexandra Township's community station focus on audience participation. New programming stems from the suggestions listeners make when phoning into the stations, or when they are working there as volunteer staff. Critical issues facing the communities are discussed-and problem solving happens in real time-on the air.

Outreach is daily and continuous-the community radio stations are vital parts of the neighbourhoods where they operate. They don't just "cover" issues-they lead the residents in collective decision making.

A KEY CHALLENGE: CAPTURING IMPACT

Recognition of the role of communication in achieving social change is not necessarily new nor surprising, but it receives comparatively little funding. While the case for this kind of programming--for the reasons already given--is building, there remain significant obstacles to it attracting major support.

Much of this work involves stimulating dialogue and debate within communities and the public, and--when it works best--ensuring that the engine of change is the community and public itself. As a consequence, much of this work is unpredictable and risky. Because dialogue and debate are the immediate objectives and are difficult to measure or attribute to any particular intervention, and because it is recognized that social change is likely to take a long time, this work is very difficult to assess and evaluate.Indeed, many of the communications initiatives that are currently funded--particularly around behaviour change--attract support less because they are perceived as addressing the main problem, but more because they can be claimed as having changed something. In the field of HIV/AIDS, for example, much of the funding for communications initiatives has gone into attempts to change individual behaviours. Much of this work has had substantial impact but it has not, as many of its practitioners would acknowledge, sought to change the underlying factors that are driving a still escalating epidemic: poverty, social exclusion, prejudice and discrimination, migration and poor health systems.

Such problems are fundamental. Communication for social change programming can constitute only part of the real solution; it can help enable people to shape their own agenda, articulate their own priorities and aspirations of how to address the epidemic, and ensure that donors are following and responding to public and policy debates within developing countries as well as shaping such debates. Evaluation of impact in this area remains difficult but not, we conclude, impossible. It does, however, mean that we must develop new methodologies.

MEASUREMENTS AND EVALUATION

Donors have a right and an obligation to demand evidence that their funds have been spent wisely, that they have achieved what they were meant to, or that there are good reasons for any changes or lack of achievement. However, there are other reasons why impact needs to be measured.

1. *Accountability*-understanding the impact of communication interventions is an essential component of being accountable. The primary accountability is to the people engaged in the communication intervention. Being involved with them in aspects of their lives requires that accountability. They are also the people, proportionate to their means, who will invest the most resources.
2. *Progress*-understanding what is happening and whether it is what people want to happen.
3. *Improvement*-information from any measurement and evaluation is crucial to both large strategic decisions and to fine tuning communication interventions in order that better value is gained from the investments that are made.
4. *Motivation*-a sense of achievement is crucial to motivation. Good motivation is an essential element of any endeavour, including communication for social change programs. The people involved draw energy and drive from knowing that progress is being made. Not knowing can lead to the opposite.
5. *Credibility*-Good data on the impact of communication for social change interventions can only enhance the credibility of this field and the investments-from local to international-that are made.

The long-term goal of all development action is to see positive change in the issues of concern. We all want less poverty, increased employment, better gender equality, to eradicate HIV/AIDS, more girls in school, higher educational achievement, lower child and maternal mortality rates, better nutrition, fewer accidents and no violence. That is the crucial measure of success.

Such changes can take five years or a decade, but generally much longer. People involved in communication for social change initiatives need more immediate data that indicates whether what they are doing is making a contribution to the overall change process.

It is not possible to run a program for 15 years before assessing impact and then finding that the wrong things were done. More immediate information on the contribution of communication to change is required.

Although communication for social change activities tend to have less specific and immediate objectives and targets, they nevertheless need to develop a similar set of indicators both to measure and indicate progress and to drive the nature of the programming. We are at the start of this work, but the Cape Town meeting, drawing on the information, analysis and perspectives above, made some suggestions of indicators.

Expanded Public and Private Dialogue and Debate

Dialogue and debate are crucial. They indicate that people are engaging in the issues of concern, are motivated to look at them, and that at least some of the parties to the debate and discussion are challenging the orthodoxy that may be contributing to the matters of most concern. For example, the role of women in politics; the need for a more open approach to sexual health issues; equal rights for boys and girls; and land redistribution. Increased accuracy of the information that people share in the dialogue/debate Accuracy of information is important.

There are two types of information. First where there is specific, proven data such as would exist in relation to a particular medical issue. Second, accurately reflecting the background information, perspectives and views of the parties to a debate over a more complex issue such as girls in school.

The more accurately the data and the perspectives are reflected in the dialogue-from among friends to public policy debate-the more likely is the chance of positive change. The means available that enable people/communities to feed their voices into debate and dialogue.

Increased leadership and agenda setting role by disadvantaged people on the issues of concern Whatever the focus of the communication for social change action the people at the centre of the issue[s]-those whose everyday lives are most affected-should be involved in the major decisions related to the initiative.

This will ensure relevance and meaning-a vital component for any intervention.

Resonates with the major issues of interest to people's everyday interests Communication for social change interventions need to be positioned in ways that resonate, make sense to them, to which they can relate. Of course this is a basic tenet of all communication, but it can be easily forgotten in the midst of complex detail relating to an issue such as breast feeding and HIV/AIDS.

If the positioning of the issue does resonate there is a greater chance of momentum and action. And it is not possible to focus on all the many and varied aspects of a concern. Rarely can the issue that resonates be chosen in advance. It will emerge and then needs to be accentuated.

Linked people and groups with similar interests who might otherwise not be in contact One of the main turning points for any change process is when different groups form alliances with a common overall objective and a loose coordination framework. Each group does its own thing, but in the knowledge that it contributes to a greater effort. Therefore activities that link people together and help working alliances can be interpreted as contributing to positive change.

CONCLUDING OBSERVATIONS

Throughout the NGO community in industrialized and in less wealthy nations, the potential both to apply communication for social change methodology and to encourage its use is great. The change communication principles seem obvious to those of us in development, philanthropy and social services. They speak to the very essence of our work-that is, to helping create locally-based solutions to critical social ills.

Yet throughout time, obvious "fixes" have been the ones most often overlooked. "Of course innovative communication techniques are essential" we hear frequently. "Of course we have to empower those 'on the ground' to have greater control of their own stories and how they are communicated. Of course 'horizontal' communication is more effective than top-down," we all opine.

Yet "how" remains a mystery in far too many instances. Or more precisely, we're not sure "how to make it work."

Key to answering the "how" question, we believe, is in finding smart practitioners and thinkers throughout the world who are able to reach others, train others, test the change communication principles, encourage ongoing site-based work, and evaluate its effectiveness. The strategy for moving this initiative forward has five prongs:

1. Reaching clarity of terms and defining, or perhaps refining, the field;
2. Identifying and describing the skills, attributes and resources necessary for communication for social change. During the Cape Town conference, participants discussed both the form and content of the skills development process.
3. Developing the systems and exchange mechanisms needed to spread the change communication work globally;
4. Maintaining the network of supporters and enrolling others; and,
5. Using concrete measurements to evaluate effectiveness and the reach of communication for social change.

We are well along on the first prong. We believe we have many good ideas for the second and third ones. Each day we're thrilled by another expression of interest that we receive; the word is getting out, which only fuels our evangelical spirits. And, as this paper suggests, there are different ways of doing evaluation that should further the communication for social change agenda.

Yet, many questions remain: can we create a "transfer of knowledge" or type of curriculum that can be transported worldwide easily and economically? What's in such a curriculum? Who are the trainers? How will they receive the information? (Is, for example, Internet-based training a viable option?) Can we establish regional centers of learning that are based on local realities? How do we reach people in those areas of the world most in need of this knowledge but who have the smallest number of resources to access such training?

Or should we, perhaps, be worrying less about skills and more about personal attributes? Going forward we must debate answers to these questions and test possible solutions on a community-specific basis.

Bibliography

Arant, David: *Perspectives: Ethics, Issues and Controversies in Mass Media,* St. Paul, Coursewise Publishing, 1999.

Berry, David: *Ethics and Media Culture,* Woburn, Focal Press, 2000.

Charles, Ramirez: *Latin Looks: Images of Latinos and Latinas in U.S. Media,* Boulder, CO: Westview, 1996.

Daniel, Webster: *The Media in America,* Santa Barbara, ABC-CLIO, 1995.

Earl, R.: *Writing for Mass Communication,* White Plains, NY: Longman, 1996.

Ericson, Richard: *Crime and the Media,* Brookfield, Dartmouth Publishing, 1995.

Fiske, John: *Media Matters: Everyday Culture and Political Change,* Minneapolis MN: U. Minnesota Pr., 1996.

Gordon, A. David: *Controversies in Media Ethics,* White Plains, Longman Publishers, 1999.

Jewkes, Yvonne: *Media and Crime,* Thousand Oaks, Sage, 2004.

Langman, Larry: *The Media in the Movies,* Jefferson, NC: McFarland & Company, 1997.

Norris, Pippa: *Women, Media and Politics,* Oxford, Oxford University Press, 1997.

Ripley, Jr. Casey: *The Media and the Public,* New York, H.W. Wilson, 1994.

Robert, V.: *Mass Media,* New York, Garland Publishing, 1987.

Sohn, Ardyth: *Media Management: A Casebook Approach,* Mahwah, Lawrence Erlbaum Associates, 2003.

Teeter, Jr.: *Voices of a Nation: A History of Mass Media in the United States,* Needham Heights, Allyn & Bacon, 1997.

Index

◆◆◆